TEACHING PSYCHOLOGY ONLINE

Intended as a resource for psychology educators ranging from teaching assistants to experienced faculty, this book shows readers how to effectively create and manage an online psychology course. Guidelines for preparing courses, facilitating communication, and assigning grades are provided along with activities and assessments geared specifically toward psychology. Pedagogical theories and research are fused with the authors' teaching experiences to help maximize the reader's abilities as an online psychology instructor. The book focuses on psychology education at the undergraduate level but it also includes material appropriate for graduate students and professionals. Readers will find helpful examples from all the major content areas including introductory, social, developmental, biological, abnormal and positive psychology, and human sexuality.

Every chapter is organized around three sections. The *Purpose* part introduces the key concepts, theory, and research. The *Implementation* section reviews the "nuts and bolts" of online teaching, and the *Troubleshooting* section addresses key problems and potential solutions. "Text boxes" highlight important tips. The website, http://www.TeachingPsychology Online.com, provides additional tips, links to related articles and other resources, and examples of online psychology assignments from across the discipline. The book addresses: launching your online course; enhancing student/instructor communication; modes of multimedia and how to integrate them into your course, including lecture videos, podcasts, blogs, wikis, and social networking sites; creating activities for online courses; assessment and grading; and online education trends including doctoral-level education.

Ideal for instructors teaching *any* psychology course, from introductory to upper-level undergraduate, to graduate courses, this text can be used for developing online courses in applied areas such as counseling, health, and industrial psychology as well as for courses in social, cognitive, and developmental psychology. Instructors of any technical skill level can use this book, including those familiar with Blackboard to those who are just getting started. Whether you are a seasoned pro or new to teaching psychology online, the tips in this book can help improve your instruction, reduce your prep time, and enhance your students' success.

Kelly S. Neff has taught psychology online to thousands of students, and has extensive experience with designing and launching online courses. Her online courses have attracted a global following and have enticed many people to try online learning.

Stewart I. Donaldson is Dean and Professor of Psychology at Claremont Graduate University, USA. He has designed several distance education programs and has taught thousands of students and professionals participating in online courses and other e-learning experiences.

TEACHING PSYCHOLOGY ONLINE
TIPS AND STRATEGIES FOR SUCCESS

KELLY S. NEFF

STEWART I. DONALDSON

Psychology Press
Taylor & Francis Group

NEW YORK AND LONDON

First published 2013
by Psychology Press
711 Third Avenue, New York, NY 10017

Simultaneously published in the UK
by Psychology Press
27 Church Road, Hove, East Sussex BN3 2FA

Psychology Press is an imprint of the Taylor & Francis Group, an informa business

Library of Congress Cataloging in Publication Data
Neff, Kelly S.
    Teaching psychology online : tips and strategies for success / by Kelly S. Neff, Stewart I. Donaldson.
    p. cm.
    ISBN 978-1-84872-922-3 (hbk. : alk. paper) – ISBN 978-1-84872-923-0 (pbk. : alk. paper)
    1. Psychology—Study and teaching (Higher) 2. Psychology—Web-based instruction.
    3. Psychology—Computer-assisted instruction. I. Donaldson, Stewart
    I. (Stewart Ian) II. Title.
    BF77.N44 2012
    150.78'5–dc232012027581

ISBN: 978-1-84872-922-3 (hbk)
ISBN: 978-1-84872-923-0 (pbk)
ISBN: 978-0-203-07399-5 (ebk)

Typeset in Minion and Scala Sans
by EvS Communication Networx, Inc.

SUSTAINABLE
FORESTRY
INITIATIVE

Certified Sourcing
www.sfiprogram.org
SFI-00555
The SFI label applies to the text stock.

Printed and bound in the United States of America by Walsworth Publishing Company, Marceline, MO.

Contents

PREFACE

Technology is changing the face of our world in unprecedented ways across nearly every aspect of our lives, from how we communicate with one another, to the foods we eat, to the demands of our professions, our access to creative outlets, to the media we consume, and how we spend our free time or pursue relaxation. With these rapid developments that surround us, it can be natural to feel intimidated or uncertain about what the future holds and how society may be shaped and molded by these forces in the 21st century. It can also feel exhilarating to know that we are living in times where there is potential for human beings to progress and develop beyond the classic paradigms we have held in place for so long. Many traditional social institutions have been affected for the better by the integration of emerging technologies, such as breakthroughs in health care, transportation, and energy. But no institution better demonstrates how technology is pushing for progress and life without boundaries like our education system, and higher education in particular. The online classroom has changed the face of higher education as we know it. In less than a decade, the percentage of undergraduate students enrolled in online courses rose from 8% in 1999 to 20% in 2007. Considering how many undergraduate students there are in the United States, the fact that 20% engaged in an online course (and this was 5 years ago!) speaks to the immense popularity and incredible potential for growth that online courses offer to our nation's academic institutions.

In light of this rapid expansion, perhaps it is not surprising that there are few academic resources for instructors who are teaching online, especially in psychology. When coauthor Dr. Neff launched her first online course in

2008, she learned to teach online mostly by trial and error, as well as from advice from other online instructors. There was no "go-to" resource to help ease the transition for new instructors, and no real guide to help navigate the pitfalls. The authors thus developed this book project not only out of a need experienced in our own teaching careers, but also in response to the surprising absence of a peer-reviewed literature on how to best train and educate online psychology instructors. The available materials are often fragmented, and not targeted specifically at the discipline of psychology. This book provides accessible and insightful guidance for those instructors looking to launch their best possible online course. Our goal is to mitigate and reduce the pressures and anxieties of online teaching, by taking a positive, hands-on approach. We embrace the values of online education, and strongly believe that anyone who teaches psychology can also teach psychology online, using the guidance and tips presented in this book.

This book best prepares online psychology educators because unlike nearly all available online teacher training materials, it is *specific* to the discipline of psychology. As one of the most popular college majors and online areas of study, it is important that online educators have access to the training and support that they need. This book can be adopted by instructors teaching *any* psychology course, from introductory psychology and other lower level classes, all the way up to specific seminars, upper level courses, and graduate courses. This book also cuts across subdisciplines, and can be used by instructors teaching applied programs like counseling, health science, industrial/organizational psychology, program evaluation, and child development, as well as instructors teaching basic science in areas such as social psychology, cognitive psychology, positive psychology, and sexology. Instructors of any technical skill level will also be able to use this book, including those who are familiar with Blackboard and technology, as well as those who are just getting started. Not only does this book feature important guidelines for preparing courses, facilitating communication, and using technology, but it also provides activities and assessments geared specifically toward the teaching of psychology. As the only online teaching book focused exclusively on psychology, this book will guide you through the entire process of online teaching, including planning, preparing, and launching your course, facilitating communication, using technology, and assigning grades. This book will also suggest content and activities that will facilitate a successful psychology course, including discussion questions and group assignments. We hope that the book will encourage some level of standardization across psychology departments to help delineate guidelines for training faculty, setting up online courses, and assigning grades. Consistency in the way that the subject is taught can help students more easily transition from course to course or from program to program, leading to more positive learning outcomes.

This book focuses broadly upon psychology education at the undergraduate level, and also features a special chapter on advanced applications to graduate students and professionals. Dr. Neff draws from her background of teaching online undergraduate courses, while Dr. Donaldson draws from his extensive experience delivering online education to graduate students and working professionals across the globe. The reader will note that this book fuses pedagogical theories and research with the authors' own online teaching experiences. As with any newly emerging research area, the available peer-reviewed literature is somewhat limited, and therefore, anecdotes and tips from the authors are provided to help supplement and enhance the reader's experience, such as advice for managing student email overload, tips for creating effective grading schedules, and anecdotes about dealing with student concerns and issues. Throughout the text, the authors address the numerous components of teaching online, including teaching philosophies and styles, procedural elements of course implementation, and technical instructions, where applicable.

This book features a synthesis of theory, research, and anecdotes designed to maximize your abilities as an online instructor. Whether you are a seasoned pro in the online arena, or considering whether or not to prepare your first course, there are tips and tricks in this book that can help improve your instruction, reduce your preparation time, and enhance your students' success. This book should scaffold your knowledge such that each chapter builds and enhances the knowledge presented in the previous chapter. Every chapter is organized according to three central components: purpose, implementation, and troubleshooting. The *purpose* part of the chapter serves as an introduction to the key concepts, featuring theory, research, and practical information about how and why these concepts matter for your course. The *implementation* section gets down to the more procedural and technical nuts and bolts of online teaching, whether you are developing good discussion questions or creating a video lecture. Finally, the *troubleshooting* section at the end of each chapter will address key problems that arise in that particular area, as well as techniques for potential solutions.

The chapters in the book follow the natural progression of the key elements of teaching psychology online. Chapter 1 introduces the current trends in online psychology, focusing on the wide range of applications to undergraduate, graduate, K-12, and organizational training. Chapter 2 focuses on planning, preparing, and launching your online course, with tips for successfully navigating the pitfalls and starting off on the right foot! Chapter 3 addresses communication between students and instructor, a key component of online learning, including how to build and foster an online learning community. Chapter 4 highlights the various modes of technology and multimedia and how to integrate them into your course, including online lecture videos, podcasting, blogging, wikis, social networking sites, as well as a discussion of the course management system itself. Chapter 5 focuses on best practices for creating activities for online psychology courses, as advised by both research and theory. Chapter 6 deals with assessment and grading, including rubrics for discussion and online testing questions and concerns. Chapter 7 steps away from the more technical elements to look towards future directions and trends in online education, with a focus on applied learning, non-traditional students and doctoral level education. Throughout the book, text boxes are provided that organize and highlight important tips and information. An accompanying website, http://www.TeachingPsychologyOnline.com will provide readers with updated information, new tips and tricks, technological developments, and links to peer-reviewed articles and other resources as they become available.

ACKNOWLEDGMENTS

Finally, we would like to thank Debra Riegert, Jessica Lauffer, Hannah Slater, and the team at EVS for helping us develop this manuscript and steering it through the production process. Special thanks to David Fetterman (Fetterman & Associates, San Jose, CA), Kenneth C. Elliott (University of Maine at Augusta), David W. Carroll (University of Wisconsin-Superior), Blaine Peden (University of Wisconsin-Eau Claire), and Suzanne C. Baker (James Madison University) who provided very helpful peer reviews.

CHAPTER 1

INTRODUCTION TO TEACHING PSYCHOLOGY ONLINE

WELCOME!

Welcome to the future of psychology training and education! By deciding to read this book, you have embraced the reality that psychology education is in the process of expanding beyond the traditional classroom-based setting into the great digital universe. Classroom-based instruction is likely to always be an important component of higher education, but new teaching modalities are emerging that are pushing psychology instruction at all levels into a new realm that is unique to the 21st century and to our current context. Consider that in the mid-1990s, the notion of online education was almost unheard of. The proposition that an individual could obtain a college degree, or at least complete part of his or her coursework, by sitting at a computer terminal probably seemed absurd. In 2012, we are undergoing one of the largest transitions in education, with far-reaching implications for the delivery of not only undergraduate psychology education, but also for K-12 education, graduate education, professional development and lifelong learning, as well as workplace development and training. Perhaps in 2025, a time without online education will seem as equally preposterous as the idea of online education would have done in the mid-1990s. Quite simply, we are in the midst of one of the greatest transformational periods in the history of education. The tips, tricks, and advice featured in this book will help you more easily navigate this new virtual landscape, and guide you to create, launch, and succeed as an online psychology educator.

WHY WE WROTE THIS BOOK

The authors of this book have diverse but complementary experiences as psychology educators. Dr. Kelly Neff has spent several years teaching undergraduate psychology online, and has developed, created, and launched her own courses. She possesses insights into the process of combining online components into traditional course formats, and has witnessed first-hand how learning online can boost student achievement. As a doctoral student and first-time online educator, Neff learned quickly that excellent online instruction requires a deeper understanding than simply posting course materials online. Using techniques to motivate student achievement through mentoring and communication, Neff has developed highly successful courses which attract hundreds of students per year across the United States, Europe, and Asia. Neff hopes that new online instructors who use this book can avoid many of the first-time glitches and problems that she experienced. In fact, this is the one book that Neff wished she *could* have read when she started teaching online!

Dr. Stewart Donaldson has taught psychology at the undergraduate, graduate, and professional training levels for more than 25 years. Five years ago, Donaldson developed a distance education certificate program and a wide range of online courses, online workshops, online professional talks, and online conferences for graduate students and working professionals. Donaldson's distance education offerings in applied psychology have been attended by thousands of participants from all across the globe. He and his online support team have learned many valuable lessons about how to teach psychology online. He is thrilled to join forces with Dr. Neff to share what he has learned about teaching psychology to students distributed across time and space.

The authors developed this book project not only out of a need experienced in our own teaching careers, but also in response to the surprising absence of a peer-reviewed literature on how to best train and educate online psychology instructors. The available materials are often fragmented, and not targeted specifically at our discipline of psychology. One reviewer of online faculty training argues that "online faculty development is still in its infancy" (Lowenthal, 2008, p. 351). Others have noted that due to the growth in the number of online students, some institutions offer online instruction "without necessarily having staff competent in all aspects of online pedagogy" (Sims, Dobbs, & Hand, 2002, p. 136). This type of "sink or swim" philosophy can create unwarranted pressure for instructors who are seeking to enhance their traditional course offerings using online components, or for those who are looking to create brand new online courses. This book provides accessible and insightful guidance for those instructors looking to launch their best possible online course. Our goal is to mitigate and reduce the pressures and anxieties of online teaching by taking a positive, hands-on approach. We embrace the values of online education, and strongly believe that anyone who teaches psychology can also teach psychology online, using the guidance and tips presented in this book.

This book best prepares online psychology educators because, unlike nearly all available online teacher training materials, it is *specific* to our discipline. Not only does this book feature important guidelines for preparing courses, facilitating communication, and using technology, but it also provides activities and assessments geared specifically toward the teaching of psychology. As the only online teaching book focused exclusively on psychology, this book will guide you through the entire process of online teaching, and will help suggest content and activities that will facilitate a successful psychology course. Because, let's face it, psychology is a special discipline, and teaching it well usually involves a unique set of skills and a comprehensive knowledge base.

Psychology Is FUN and Important to Teach!

For a variety of reasons, psychology courses are some of the most fun, engaging, and valuable courses to teach. First, psychology has been extraordinarily successful at attracting the next generation of social scientists into the discipline. The growth of interest in psychology during the past three decades is striking, as psychology has become one of the most popular majors on college campuses across the United States (Donaldson, Berger, & Pezdek, 2006). Second, psychology is relevant to everyone's lives, from undergraduates, to graduates, to professionals, to instructors. With a broad range of topics, including human sexuality, political change, happiness, organizational leadership, power dynamics, health and wellness, persuasion, and financial decision making, the discipline is extremely appealing and exciting to learn about. For example, at Harvard University, positive psychology has overtaken economics as the most popular course on campus. It is hardly surprising then, that many career opportunities are afforded to students who are trained in psychology (Donaldson et al., 2006). Knowledge and application of the latest psychological findings can benefit a wide variety of professionals across disciplines and lead to improved workplace performance.

WHY TEACH PSYCHOLOGY *ONLINE?*

There are a number of benefits to transitioning psychology courses to the online classroom, or to using online materials to supplement your traditional courses. First, teaching online provides access to a larger, more diverse student population. A traditional classroom is limited to only those people who reside within a reasonable commuting distance from the institution, who can also afford to pay for transportation and arrange for childcare/time away from work. Individuals who share the same geographical location may also share similar attitudes and cultural/social norms. Given that teaching psychology often involves critical analysis of culture, society, and ideas, when all students in the class are from roughly the same background it can sometimes limit the depth and breadth of in-class discourse. However, an online class provides access to a larger, more diverse student population than could be possible with a face-to-face lecture. Online education therefore levels the playing field in terms of socioeconomic status, where students can join the course without sacrificing work hours, childcare responsibilities, and transportation costs. The online teaching of psychology also eliminates the requirements for geographic proximity, broadening the student body to include students across state lines, in different cultures, and even from different countries. In the authors' experiences, the integration of students from across the world into a single psychology course adds tremendous insight and excitement for students.

Furthermore, online courses enable instructors to facilitate student interaction at a much more competent and comprehensive level than evidenced in the classroom. Imagine a large lecture hall with 100 students. In your experience, how many of these students will raise their hand and speak out during your lectures? If your experience is anything like that of the authors, then probably not many students will engage in an active way. Face-to-face lecture courses do not always enable student interaction in a comfortable, stress-free setting. Often, only certain extraverted, confident, secure students will elect to participate and share their views in front of so many of their peers, leaving the shy or insecure students with little opportunity to create discourse. The online learning environment removes the social pressure and anxiety from classroom interactions. On the online discussion board, it is almost impossible to distinguish the shy "back row" students from the talkative "front row" students. Suddenly, all students have equal opportunities to voice their thoughts in an open forum without embarrassment or fear of reprisal. This is one of the most common positive features for students of online courses: They appear to enjoy chatting online about the course material! And why wouldn't they, considering that this current generation of college students (and all those after it) have grown up utilizing online communication as their premier source of social interaction? Suddenly, psychology courses can transition from a faculty member delivering a lecture, to a large group of students creating new ideas, analyzing theory, thinking critically, and developing their own conclusions.

Online courses are not only great for stimulating growth in psychology students, but they are also wonderful for an academic psychologist's schedule. If your online course is implemented using some of the tips in this book, then you should have more time to yourself to focus on publications, presentations, and other academic projects. You may spend less time in an office, less time in a car/bus/train commuting, and save money on your transportation costs. Just thinking about that extra time to yourself probably makes you giddy with excitement. However, it is important to remember that online teaching can be a process of trial and error, and over time, you will probably figure out the strategies that work best for you!

Finally, teaching online is not only time and cost effective for you, but it is also very efficient for your academic institution. During these times of massive budget crises, particularly at public universities and community colleges, this argument alone should be sufficient to prompt administrators to provide online course options. Online courses require no facilities and maintenance services; they do not require electricity; nor do they require any infrastructure at all other than what is afforded by the registrar and the technology services that support the online interface. It is possible to enroll many more students into a single online class than is possible with a single face-to-face lecture. This phenomenon reflects supply and demand. An online course in California can appeal to not only those students who live close to the university, but also to students across the nation and world. Suddenly, many more students can be accommodated into a single classroom, at minimal additional cost to the institution. A highly rated online psychology instructor can become a successful, marketable brand, bringing in a variety of students from multiple institutions.

THE DIFFERENT ONLINE APPLICATIONS OF PSYCHOLOGY EDUCATION

While the majority of attention in the online teaching literature has focused on courses delivered to college undergraduates, psychology can also be taught online at any level or age range. Many opportunities are arising, including K-12 education, graduate education, and professional training initiatives. Psychology and its related components are taught across a variety of contexts extending far beyond college undergraduate education, and thus there are benefits to transitioning these to online education as well. Consider the following avenues for application (chapter 7 of this book will focus on advanced applications to professional training and beyond).

K-12 EDUCATION: MOVING ONLINE?

A burgeoning trend in K-12 education involves the integration of online education components. A February 2010 report published by Simba Information and Market Data Retrieval shows that about one-third of public K-12 schools in the United States already have some kind of online education program, and an additional 20% will offer these programs during the 2011–2012 school year. This means that by 2012, over half of all public schools in the United States will feature online learning components. In New York City, for example, a project known as *Innovation Zone*, or *I-Zone* was proposed for the Fall 2010 school year that would see nearly 80 public schools deliver a large amount of formerly classroom-based instruction online (Gonen, 2010). This type of instruction takes many different forms, including using online instruction for independent study and Advanced Placement courses in high schools, a blended learning model where online instruction will be delivered in the classroom, and elementary and middle schools piloting software that enables teachers to tailor math and reading lessons to the educational needs of each student.

ONLINE GRADUATE EDUCATION

Online graduate programs are currently on the rise, with over 600 online graduate degree programs currently offered in the social sciences alone (according to the website www.Gradschools.com). These programs include courses offered by some of the most prestigious universities in the United States, such as Harvard, MIT, and Stanford. Online graduate degrees in psychology exhibit the same depth and breadth as traditional offerings, including programs dedicated to clinical psychology, sex therapy, organizational psychology, educational and school psychology, developmental psychology, social and personality psychology, applied behavior analysis, sports psychology, and psychoanalysis. While the majority of online psychology degrees feature master's programs (around 400), there are also nearly 200 online doctoral programs in psychology, including those offered by Philadelphia University and Arizona State University. Instructors working with online graduate programs in psychology can definitely benefit from the many tips and tricks in this book, with a particular focus on the advanced applications chapter.

Psychology and Organizational Training

Psychological principles are also often utilized in workplace training initiatives meant to open up dialogue, promote respect and tolerance, and educate employees about harassment or other policies. As educators, it is important that we do not overlook these training sessions as an arena to provide high quality online education. For example, Zembylas (2008) argues that an online program to reduce cultural discrimination and increase diversity can utilize online communication and engagement to promote the reframing of previous beliefs and stereotypes. The creation of an online learning community is especially important for these types of training programs as a means of encouraging support, shared goals, and dialogue about the issues at hand.

Likewise, universities that offer professional development or certificate training in psychology can also benefit from offering these online. From an applied online course in grant writing, to an online certificate in hypnosis, advanced training in psychology has certainly made the jump to the online arena. Based upon this discussion then, it is clear that online psychology education can extend far beyond the undergraduate Psych 101 realm to include K-12 participants, graduate degree programs, and diversity/career training sessions.

Roadmap of this Book

This book features a synthesis of theory, research, and anecdotes designed to maximize your abilities as an online psychology instructor. Whether you are a seasoned pro in the online arena, or a newbie just dipping your feet in, there are tips and tricks in this book that can help improve your instruction, reduce your preparation time, and enhance your students' success. This book should scaffold your knowledge such that each chapter builds and enhances the knowledge presented in the previous chapter. Every chapter is organized according to three central components: purpose, implementation, and troubleshooting. The *purpose* part of the chapter serves as an introduction to the key concepts, featuring theory, research, and practical information about how and why these concepts matter for your course. The *implementation* section gets down to the more procedural and technical "nuts and bolts" of online teaching, whether you are developing good discussion questions or creating a lecture video. Finally, the *troubleshooting* section at the end of each chapter will address key problems that arise in that particular area, as well as techniques for potential solutions.

This book begins by highlighting the basic procedural elements required to create, prepare, and launch a successful online psychology course. What special considerations are required when creating an online version of your course? The importance of good planning and careful execution are presented at length at the beginning of chapter 2. The chapter then goes on to discuss the many decisions you will be required to make, including selecting hybrid versus fully online courses, creating your course schedule, assigning due dates, choosing the right class size, and delivering an effective course orientation and syllabus. Potential problems that you might encounter in the new learning environment are discussed next, with solutions provided for dealing with emails, and with the change that is sometimes exhibited when students learn online, known as *online disinhibition*.

Once you are able to prepare and launch an online course, chapter 3 hones in on your next step as an instructor: facilitating excellent communication between students. Theory and research surrounding the notion of an "online learning community" are discussed, along with potential implications for your courses. How does one create an online learning community? How does one facilitate successful online discussions? These questions will be addressed using research as well as the author's anecdotes and experiences. Using the techniques set out in this chapter, professors can ensure that online discussions maintain the same or a better level of quality, critical thinking, and insight compared with face-to-face discussions. Troubleshooting tips are discussed with a focus on how you can best communicate and give help when your students are in need.

Now that you are able to launch your course and communicate with your students, it is time to consider the wealth of available technology that can supplement and enhance your course. To highlight the importance of technology and multimedia, chapter 4 begins with a discussion of the current media use habits of our students. Technical descriptions are then provided regarding the use of Blackboard and Moodle, the two most commonly used course management systems (CMSs) in higher education. Then, you will receive step-by-step tips for integrating multimedia into your course, from creating and posting online lecture videos, to making audio podcasts, writing blogs, designing collaborative wikis, and integrating your course into social networking websites. Finally, the chapter will address two issues that many online psychology instructors should remain aware of, pertaining to the ownership of the intellectual property of your online course, and the use of copyrighted material.

At this stage, you should be feeling comfortable with the procedural elements involved in creating a course, communicating with students, and integrating technology and multimedia. Chapter 5 will focus your attention on best practices for creating activities for psychology courses. First, this chapter addresses how activities can be translated into the online learning environment, and how teaching theories like Bloom's taxonomy can help inform activity development. Then, this chapter presents the types of possible activities and how to implement them with success. What happens if you get stuck or can't come up with an idea? Links to web-based resources and databases that house these activities will be offered to readers, with resources from across the discipline (including social, positive, developmental, sexuality, biological, and statistics).

Once you are able to create, implement, and grade online psychology assessments, you should be ready to take on the task of administering online assessments including papers, quizzes, and tests. Chapter 6 discusses the creation of learning objectives in psychology, and how the assessment, testing, and grading of online psychology students leads to new challenges and opportunities for professors. One of the central issues here surrounds the accuracy and legitimacy of online testing and online discussions. The authors argue that through using the tips presented in the chapter, online testing can function similarly to face-to-face testing and provide a satisfying and acceptable method for assessing student performance. What are the best types of online test questions? How should they be disseminated? These issues are addressed here, as well as troubleshooting potential pitfalls of plagiarism and academic dishonesty.

In the final chapter, we will step back from the procedural and technical elements to broadly explore future directions of online psychology education. How is online education opening up new frontiers for nontraditional students? How can online psychology be harnessed to deliver quality graduate and doctoral level education? Then, let us consider the not so distant future and the changing landscape of education at all levels. What kind of impact will online learning have upon our future academic departments, institutions, and funding? How can we effectively train other instructors to become great online teachers? This chapter closes with an analysis of future trends, including how the shifting demographic and economic factors in the United States are paving the way for the future of online psychology education.

CHAPTER 2

PLANNING, PREPARING, AND LAUNCHING YOUR COURSE

Get excited! It's time to plan and prepare your online psychology course. As you proceed through the book, you will notice that the many tips and tricks provided have been compiled from a variety of sources. The authors conducted an extensive literature review in hopes of uncovering published research on online pedagogical strategies, especially those specific to the social sciences and psychology. However, in this newly emerging area of research and thinking, often there is quite simply a lack of peer-reviewed evidence to best guide our readings. Where existing research and theory is not available, the authors share their opinions, based upon past online teaching experiences. Please note that we (the authors) certainly cannot claim to know everything about teaching psychology online! Opinions, thoughts, and past experiences are provided for you to use as illustrative tools for how to solve problems, approach certain situations, and create and implement content. In other words, while we believe that we give good advice (we hope!), it is nonetheless up to you to create your own path in your online career. Some strategies might work wonderfully for you; and in other instances you might discover your own method that builds from something that you read, but that works even better. Always do what feels right for you, and trust your gut—it is your course and your career after all!

In the same vein, also try to keep an open mind as you read these subsequent chapters. Please don't feel daunted or intimidated about teaching psychology online. This book is filled with a wealth of information, but you are by no means required to use all of it in your course! Try to experiment to find out what elements are best incorporated into your course, but don't let yourself become overwhelmed if you feel as though you are trying to fit square pegs into round holes. Yes, it's true that online courses require preparation, technical skills, and attention, but this is no different from what is required in a traditional face-to-face course. We strongly feel that while online teaching may require a slightly different, revised skill set, your online workload will probably be equivalent to the work required to create and launch a traditional lecture. We hope that by reading this book, the experience will become less stressful, and your time commitment will be smaller than when you create and administer your face-to-face lectures. As with all pedagogical efforts, practice makes better, and the more effort you put into honing your online teaching skills, the easier the process will become.

PURPOSE: PREPARATION IS VITAL

Imagine a common experience: You arrive to your lecture on the first day of class. The intention is simple: Make a good first impression, distribute your syllabus, and explain to the students what is expected from them in order to successfully complete the course. Now imagine you just woke up with cold sweats after having a nightmare about your first day: The syllabus is written in a different language, or worse, you've forgotten it all together. You come across as disorganized, confused, and become a laughing stock with the student body. In this nightmare situation, you are faced with challenging levels of damage control if you are to reestablish yourself as a confident, competent leader and educator.

While first day jitters are common, a full-on nightmare situation like the one described above would rarely happen to a seasoned professor. However, even the most experienced instructor can experience difficulties in an online course if the materials are not prepared and presented according to a detailed plan. Consider the many reasons why an online course requires detailed attention to planning. First, the traditional classroom environment is a familiar setting that the majority of your students have participated in since kindergarten. They are accustomed to sitting in a room, staring up at the teacher, who is telling them what they need to know. They write down what the teacher says, read the book, and take a quiz. This is a usual learning pattern that many students have followed for years and years. Online, you are creating a new learning environment and must set boundaries, rules, and expectations for that environment that may feel unique and unfamiliar to both yourself and your students (at least, in the beginning). With no teacher in the room to stare up at, many online students are required to take a much more active engagement in their learning.

Second, traditional students attend class each week—this is how instructors are able to measure their levels of commitment and engagement in the course. Online students, on the other hand, never physically attend class. Therefore assignments (such as discussions, papers, and quizzes) become central to your ability to gauge student commitment and performance. If the student does not complete any assignments in a week, as an instructor you might equate this with cutting a week's worth of class. As such, from the beginning of class students ought to be aware of (a) what is expected of them, (b) how they are to complete their assignments, and (c) when those assignments are due.

Third and finally, in the classroom it is easy to communicate to rectify mistakes. A student asks a question, you answer it verbally, and then if other students did not pay attention to your response, their subsequent mistakes are their own responsibility due to lack of attention or attendance. Online, students often ask the same questions via email, and unlike the traditional classroom, you may receive the same question 20 times in 15 minutes. Personal emails are often required because mass emails or mass discussion posts directed to all students do not always rectify individual problems. Not every student checks his or her email or the discussion board regularly, and some students have specific issues or questions about grades or course status. Therefore, mistakes in your syllabus and assignments must be rectified before the start of class to avoid communication problems.

A successful online course is most likely one that is created and uploaded by the time that the course starts. While it is possible to create course materials and post them on a weekly basis, students who choose to work ahead may become frustrated with this approach. Further, if you are not able to keep up your share of the weekly work, you could end up creating false expectations. Even if you intend to maintain a weekly uploading schedule, events that are out of your control can happen such as sickness, family issues, heavy workload, or internet/technical problems that can skew your schedule. Launching the course *before* the first week of class ends is one of the best ways to minimize complications during the semester. When you first create your course, consider adopting the *test, test, test* philosophy.

Although it applies to your students as well, the test, test, test philosophy is specifically aimed toward you, the instructor! For the course to function properly, you may have to do a share of homework, too! And for the online instructor, homework happens *before the course has even started*. So, what is a good strategy for you to test, test, test? Well once the course has been scheduled, choose your assignments, and decide on strict due dates. Try to adopt a student's perspective and engage with the materials as if you were seeing them for the first time. Ask yourself some key questions: "Does this make sense?" "Is this assignment ambiguous?" "Are the expectations clear?" If you think that there might be problems, then your students may very well have problems.

Consider the following example: You create a discussion board for your online Introduction to Psychology class. You want the students to discuss gender stereotypes, so you create the following prompt: "*What is a gender stereotype? Who uses gender stereotypes? How do gender stereotypes play out in the real world? Give an example from your past experiences.*" While this prompt may make sense to the instructor, it is missing a few elements that online students might look for. First, how many discussion posts are required? How long do posts need to be? Do posts need to address all parts of the question? Do posts need to be in response to another student's comments? These are procedural issues that you might want to explicitly clarify when you create an online assignment. A better prompt before your discussion question would look something like this

---

2.1 SAMPLE DISCUSSION PROMPT

Please make two posts. Each post must be one paragraph long (4 sentences or more). One of your posts must be in response to another student's comments. You can create a new thread or respond to a preexisting thread. Across your two posts, you must answer all parts of the question to receive full credit.

While this is the format that the authors prefer to use, there is a vast array of other formats for discussion assignments, which are discussed in chapter 5. Regardless of the format that you select, try to remain consistent across your assignments to adhere to student expectations and avoid confusion. In the case that you want to create an assignment that does not adhere to the regulations that you had previously outlined, you may want to explicitly state: "*The rules for this discussion board are different from your previous discussion board assignments.*"

IMPLEMENTATION: CHOOSE YOUR OWN ADVENTURE

One of the greatest benefits to online teaching and learning is that it enables the instructor to have greater latitude for deciding course structure. In a traditional classroom, similar teaching and assessment methods are often deployed: More often than not, these involve some combination of exams and papers, due at specific intervals during the semester. In the virtual learning environment, assignments are usually due every week to ensure that students stay on track with their learning. Thus, the instructor can decide which types of assignments will be assigned to certain course materials; for example, a quiz one week, a discussion the next, then a video or a blog. This ability to specifically tailor course assignments enables you to create a unique online course, different from all other psychology courses offered in your subject areas. As an online instructor, you have the opportunity to really put a special stamp on your course and the way it is taught. In the following section, several key components of online course building will be discussed. You are by no means required to integrate all of these elements in your course, but it is hoped that this discussion provides useful insight into the many procedural and technical elements implicated in the course creation process. Just remember, as the course creator and instructor, many of the decisions regarding these are yours alone; so choose your own adventure (and choose wisely)!

BLENDED VS. FULLY ONLINE COURSES

One of the first issues to consider when planning your online course is whether your course will be fully online, or whether it will be comprised of online and traditional classroom elements. Courses that combine traditional classroom meetings with online components are known as *blended* or, hybrid classes. What distinguishes a fully online course from a blended course? In their survey of online education in the United States, the Sloan Consortium defines an *online course* as one where 80% or more of the course content is delivered online, usually with no face-to-face contact (Allen & Seaman, 2010). According to the Sloan report, a *blended* (or hybrid) course is one where 30 to 79% of the course content is delivered online. Blended courses typically feature online discussions and a reduced number of face-to-face class meetings. Blended courses are different from *web facilitated* courses, which deliver 1 to 29% of their content online and use technology (such as posting a syllabus on a course management system) to better facilitate their face-to-face course.

Are blended courses better for students than fully online courses? A number of research studies comparing the performance of students in blended versus fully online courses have not demonstrated any significant differences between the two formats. In their meta-analytic review of 10 studies comparing blended and online courses, Means and colleagues (Means, Toyama, Murphy, Bakia, & Jones, 2009) found that seven studies showed no significant differences in student performance across online and blended formats, two studies showed statistically significant benefits for online instruction over blended instruction (Campbell, Gibson, Hall, Richards, & Callery, 2008; Poirier & Feldman, 2004), and one showed benefits of blended instruction (Keefe, 2003). Authors of the meta-analytic review warned that differences in course content and quality of instruction across the studies being compared were most likely responsible for the variation in the success of online or blended courses. However, when the same review compared 51 effect sizes regarding the difference in student performance between online and face-to-face instruction, 11 were significantly positive in favor of better outcomes for online or blended learning over face-to-face learning, while only two were significant in favor of face-to-face learning over online or blended learning.

Taken as a whole, this meta-analytic review commissioned and published by the U.S. Government (the most comprehensive review conducted to date on student performance across online, blended, and hybrid courses) showed that students tend to perform better in online or blended courses in comparison with face-to-face courses, while differences between online and blended courses are marginal. An experimental study by Parker and Martin (2010) demonstrated that students in fully online courses report higher levels of interactivity, usefulness, and synchronicity than their counterparts in blended courses featuring the same material.

Research and evaluation is vital to determine which types of courses are best suited to online, hybrid or face-to-face formats (Sprague, Maddux, Ferdig, & Albion, 2007). Which psychology courses should be taught as a traditional, blended, or fully online course? In terms of investigations into the effectiveness of online, hybrid, and face-to-face psychology instruction, research is particularly sparse. Dell, Low, and Wilker (2010) compared online and face-to-face instruction across human development and educational psychology courses. They found no significant differences in the quality of work submitted by students in the online versus traditional class. Rather, the authors argued that the platform (online or face-to-face) was not as important for student performance as the instructional strategies employed, a finding echoing past research by Bernard and colleagues (2004). These suggested strategies include effective interaction with the instructor, active learning, application of knowledge, facilitation of self-regulations, and high expectations. In an older study by Waschull (2001), students who chose to take an introduction to psychology class face-to-face got better grades than students who chose to take the course online. However, these results should be interpreted with caution since the online section of the course featured no online discussions whatsoever (only written lectures, relevant websites, and article assignments). Locating other studies that compare psychology courses across face-to-face, blended, and online formats has been challenging.

Now think about your own psychology course: Would you prefer to teach a blended, fully online, or face-to-face web facilitated section?

Sometimes, the instructor will be given the choice of which type of class to teach. Other times, the college or university will decide whether the course will be online, blended, or traditional, and then assign instructors accordingly. Blended courses certainly have value in their ability to bridge the gap between the classroom and online learning environments. In a blended course, students may attend lectures, and then return home to complete selected modules online. Professors can assign quizzes and tests to be given in the classroom or taken online.

One of the benefits of experience with teaching online is that traditional lecture classes can be easily transformed into web-facilitated or blended courses. For example, Dr. Neff recently taught a Psychology of Sexuality course featuring over 100 students that was just too large to facilitate open communication across all of the students in the classroom at once. Particularly given the sensitive subject area, some students did not want to discuss topics while physically in front of their peers. The solution to facilitating student interaction became clear: Assign online discussions as a way of engaging those who did not feel comfortable talking about sensitive issues in front of their peers! Indeed, by the end of the semester, many students were thankful for this opportunity, stating that the online component allowed them to participate in a way that would not have been possible otherwise.

Scheduling

As an instructor, you get to make the fundamental decision of when materials will be covered and assignments will be due. Once you decide on your course schedule, try to stick with your plan (just as you would in a face-to-face course). There are many ways to schedule an online course. Based upon their experiences, the authors have found it most useful to divide the course material into separate 7-day weeks, corresponding with each week that the course will be offered. So, if you are teaching an 8-week online course, you might have 1 week of introduction or orientation, followed by 7 weeks of material, and possibly finishing with a final exam (if you decide to have a final exam). If your college or university has a final exam schedule, then your final exam might not fall during your last week of the course, but during the predetermined final exam week. If you do not have a final exam schedule, you might want to consider assigning 1 week of orientation, 6 weeks of course material, and 1 week for final exam review and assessment. Alternatively, if your materials do not fit into a 6-week time span, you could assign 1 week to orientation, 7 weeks to material, and hold the cumulative final exam at the end of the final week. Remember, your online class does not need to have a final exam unless your college or university allots the time for a final or recommends that you assign a final. The decision is totally yours.

The division of the weekly course material also happens entirely at your discretion. Consider grouping similar elements into the same week, especially if your class is short and you need to chunk material. So, for a 6-week psychology of sexuality course, the instructor could assign all of the material on sexual behavior (sexual expression and the paraphilias) into 1 week, and then all of the material relating to sexual health (such as sexual dysfunction, STI transmission, and contraception) into the next week. This enables consistency and allows for exercises connecting a range of similar topics during the same week. However, in a 15-week psychology of sexuality course, each of these topics could be covered in a different week (1 week for dysfunction, 1 week for contraception, etc.). When you schedule your online course, try to consider the amount of time you have, the amount and type of material, and the varieties of online assignments you envision as corresponding with each week.

When scheduling the course, you may also want to factor in time for holidays and breaks. If you know that there is a week allotted to spring break, or a break that lasts a few days or more, you could potentially avoid assigning materials to be covered during that week (if your schedule permits). Even though students technically could complete the material during the break, they might appreciate adhering to the same vacation schedule as their counterparts in face-to-face classes. This way, they should not harbor ill will at being "required" to work during the holiday, when everyone else is on vacation. Likewise, some students relish holidays and breaks as a great time to catch up on work, or work ahead. Thus, a lull from course assignments during the holiday or break could enable those students to work through the course material at their own pace. Likewise, when there is just one holiday during the week that the school observes (such as Veteran's Day) then it is probably not necessary to cancel class materials for that entire week.

DUE DATES

Online students seem to benefit from having a specific assignment schedule that explains what is expected of them, and when their work is due. For example, in a survey of learning attitudes in a sample of online students in a large-sized class, Berry (2009) found that 25% of students reported that remembering deadlines and due dates was one of the most difficult aspects of online learning. Choosing a specific day when all assignments are due and informing the class repeatedly of this throughout term ("Remember, you have an assignment due every Thursday") could help to create that level of steady consistency and encourage students to adjust their schedules accordingly.

How would making all assignments due on one day per week play out? Imagine that during the first week of class (which usually begins on a Monday) an assignment is due on Friday. After the assignments for the first week are submitted, the second week of course materials would begin on Saturday. Assignments from Week 2 would then be due on the following Friday, and so on.

While Friday is often an intuitively appealing due date to select, as the instructor you can choose any day of the week as your due date, so long as you make it well known to your students. Consider how long it takes you to grade these assignments. If assignments are due on Friday, you might spend your whole weekend grading these so that they are ready for Monday. In the authors' experience, Wednesday works well as a due date. Assignments submitted online on Wednesday can be graded on Thursday and Friday, freeing up the weekend for other work or life activities and enabling students to review their grades quickly after that module. If your workload permits, try to grade all online assignments within 1 to 2 weeks after they are due. Recall that grading online assignments can often be time consuming, and students may expect to see their grades posted within a few days after their assignment due date. If you do not indicate when assignments will be returned, you might start to receive multiple emails after a few days, such as, "Did you receive my assignment? I haven't seen a grade and so I am not sure it was processed correctly, please help!" If you plan to take one month to return all assignments that is fine too—but just try to make sure your students are aware of this.

Another factor to consider when scheduling your class is not only the day of the week that the assignment is due, but also, the specific time of day. You will find that no matter what time of day you select, a large percentage of online students will wait until the very last minute to submit their assignment. The authors have found that 11:59 p.m. works as a suitable submission time, meaning that so long as the assignment is submitted at some time on the date that it is due, it is accepted. According to Berry (2009), online students tend to prefer to submit their assignments in the evenings, with 41% reporting "evenings" (5–9:00 p.m.) as their preferred submission time and 33% indicating "late night" (9:00 p.m.–midnight). The evening preference has also been mirrored in the authors' previous courses, with approximately one-third of students submitting their assignments during the last hour, after 11 p.m. During your course orientation, discussed later in this chapter, try to remind students that if they wait until the last minute to submit, and then experience some kind of technical problems, that they might not receive an extension. This could help deter at least some students from waiting until the last minute to submit their assignments.

Also recall that this is cyberspace, and not all students are in the same time zone as the instructor. This happens frequently in online courses as some students live in other parts of the United States or even in other countries. Just this past semester a student living in Honolulu (us, jealous?) tried to submit her first assignment at 11:55 p.m. Hawaiian time, only to realize that she was 2 hours late, as the assignment was due in Pacific time. Being her first error, the instructor took off a few points for lateness but did allow her to submit and gave her partial credit. However, a repeated offense could have been met with no credit.

On the subject of late assignments, the authors have found that online courses can benefit from strict lateness policies. As mentioned earlier, the timely submission of assignments is one of the key ways to gauge student engagement and progress in online courses. Thus, when a student does not submit his or her assignment on time, this is an indication that the student may not be keeping up-to-date in the course. You can use your course orientation to solidify the importance of the timing of the due dates. Sometimes, students will receive one reprieve for their first lateness offense (such as our Hawaiian friend, above) but afterwards late assignments might not be accepted unless a valid, verifiable excuse is provided. It can be much more difficult to validate excuses for online students, and therefore, making assignments available weeks in advance is a great way to ensure that students have ample time to submit. Assessment and due dates are discussed in greater depth in chapter 5.

CLASS SIZE

Another factor to consider when planning your online course is the size of your class. Sometimes the instructor can dictate the class size, whereas other times, the college or university has the final say. Unlike face-to-face instruction where the professor can instantly clear up discrepancies and problems, online courses often require individual emails and discussion board posts to make the same corrections or solve the same problems. Now consider the increased workload required to teach a large online class of 150 students or more, versus 30 students. Online educators such as Berry (2009) have argued that there are "substantial" differences present when teaching greater than 150 students, compared with teaching only 20 or 30. If you find yourself teaching a large class, Berry (2009) suggests four ways to better cope with your increased workload: (a) shift to a learner focus, (b) build trust and personalize the course, (c) establish deadlines, and

(d) deal with online testing. Although these components matter for any online course, they are especially relevant when the number of students exceeds 150.

1. *Learner Focus*: Just as a professor who lectures creates his or her own lecture notes to guide the lecture, so too can the online professor create learner notes to help guide the student's learning and studying, including guidance on specific topics ("This theory is derived from Festigner's cognitive dissonance theory") and comments ("While this was not discussed in the textbook, you should be familiar with the concept of attitude change from introduction to psychology").

2. *Building Trust*: Students in a large class will have confidence in their instructor's ability to reliably and consistently communicate and solve problems. This level of trust can help to inhibit students from sending frequent unnecessary emails, panicking when a problem arises, or feeling isolated and neglected. Berry argues that trust can be established through three routes: (a) providing a current photo and biography of the instructor, (b) communication through email, and (c) learner notes. The authors agree with this assertion and would consider adding the following to this list: (d) video or audio recording of the professor's lectures or comments, (e) individual feedback on each student paper submitted, and (f) impromptu mentoring and advising, where applicable.

3. *Deadlines*: When online students know when their assignments are due, they will be able to plan ahead and should experience less confusion. With so many students in a large class, publicizing deadlines early on ought to reduce the number of excuses and level of confusion when assignments are due.

4. *Online Testing*: Online testing, discussed in chapter 6, can be an especially arduous task when conducted incorrectly in a large class. There are a number of strategies to engage in which can help make testing easier for large classes, including using multiple choice question formats, making quizzes and tests available weeks in advance, and randomizing questions knowing that students may discuss the exams with their peers.

This discussion begs the questions then of what *is* the ideal size for online psychology courses, 20 students or 200 students? Currently there is no consensus regarding an ideal class size for online instruction in psychology—online class sizes vary considerably across universities and across departments. Currently the American Psychological Association does not provide guidelines for the ideal online class sizes in psychology.

However, a 2008 article in APA's *Monitor on Psychology* reminds us that many face-to-face Introductory Psychology courses are huge and impersonal, often containing several hundred students. Therefore, large online Introductory Psychology classes can often be more interactive and immersive than face-to-face ones (Munsey, 2008).

Depending upon the method of instruction, anecdotal reports have been recorded of successful online courses ranging from 12 to 500 students. Colwell and Jenks (2004) recommend that courses should begin with 20 students at the undergraduate level, and between 15 to 18 students at the graduate level. This is selected as the optimum class size because it provides a sufficient number of students to facilitate discussion, but not so many students that the sense of online community is lost. According to this perspective, additional students should be divided into separate groups of 20. Further, Colwell and Jenks argue that instructors who teach larger sections should be compensated and provided with assistance with grading and communicating (such as an online TA or graduate student). Boettcher (1999) echoes a similar perspective, arguing that the ideal starting point for an online class includes approximately 10 to 14 students.

Generally, the ideal size of an online class relies upon a number of factors. First, Boettcher and Conrad (2004) suggest that instructors should consider the "usual suspect" variables that underlie ideal class size in traditional courses, such as level of content, difficulty, institutional goals, learning objectives, student abilities, and training. They further suggest that additional variables come into play that are unique to online education, including but not limited to: faculty and student expertise with technology, student expectations with online learning, establishment of a virtual community, and faculty willingness to accept a heightened workload. Given that there are currently no discipline specific guidelines for psychology, it seems the best advice for new online psychology instructors to start small (if possible) to increase familiarity and comfort with technology, and develop good habits that can be carried into larger versions of the course (Boettcher, 2010). Crucially, the majority of researchers suggest as the number of students increases by groups of 20, it becomes necessary to separate them into smaller groups to ensure the establishment of virtual communities and effective discussion communication.

The authors maintain extensive experience teaching large online classes. Dr. Neff has taught courses ranging from 45 students at the minimum to a combined course of 150 students at the maximum, while Dr. Donaldson has engaged in professional training courses with several hundred simultaneous participants. It is undoubtedly true that as the number of students in the course increases, so too does the instructor's workload. This is due mostly to the time it takes to communicate with each individual student via email and discussion board. For example, Dr. Neff's first ever class held only 45 students, the minimum size at her academic institution. The following semester, Dr. Neff's course doubled to 90 students, leading the college to offer a teaching assistant/online teaching trainee to assist with administration and grading. In an unexpected twist, training the TA became an additional task, often resulting in several emails and phone calls per week (sometimes per day) from the trainee that required detailed responses. Questions like "How do I create my web page?" which were really irrelevant to the course itself, but related to technology in general, were asked regularly. In this respect, the time spent training the TA could have been spent on grading all those additional assignments. Based on this anecdote, if possible try to gauge your TA's level of technical expertise before you hire him or her, or encourage your institution to offer technology training seminars to all potential TAs.

The author's most recent course was a combination of two sections that exceeded 150 total students. Due to the increased comfort level having developed the course and taught it for three years, this appeared to be a perfectly manageable group of students, so long as they participated in the proper course orientation. Although much of the literature suggests grouping students into minisections of 20 for discussion, she chose to let the entire 150 person strong class interact together to investigate the possibility of large online class sizes. The results were promising. Students multitasked their discussions in an innovative way, conducting several different conversations with several different students on several different topics simultaneously.

Perhaps large discussions are more possible now than ever before, as students have become increasingly accustomed to multiple online interactions, thanks to their frequent usage of social networking websites that facilitate communication, like MySpace, Twitter, and of course, Facebook (these are discussed at length in chapter 4). Imagine that 20 years ago, the average American used to have around 50 friends, and an advanced primate's brain supposedly cannot process more than 99 social relationships simultaneously. However, one look at a student's Facebook page shows how their social worlds have flipped upside down. Some college students right now have thousands of online friends. Being able to manage this many interactions means that some members of the newer crop of online students may be more comfortable with and accustomed to large online class sizes. So in the future, researchers might find a discussion group of 20 to be a conservative estimate for the ideal threshold to establish a sense of community and engage in online discussion. Additional research must be conducted to determine if this effect holds true for incoming psychology students.

The answer to the question of *"What is an ideal online class size?"* remains relatively unclear. For psychology courses specifically, the answer is even more ambiguous. Many introductory courses are massive in size, while other upper-level psychology classes can be very small, so perhaps a similar standard should be applied to the teaching of psychology online. The first step then ought to be considering how large the in-person course is, and gauging whether a transfer to that size in an online class reflects a good fit. Second, Boettcher and Conrad (2004) recommend weighing the expectations of students, faculty, administrators, and society when deciding the size of your online course. For students, how much interaction is appropriate? For faculty, how much of a time commitment will be required? For administrators, what is the desired course size consistent with institutional policies? And finally, in terms of society, what is the best balance of class size that enables lowered costs and enhanced learning outcomes?

We hope that in the immediate future a greater amount of comprehensive research will be conducted to determine ideal class sizes, for psychology as a discipline and beyond. For now, trust your gut: if you become overwhelmed by the emails, discussions, and grading, it might be worth reducing the size of your course in subsequent semesters. Likewise, if you can handle more students, enlarge your class: Your students will be happy for the opportunity to study and your administration will be happy for the extra revenue!

ONLINE ORIENTATION

All courses require some kind of orientation, and certainly, online courses are no exception. Due to the requirement for students to be efficiently familiar with their course management system (CMS), email, and software to succeed in the course, an orientation to the technology featured in the course is especially useful. Students who are new or unfamiliar with the virtual learning environment may require additional steps to increase their comfort with technology. Orientation should incorporate the key elements of the course to leave little room for confusion or ambiguity. The overarching goal of orientation is to provide students with the technical and procedural abilities to successfully complete the course. It is often difficult to instill these during a 1-week training period but instructors can always do their best to ensure that this happens. A good online course orientation should address a series of vital components that scaffold upon each other, building an understanding of the course interface and what it entails.

While there is no exhaustive list of what should or should not be included in an online course orientation, based upon their teaching experiences, the authors recommend addressing some or all of the following components: access, software, policies, assignments and grading (see text box below). While it is true that many of these components will be covered in your syllabus, you might want to consider that (a) students do not always attentively read the syllabus and (b) students need some interactivity to ensure their online knowledge retention. While your orientation should contain some of the procedural elements featured in the syllabus, it can also go beyond the syllabus by providing skills, tactics, and solutions to common problems. You probably want students (especially those new to the online environment) to feel comfortable and confident in their ability to successfully utilize the technology presented in the course. After your orientation, students could benefit from engaging in a lengthy "manipulation check" (discussed below) to ensure that they retain the knowledge of these components and can apply it to the online course environment.

2.2 ONLINE ORIENTATION

Access
To CMS
To Email
To Environment/Discussion Boards
Software

CMS
PowerPoint
QuickTime

Policies
Academic Honesty
Netiquette
Due Dates
Late Assignments

Assignments
Frequency
Due Date
Type
Grading
Rubric
Extra Credit

Access

Gaining access to the course and its components is of central importance for online students. First and foremost is the course management system (CMS) itself. Whether you use Blackboard or Moodle (CMS is discussed in chapter 4), students should be familiar with how to enter the interface and gain access. Where can they locate their login name and password? Do they have to contact technical support or admissions and records to have their account set up? Who should they contact if they cannot log on to the CMS? Students who cannot overcome the initial hurdle of access may drop the course before they can even access the course materials, meaning that they will never actually see the virtual learning environment. This is why you might want to post your orientation (whether it is a video, audio, PowerPoint, or other type of learning module) in other places where your students can see it, including via email, YouTube, Facebook, and your own personal webpage. Also try to include problem-solving information in the first phase of your orientation: "What happens if I can't find my password? What happens if I log in and can't find the course?" Often, academic institutions have online technical support departments for student referral. However, these divisions sometimes take 24 to 48 hours to one week to respond, and sometimes students are better off directing their questions specifically to you.

Consider that for most online courses, students are required to have a university or college sponsored email address to receive correspondence and log-in information. However, some students (particularly new freshman) sometimes have issues even activating these new emails. It could become frustrating for you, and for them. You might send an email through your course that is directed toward their college email address, which they may never access. And in return, "SurferDude89" might be sending you emails asking when his paper is due, that are going straight to you junk email box. To avoid this miscommunication, you could ask students to activate and use their @college email address for their communication in your course. Explain that if they rarely check that account, they can set their preferences (usually options: email forwarding) to forward your messages to the account that they do check. If they are forwarding, preferably this will be to an email address that they can access from a mobile device such as their phone or laptop, this ensures that they will be able to view your emails promptly, if not, instantly!

Once your students are able to access the CMS and their @college email address, their next main point of access is the virtual learning environment itself. There are usually specific components the instructor will want students to access, including assignments, documents, tests, and crucially, the discussion board. Immediate accessibility training for the discussion board can be helpful because the discussion board functions like the heart-beat of the online class organism. It is through the discussion board that students create their online community, communicate with the instructor and their peers, and submit assignments. Therefore, the discussion board should probably be one of the *most* easily accessible components of your CMS interface. This might mean that it is the first button on the list, or that it takes a place of prominence on your interface, or that it is highlighted by bold text. Regardless as to the method for highlighting the discussion board, it should be helpful to inform students via orientation specifically where they can find it. For example, "You can find the discussion board on the top left-hand side of the screen by clicking on the chat icon." As part of your manipulation check, students could be required make posts on the board, discussed later in this chapter.

Software

After you have ensured that your students can access the course via the CMS, their @college email, and the discussion board, one potential next step is to review the kinds of software they will be responsible for using. Your students may need to learn how to use a number of different types of software, including their CMS as well as MS Office (PowerPoint, Word), Quicktime videos, Adobe (PDF, Flash), and if your university subscribes to it, Turn-it-In.com or other antiplagiarism software. This software might be required in addition to Wikis, Facebook, and YouTube. Depending on the composition of your course, students may need to know how to use many other types of software (discussed in chapter 4) and ought to be provided with relevant orientation.

One of the greatest challenges to your software orientation is that due to the depth and breadth of available e-options in Web 2.0, your students are bound to be using different types of computers, different web browsers, different A/V software, and different word-processing software. One of the best ways to avoid controversy and confusion early on is to explicitly (and exhaustively) state exactly which kind of software students are required to use. Start with the format that you utilize to post your lecture information. For example, if you use PowerPoint slides, explain that all students will need access to MS Office with PowerPoint, or direct them to the website where they can download the free PowerPoint viewer. The same technique can also be applied to lecture notes disseminated via Adobe PDF. You can ask students to download the most up-to-date version, and provide them with the website (all up-to-date software websites are provided on the website companion to this book). Similar problems or difficulties can arise with streaming videos. Generally you want your students to have capacity to stream MP4 (Quicktime) videos. Quicktime is also a free download for people with PCs or Macs. In terms of the web browser itself, some course management elements experience problems with beta versions of Internet Explorer, so if this is the case, try to steer your students away from these and toward Firefox or Safari. While some software may be more useful than others at the time of press (such as Firefox over Explorer) these can fluctuate. What matters is not so much the software that you choose, but how you provide accessibility in the form of free downloads, training, and troubleshooting for your students. Many courses also provide antiplagiarism software (such as Turn-it-In.com). While this is discussed at length later on, you may want to inform students that they will be required to submit papers and assignments directly through the software, and provide an explicit link to their submission page.

Policies

After engaging in the procedural and technical elements of orientation, another useful step is to outline your course policies. While these will probably be documented at length in the course syllabus, consider highlighting the most important, relevant, or crucial points. For example, you might want to begin with the academic honesty policy. Some universities that feature online teaching may even offer an online version of the academic honesty policy designed to address the specific concerns of online learning. Of these, the biggest concerns are e-plagiarism (such as copying from wikis or other websites), forms of cheating (such as ensuring that the students themselves are taking the course, and not someone else who may have already taken the course), and falsification (such as lying to the instructor about quiz lockouts or other excuses). It should be made clear that the instructor will be very alert to these offensives, and that consequences are unavoidable. As a side note, the nature of the consequences depends on the institution and its governance. For example, the California Community College system recently relayed a finding that a student who cheats on a test or paper should not be given a grade of zero in the whole course, only on that assignment on which they cheated. So if a student submits a paper to Turn-it-In that comes back as 80% copied from other websites, a zero would be an applicable grade on the paper but that student should not automatically be given a failing grade. Please check with your school administrators because these regulations can vary tremendously!

After detailing academic dishonesty, a session on *netiquette* might be particularly useful for students who are new to online learning. Quite simply, the term *netiquette* (a combination of the terms *network* and *etiquette*) refers to regulations that dictate what should or should not occur with respect to online communication (Shea, 2004). Certain types of rude or disrespectful communication are not acceptable in the online class-room. You could give examples of unacceptable personal remarks, such as "Barbara, anyone who says that is a complete moron, you must be stupid" and more respectful ways of expressing them, including "Barbara, I appre-ciate your comment but I disagree because of x, y, z." It is also important to encourage students to think before they write, and imagine if they would make the same comment to another student's face, or in the physical pres-ence of the instructor.

Finally, procedural policies regarding due-dates and lateness can be relayed at this point. It is important that these are explicitly stated in the orientation materials to ensure that students take these deadlines seri-ously. One of the biggest problems for many first time online instructors are issues regarding late assignments, such as email bombardment includ-ing, "My internet crashed right before I was handing in the assignment, that's why it was late!" with a follow-up that "It's not my fault!" In the expe-rience of the authors, failure to immediately nip this attitude in the bud may lead to its reemergence throughout the semester. In your orientation, clarity can be a useful approach to take, such as postings that: "TECHNI-CAL PROBLEMS ARE NOT AN EXCUSE FOR LATE ASSIGNMENTS" with a subtext that "assignments are available days/weeks in advance of the due date, computer or internet problems that hinder submissions are not a valid excuse for a missed assignment." Or, put another way, "*You are responsible for submitting assignments on time, regardless of any technical problems you may experience.*" (Imagine an Uncle Sam portrait pointing YOU to drive the point home!) If students know from the very beginning that they will not be able to utilize this excuse, they will probably try less frequently. In a perfect world, they would not try at all, but some students simply cannot resist asking for extensions! In addition to the due-date pol-icy, this also might be a good time to explain your take on lateness. Some instructors will accept late exams or papers and mark them down one grade point for each day late, while others will not accept any late assign-ments. The online environment lends itself well to the latter approach. An assignment can be made unavailable the second that the due date expires, meaning that all students will be required to submit assignments on time, or not at all.

Assignments

After highlighting the procedural policies relating to assignments, this might also be a good time to state what the assignments are, and when they are due. First, go ahead and highlight the frequency of assignments.

So, if assignments are due every week, you could tell your students which assignments are due each week. Imagine that each semester, the instructor can create and post a new online orientation video providing the specific dates when the larger assignments are due. This leaves little room for confusion or discrepancy for students who watch your video, especially because students can be tested on this information in the orientation quiz. Highlighting assignment due dates can help to define student goals and expectations. If the instructor clearly tells students what is expected from them (that, for example, each assignment is submitted by the Wednesday evening when it is due), they will appreciate that structure and allow it to guide their studying. Finally, in an orientation video, you can describe the different types of assignments and how they will be submitted. Will papers be submitted to Turn-it-In? What is required of discussion posts? Are the exams timed? These are all questions that, if answered at the beginning, should make your life and workload more pleasant later on. The types of assignments and assessment that you can assign are discussed in chapters 5 and 6.

Grading

The final procedural element for online orientation is the dissemination of the course grading policy. All students seemingly want to know what it takes to get an A, and online courses are definitely no exception! While online grading rubrics and strategies are discussed in chapter 6, consider providing your selected rubric of choice at orientation. This could deter students from slacking during the first few weeks of the course, if they are aware that the first assignment counts as much toward their grade as the final assignment. Also at this time, decide if you are going to provide extra credit. It is probably better to make this decision at the start rather than at the end of the semester, when the instructor may or may not be receiving constant whining emails from students who have a C but want their grade bumped to A, and would like to revise the 12 assignments that they neglected to submit earlier. Due in part to online disinhibition (discussed later in this chapter), you will find that some students are bolder (and slightly more absurd) with their requests for extra credit as the semester goes on. One of the best ways to handle this is to decide at the start of class (a) if there will be extra credit and (b) what the extra credit will be. A great strategy is building extra credit directly into the course, such as dropping everyone's lowest quiz grade or lowest discussion board posts. Also at this juncture, the instructor can let students know no additional extra credit beyond this will be offered. This way, when the grade-grubbing email crew potentially begins to light up your inbox at the end of the term, you can calmly explain that they have already received extra credit and that no additional extra credit is offered. The authors find that this works very well, and greatly reduces frustration with student grading at the end of the semester.

Having reviewed the central components for your online orientation, let us consider how to disseminate this information. Is it even possible to fit all of this information into a 10- or 20-minute video or is a learning module, a website, or a PDF document more effective? Online orientation seems to be most beneficial when it mimics the first day of class in a traditional classroom. This structure taps into a familiar, shared experience of the students where the professor sits them down and explains everything they need to know! For this reason, an orientation video posted on YouTube, the faculty website, and the CMS appears to be one of the most useful methods for orientation delivery. Creating orientation videos can be easier than you would expect, especially when using the tips provided in chapter 4. Consider using the template provided in this chapter (access, software, policies, assignment, and grading) to create a script or outline as a base for your video. Then practice a few times, and start by recording onto your computer where there is minimal investment if your attempt fails. If you really find you are struggling, write down exactly what you want to say and read it, or consider providing an audio recording or podcast, discussed in chapter 4.

Crafting an online orientation with a personal touch can also benefit your general ability to establish rapport, again because it seems to maintain a shared expectation of "meeting" their professor on the first day of class. Seeing the professor's commitment to their specific class should lead to greater student investment when compared to being emailed a document or link to materials online. In addition to establishing rapport, a video serves as a great orientation because it can be disseminated across a variety of media outlets: Posted on your website, YouTube, Facebook, emailed, in addition to being available on the CMS. Since some online students prefer to receive written rather than oral instructions, consider also sending along your video script or outline, or at the least, your syllabus, to the class at the same time as your video. Then encourage students to study from both because there might be a quiz.

Manipulation Check

Going through all the trouble of creating a comprehensive, excellent orientation might seem pointless if its effectiveness is not going to be measured. Considering that part of orientation revolves around increasing student efficacy to learn in the virtual classroom, review activities could measure knowledge, and also, the ability to engage in activities. Consider your orientation manipulation check as a win-win situation. To ensure that students take your course seriously, orientation exercises could count as your central assignments during the first week of class. Failure to successfully complete the orientation exercises might result in students who begin the course feeling uncomfortable and unfamiliar with the virtual classroom itself. Then, a mistake when posting on the discussion board or a locked-out quiz may result in that student unnecessarily losing points from his or her grades. The content and delivery of orientation exercises themselves can vary from course to course and instructor to instructor. Generally, four types of activities discussed below can be utilized to assess competency in the central components of the virtual learning environment: Making a post, taking a practice quiz, submitting a sample paper, and creating a video or audio clip.

Making a Post

Students can benefit from detailed instructions and training on when and how to make their posts on the discussion board. Depending upon the student's level of expertise, posting may seem extremely easy or slightly more difficult. After directing students to the location and mechanics of the discussion board during orientation, the instructor can provide an exercise and require students to (a) create their own string and (b) reply to a classmate's post. The content of the exercise itself can vary. For example, you can combine the post assignment with ice-breakers to make students more comfortable, or other activities like student introductions, or first impressions of the class. Successful orientation prompts could include questions about "Why did you decide to take online courses?" Or, "What do you think is the best definition of 'Social Psychology' and why?" Alternatively, the instructor could take a more humorous route and ask students to "share a fun and interesting fact about yourself" or provide a link to a favored website or funny video. Posting a link is another feature of the discussion board that is sometimes underutilized by students, so an orientation activity to promote link posting would be valuable if students will be asked to do this later on in the course.

Taking a Practice Quiz

Another central component to online learning is testing, discussed at length in chapter 6. For orientation, consider that you want students to be able to explore and examine the testing apparatus without feeling conscious of how it may affect their grade. Especially on timed quizzes and tests, some students may panic if they become confused or have difficulties with the technology involved. So, for orientation, it might be beneficial to require students to complete at least one quiz and set a specific due date for that quiz. If you intend to use timed quizzes and tests, then consider setting a timer here so students become accustomed to this style of testing. If you intend to use multiple choice questions or true/false questions during the semester, then you could choose the same style for the orientation quiz. Also before students begin the quiz, consider reiterating your testing rules at the outset. For example, depending on your chosen CMS and software, testing rules can look like the following:

2.3 QUIZ RULES

To avoid being "Locked Out" of your quiz:
- Do NOT press Save, Forward, Back, or Print during your quiz.
- Do NOT click outside the testing window during your quiz.
- Do NOT open other programs, or have other browser windows running.
- Do NOT take the quiz on your cell phone.

After providing these instructions, consider the content of your orientation quiz. There are many best practices here that instructors can benefit from. First, you could create a quiz based solely around the orientation materials themselves. This has the function of being a manipulation check for your orientation. Consider multiple choice questions: "What day are assignments due in this class?" with response choices of "Monday, Saturday, Wednesday, or Friday" or, "Extra credit is offered in the form of: Dropped quiz, extra paper, etc." This can show the students how seriously you intend for them to learn the orientation materials, and also demonstrates which students did not carefully pay attention to their orientation. The instructor may want to consider contacting students with poor scores and asking them to review the orientation materials again.

Another type of orientation quiz revolves around course-specific content. Often psychology courses use scaffolding, building from knowledge acquired in previous courses. Usually, Introduction to Psychology is considered a prerequisite for most higher level undergraduate psychology courses. If you are teaching one of these higher level courses (including but not limited to: developmental psychology, social psychology, research methods, abnormal psychology, cognitive psychology, program evaluation, or psychology of sexuality), consider creating a quiz featuring content which students should have retained from introductory psychology. This will serve as an excellent reminder that students continue to be responsible for such material, and again, will allow you to gauge your classes' knowledge of basic psychological principles.

Alternatively, an orientation quiz could feature course-specific questions pertaining to your subject matter, to measure introductory knowledge in the subject area and provide students with a taste of what is to come! For example, imagine a psychology of sexuality course where students complete a quiz entitled "Are you a SexPert?" featuring true/false questions pertaining to some of the interesting or difficult topics ("There are 1,000 sperm in one teaspoon of ejaculate" or "People who are bisexual eventually choose to be straight or gay"—FYI both are false). Again, the benefits of such an approach are twofold: (a) The instructor can effectively measure the baseline knowledge of the students while (b) ensuring that they have had adequate practice and training for future online quizzes and tests.

Submitting a Sample Paper

Many online classes require a written paper component. In psychology, these papers can range from thought or reaction pieces ("Share your attitudes about this subject") to critical thinking papers ("Should prostitution be legalized, why or why not?") to more theoretical papers ("Explain how theories of adolescent risk behavior have evolved?") to full-blown research papers ("Create an intervention to improve marital communication among couples in relationship therapy"). In an online psychology course, all of these are possible assignments based on course goals and learning objectives. Depending on the assignments you choose (discussed in chapter 5), consider creating a much smaller (almost miniversion) of that assignment for your orientation exercise. For example, if you plan to assign a research paper, your orientation paper could be "Write one paragraph about an intervention to improve relational communication" and so forth.

After deciding on the content of the orientation paper, consider the mode of submission. As noted earlier, many academic institutions now offer antiplagiarism software that is integrated into your CMS, such as Turn-it-In.com. If your course will incorporate antiplagiarism software, it is useful to provide detailed instructions on how to use/submit materials for it. Students will need to locate a specific icon directing them to the submission page where they have to upload their document. Sometimes antiplagiarism software can alter the formatting of the document or create other issues that you could mention. Exercises featuring antiplagiarism software can also be a great way to discourage plagiarism from the beginning of the course. Once students see how their orientation paper is dissected and analyzed, they should be much less likely to cheat or copy on their actual paper.

Creating a Video or Audio Clip

This final component might not be required for all psychology courses. However, asking students to create their own content is a great way to encourage collaboration and involvement. Incorporating student-generated content can reduce the potential anonymity and invisibility of online learning while simultaneously increasing excitement and engagement. If you decide to include user-generated audiovisuals, consider what type would suit your course. Perhaps an audio summary or analysis of a specific theoretical position would add depth when posted on the discussion board. Likewise, you may want to ask students to create a video intervention to improve adolescent exercise habits. Try to tailor your orientation exercises to the type of content and delivery you plan to utilize in your class.

For example, you might ask students to make a podcast (detailed in chapter 4). They will need specific hardware and software to do this, so consider incorporating a separate podcast orientation into the course that explains how to do this and upload it onto iTunes or directly to the CMS for the class. Likewise, you may want students to post their sample interventions on YouTube. In this case, you might provide additional instructions in your orientation on how to go about doing this. Then comes the fun part! For the final component of orientation, ask students to create a 2- to 3-minute clip of material—it can be a vocal recording, music, or visuals (either of themselves, others, or a montage)—and ask them to deliver the content in the desired modality. Meanwhile, make sure to be on hand for troubleshooting and to provide a list of common problems or issues. You may even want to consider separating your audiovisual orientation into a separate module because it can take longer than other activities. While this is not required for your course to become successful, providing well-constructed orientation materials surrounding user-generated audiovisuals should make the process relatively simple for your students (particularly those who are already doing this for fun!)

ADDITIONAL COURSE MAINTENANCE ISSUES

No Shows and Late Additions

At many institutions, the instructor is required to drop students who fail to attend the first day of class. Locating the "no show" drops in online courses may be more challenging than simply taking attendance on the first day of a face-to-face class. Even online students will sometimes send emails to their instructors asking if they need to physically attend the first day of class to ensure that they can hold their place. For a fully online course, a helpful response to this question would be, "No you are not physically required to attend the first day, but your successful completion of online orientation will ensure your place in the class." In this respect, online orientation can be used to separate out the inevitable "no shows" who have completely forgotten that they registered for an online course months earlier. One method for discovering your online "no-shows" is to set tight due dates for each orientation exercise (post, quiz, paper) usually falling within the first week of class. Then, explain in your orientation (and CMS postings, emails, etc.) that students who fail to complete these activities by the due date will be dropped from the class as "no shows." Additionally, your CMS may give you an indication of when the student last logged in to the course. If the student does not log in during the entire first week, they may also be treated as a "no show."

One potential enrollment complication that could arise relates to late students trying to add the course. If a student petitions to join after the orientation has been completed, this can be tricky. On the one hand, this student probably has a very convincing need for your course ("Professor, I am ONE unit away from graduating and I just realized this is the only class I can take to meet my requirements, and I am really interested in it, please HELP me!"). On the other hand, adding students after orientation has passed can sometimes become problematic. These students will probably have to hit the ground running, or face falling behind. New students who join the class late would have to complete, in the first week, all of the orientation exercises as well as the required graded assignments as part of the class. Some students can adapt to this workload without complaint. However, it seems that many late-added students may need extensions during the first week, leading to a potential knock-on effect of requiring extensions in the second week so that the first week's work can be conducted. Eventually this will spiral and the student will either fail to complete the work and continue to ask for extensions all the way through to the midterm, or will manage to catch up.

In the authors' experience, as many as half of the students who add after orientation eventually end up dropping the course, or fail to complete their assignments. Often the process is associated with numerous back-and-forth emails about how much they want to stay in, but don't have time to make up the work. As a rule of thumb, adding students after the orientation period has ended can be problematic and often fruitless. If you decide to add students (or if the institution requires you to), try to ensure that they remain up-to-date with assignments or face being dropped if they do not complete their assignments.

ONLINE SYLLABI

When an online instructor creates an excellent orientation, the syllabus can feel almost superfluous (or at least, redundant). The syllabus itself should contain much of the detailed procedural information covered in the online orientation (access, software, policies, assignments, and grading) as well as a specific course calendar of weekly documents and assignments, learning objectives, and information on where to find course materials. As a traditional lecturer, it can be difficult to imagine an educational situation where the syllabus does not function as the central procedural guideline for the course. For online courses, the syllabus still remains a key document (much like a written contract between the professor and students), but the syllabus is static and clings to the page whereas the orientation jumps out and interacts with the students. In this respect, the syllabus is not exactly irrelevant, but rather, the orientation delivers the material in the syllabus in an engaging, effective way. Further, the orientation exercises demonstrate how much of the information in the syllabus is retained, a feature that professors in traditional classrooms would undoubtedly also appreciate!

The place where your syllabus can really shine is in its presentation of the course calendar and weekly documents. To tailor your syllabus specific to online content delivery, consider inserting links to relevant websites for each week directly into your syllabus text. This way, a student opens your document, and clicks on the hypertext link that automatically opens the web browser with the desired materials. For example, Miller (2009) presents this course calendar from a sociology course featuring web-based content. You can see that the gray hypertext links connect users directly to the content of interest (see Figure 2.1).

Additionally, your course calendar can specifically outline when one week ends, where the next week starts, and when assignments (such as reading, quizzes, and papers) are due. While there are a number of ways of presenting this information, the authors tend to favor a traditional written format in the syllabus, followed by uploading information directly to the CMS course calendar so that students see notifications about due dates when they log in to the class. Below is a sample calendar from an online Psychology of Sexuality course (see Figure 2.2).

Note, for example, how Week 2 starts on Thursday 2/11 and continues until the following Wednesday 2/17, when the Discussion Board 1 assignment is due (in bold) along with the relevant reading. This format, when

Feb 9
Topic: Socialization: Self and Society
Text Assignment: Thompson & Hickey - Chapter 4
For Your Information:
"Jonathan Haidt: The Real Difference between Liberals and Conservatives"
http://www.ted.com/index.php/talks/jonathan_haidt_on_the_moral_mind.html

Feb 11
Topic: Developmental Socialization / Resocialization
Video Assignments:
"Growing Up Online" http://www.pbs.org/wgbh/pages/frontline/kidsonline/
To what extent and in what ways is the internet important in the lives of youth today? Is participation in social networking websites sites such as MySpace and Facebook problematical for youth and their parents? How does it possibly shape and confound identity? Do you have a page or pages on a website? To what extent do they reflect the "real" you? Have/has your parents/parent seen your site? If so, what was their reaction? If not, why haven't you shown it to them?
"Lord's Children" http://www.pbs.org/wnet/wideangle/episodes/lords-children/video-full-episode/2188/
Who are the "lord's children"—i.e., where are they from, how do they come to be, what are they forced to do, what impact does becoming one have on them? How are they commonly treated by family members when they escape? Describe efforts to resocialize them. Generally, how effective are such efforts?

Feb 13
Topic: Socialization, Role, and Identity
Video Assignments:
"U.S. Interrogator Talks Openly About Abu Ghraib 25 Oct 2006"
http://www.youtube.com/watch?v=bTeE1ykArBU
"Good, Bad, and Ugly"
http://video.nytimes.com/video/2007/04/02/science/1194817098443/good-bad-andugly
html?scp=1&sq=zimbardo&st=cse
Why do decent people sometimes do bad things? Compare and contrast Zimbardo's experiment with the case of Abu Ghraib. Consider the extent to which we "become" our roles. How likely are we to identify with the roles we play, no matter how disagreeable they might personally seem to us at first glance? In watching these videos, consider the following questions: 1. How did those (soldiers and students) who served as guards generally come to behave? 2. For what purposes were prisoners subjected to abusive treatment by guards? 3. Why did the guards engage in such behavior? 4. Do you think that you could have personally resisted becoming fully absorbed in either role? 5. What lessons about human behavior can we learn from these two video clips?
Audio Assignment: "RadioLab: Morality"
http://www.wnyc.org/flashplayer/player.html#/play/%2Fstream%2Fxspf%2F54698
What makes some of us more "moral" than others? From where does our sense of morality originate? Are humans the only species concerned with moral issues?

Figure 2.1 *Syllabus with Web-Based Content. Week Four Assignments for SOC 1013 Class.*

DATE	TOPIC	READING (due for this week!)
Week 2: Thurs 2/11 – Wed 2/17	*Sex & Culture* Sex, Media, Norms, Society ***Discussion Board 1 Due 2/17**	Text Chapter 1 and *"APA Sexualization Report"* online article (http://www.apa.org/pi/women/programs/girls/report.aspx)
Week 3: Thurs 2/18- Wed 2/24	*Sex Research* Methods, Researchers, Kinsey ***Discussion Board 2 Due 2/24**	Text Chapter 2 http://www.kinseyinstitute.com http://www.sexscience.org
Week 4: Thurs 2/25 – Wed 3/3	*Female and Male Sexuality* Anatomy, Physiology & Response ***Quiz 1 Due 3/3**	Text Chapter 3 & 4 http://www.the-clitoris.com http://www.circumcision.org
Week 5: Thurs 3/4 - Wed 3/10	*Gender* Identity, Intersex, Transsexual ***Gender Activity Due 3/10**	Text Chapter 5 http://www.apa.org/research/action/gender.aspx http://www.isna.org

Figure 2.2 *Online Sexuality Syllabus.*

explained during orientation, can be especially beneficial if the instructor selects nontraditional weekly formats (in this case, a week that starts Thursday and ends Wednesday, instead of a week that starts Monday and ends Sunday). Also, one can see how relevant websites are inserted directly below the textbook reading due for that week. These websites should also be included in the course documents section of your CMS for the corresponding week. Most CMS interfaces provide a course calendar, and it only takes a few minutes to enter each weekly due date and the start/end of each week into this course calendar. This provides multiple forms of technology that offer the same information, increasing accessibility and reducing confusion.

Other online psychology instructors utilize a variety of strategies for presenting important information their syllabi and course calendars. Again, there is no official best practice for an online psychology syllabus, other than it contains the course calendar and objectives, as well as the important components also featured in your orientation (access, software, policies, assignments, and grading). In your syllabus, it is possible to go into greater detail on these topics (if necessary) than what is provided in orientation. Remember that a syllabus is never substitution for online orientation, just as orientation is never a substitution for the syllabus. Students will benefit from the combination of both elements. The syllabus documents all policies, objectives, and assignments in written detail and provides a detailed course calendar. The orientation can operate as an audiovisual, PowerPoint, or learning module (or some combination) delivery of this information, followed by a comprehensive manipulation check. Just try to ensure consistency across your orientation and syllabus to avoid student confusion.

TROUBLESHOOTING: CAN'T WE ALL JUST GET ALONG?

This section highlights the sources of potential problems with our online courses and online students. While we hope that everything will run smoothly, this is not always the case and sometimes, problems can arise. It is important to be aware of what happens when things do not go according to plan, so that the instructor can quickly and swiftly take action to rectify the problem. Further, consider that when taken broadly, online social behavior differs substantially from face-to-face behavior. In the context of your online course, the way that students establish their identity and interact with each other will be somewhat different from your face-to-face courses. Sometimes, this different online mentality can cause problems for the instructor and students alike. The nature of these problems, and how to deal with them effectively, are discussed below with examples taken from the research literature, and from the authors' online teaching experiences.

IMPLEMENTATION PROBLEMS AND EMAIL INSANITY

Instructors can benefit from paying close attention to the many tips outlined in this chapter. For example, in addition to reviewing your entire online class for clarity and consistency, you can also benefit from checking every assignment due date. To avoid students submitting assignments late, you can make assignments "unavailable" after the due date. This means that once the due date has passed, the assignment is no longer visible to students, although it remains visible to you. This way, students are not able to submit a late assignment without instructor permission.

While this is a great strategy for avoiding late submissions, it can backfire when left unchecked. In the author's online course a few semesters ago, a quiz "disappeared" at 6:00 p.m. on the day of the due date, instead of 11:59 p.m. on the due date, when it was actually due. Unfortunately, the instructor was delivering a face-to-face lecture that evening and did return to her email until 10:00 p.m. that evening. Upon opening the email inbox, she was astounded to have accrued over 100 new messages in a 4-hour time span. Further, nearly all of them were from online students who were very upset that they had studied for the quiz, only to find that the quiz had vanished. "Did I miss the due date?", "Can I get an extension" and general "What is going on!?" set the tone for the email. There were also more detailed responses: "Professor, I am freaking OUT! I have to go to work and this is the only time I can take the quiz. It is really important to my grade and I don't know what to do!" Some students had sent multiple emails addressing their growing concerns. The course discussion board also lit up like switchboard, with multiple discussions carrying on: "Can you find the quiz? No neither can I", "Where is Professor Neff, why hasn't she fixed this?" And one in particular that expressed how everyone felt: "I am *so* annoyed about this."

Naturally, the instructor was upset when this happened, feeling as though she had created a major expectancy violation, and even worse, she had failed to address the problem for hours. To rectify the situation, she went into a kind of "emergency" troubleshooting mode. First, she immediately went into the course and made the quiz available again. Next, she sent a mass email to the entire class explaining that "for some unknown reason" the quiz had disappeared. Then, she posted several similar replies to threads on the discussion board that the quiz had disappeared but now was back, and apologies for the stress and worry caused. Due to the inconvenience everyone had experienced, the instructor then had no choice but to extend the deadline for one more day, and made triple sure that the due date and time was correct.

The silver lining to this cloud is that the author's suffering can direct the readers of the book away from making similar mistakes. What did she learn to pass on to you? First, on every day that an assignment (quiz, paper, test, discussion) is due, a conscientious instructor can benefit from going into the administrative control panel, and checking that the due date and time is correct. This only takes a minute or two but can help to deter massive drama in the long term. Second, it is probably better for an instructor to avoid scheduling due dates for online classes at times when he or she is unavailable or working on other projects. In retrospect, knowing that she was lecturing that evening, it would have made more sense to make the assignments due the following day. Academic psychologists often experience numerous work and life conflicts; planning out your online class in a way that minimizes this conflict helps you in the long term!

This example highlights one of the many ways that implementation problems can create difficulties for the online instructor and students. Other issues that can arise from implementation malfunctions can include attrition, stress, and of course, email insanity. Although there is currently a dearth of peer-reviewed research addressing online student attrition, it appears that online courses seem to have slightly higher attrition rates than face-to-face classes. This is not because students do not like learning online; rather, the authors postulate that many people sign up for online courses not knowing what to expect, and often drop the course when they learn about the workload, or due to other life–work conflicts. Further, it is possible that some students register for online courses months in advance, only to forget their intention to take the course. It appears then that some level of attrition (the authors have noticed between 20 to 30% in the past) serves as a natural and expected part of the online learning experience. However, if a class is poorly executed, attrition rates will be even higher due to confused expectations. Imagine again the nightmare situation of the professor showing up to class completely unprepared. What happens? The students lose faith in that professor. The professor is thought to be incompetent and a joke. When students lose faith, they are likely to drop the course, or find the same course taught by another professor. The situation is magnified online, where there is no social pretense to keep students coming back to that specific course. Rather, an online student who has trouble accessing materials on the first day, or has questions that are unanswered, may decide that the online class is not worth the trouble.

Stress is another consequence of a course with implementation difficulties. This stress can be especially problematic when a student is new to online learning, and has trouble opening an attachment, or using the right software, or finding the due date for an assignment. This student is not able to raise a hand to ask for help as if he or she were in a traditional classroom. Rather, the student must rely on the professor being on top of the email game. Sometimes, the student may internalize this stress and allow it to become a burden, or externalize the stress and blame the professor. This type of professor-blame does not bode well, as word travels fast online. Across "Rate my Professor," "Pick-A-Prof," Facebook as well as word of mouth, any trouble that you have with launching the course can be disseminated immediately across multiple venues with a simple message you want to avoid, summarized as "Beware, this professor sucks!" Clearly, this type of student stress resonates and translates into professor stress. As academic psychologists we like to believe that we are excellent at multitasking, simultaneously teaching, advising, researching, writing grants, all the while living life as excellent human beings to boot (well, we can dream!). Thus nothing violates our self-concept more than the feeling that we are not in control, or worse, that we are professionally incompetent. To avoid this feeling and the ensuing anxiety, it is imperative to plan, plan, plan and test, test, test!

In addition to anxiety caused by potential failings, perhaps the one of the worst consequences of a poorly planned online course is what the authors like to call *email insanity*. We are all accustomed to multiple emails per day related to our professional careers. Many of these are from students, asking questions, setting up meetings, or griping about grades. In the virtual learning environment, the frequency and intensity of emails is elevated. The majority of online professors will never have a face-to-face interaction with their students. Without direct access, students rely upon discussion boards and emails to communicate (communication in the online classroom is discussed at length in chapter 3). For those of us surgically attached to our Blackberries and iPhones, the heightened emails associated with teaching online courses may not be especially problematic. However, when a mistake occurs, such as a missing link, unclear prompt, or a disappearing quiz, email insanity can ensue. Even for the most seasoned email pro, it can feel overwhelming to discover an inbox filled with 50 or 60 emails in an afternoon, all pertaining to the same topic. While it is not entirely avoidable, you can certainly reduce the inbox overload by planning ahead and catching mistakes before your students do. Most importantly, if this happens, just remember that everything is going to be fine. We all make mistakes and your students will appreciate it when you rectify the problem!

RAPPORT AND ONLINE DISINHIBITION

We have to consider that without the physical closeness afforded by face-to-face education, online instructors may have to take special steps to create and maintain a good working relationship with their students. Indeed, establishing rapport remains an important and challenging part of teaching online. Some studies have shown that an overly formal class lacking in personality and flair can lead to online students feeling cold and unpleasant (Gibson, Tesone, & Blackwell, 2001). It is not surprising then that online students tend to report that the actual lack of face-to-face communication with their instructor is their greatest objection to online learning (Borstoff & Lowe, 2007). While research in the area of rapport in online teaching is quite limited, some online educators have argued that forming rapport with students reflects the highest level of skill required in online teaching (Hampel & Stickler, 2005). At least according to this one theoretical framework, online educators must master all other components of teaching online (such as competence with technology and online communication) before they can master the creation of their own personal style and rapport. The authors have found that while creating rapport can be a tricky process, it is not necessarily any more difficult than mastering one's technological medium or facilitating online communication. In fact, rapport seems strongly associated both with the type of medium utilized and the professor's communication style.

Rapport is necessary because of the psychological mind-space that some students enter when they become part of the virtual learning environment. Because the virtual classroom differs from our accustomed face-to-face interactions, a phenomenon known as *online disinhibition* can occur. Quite simply, online behaviors can be more extreme, less inhibited, and sometimes more revealing, than behaviors that occur during face-to-face interaction. Suler (2004) has written at length about the components of online disinhibition, including dissociative anonymity, invisibility, asynchronicity, and minimizing authority. It is important for online educators to be aware of the distinct variability in online behavior when compared with face-to-face interaction, so that in some cases, we can help to manage and reduce occurrence of online disinhibition.

DISSOCIATIVE ANONYMITY

Online behavior is often completely separate from individuals' identities. As the term *anonymity* implies, many of the interactions and experiences that people encounter online can be completely separated from their true identity. In this respect, people are sometimes dissociated from themselves, and may feel less accountable for their online behaviors. How does this relate to online teaching? The implication is clear: While a student's name is utilized in their online class experience, their face does not need to be revealed to the class. As such, online students may perceive themselves to be less accountable for their actions than their face-to-face counterparts. Online students may also be more likely than their face-to-face counterparts to share personal information or discuss controversial topics.

INVISIBILITY

As stated above, an individual's face and tone of voice are rarely revealed online. Likewise, the physical reactions of others (such as eye contact or body language) are also concealed. With written text as a key mode of communication, online students do not have to concern themselves with how they look or sound to the class, nor do they need to worry about the reactions of their classmates. They may feel free to express themselves, but they are also lacking certain social cues that we often depend upon when we communicate. Think of eye contact during a lecture: As a professor, you can tell who is paying attention, and who is asleep in the corner. In this respect, your online students are invisible except when they submit an assignment or participate in a discussion board.

Asynchronicity

Much of online interaction is asynchronous, meaning that people do not interact at the same time, but leave messages for each other (such as emails and discussion posts). Although this is evolving thanks to live-chat and other interfaces, often a person's communication is not met with an immediate response or reply. The lack of immediate feedback for one's comments distinguishes the online learning environment from the traditional classroom. If a course is totally asynchronous, a student can leave a message and forget about it, only to find a host of replies one week later when he or she can barely recall the starting point for the original post. While the synchronicity of online activities will be discussed in chapters 3 and 5, consider that a live (synchronous) class meeting can reduce student disinhibition and boost their perceived connectedness.

Minimizing Authority

In many ways the internet is the great equalizer, in that it is impossible to tell if the individual with whom you are communicating is a person of high or low status. In other words, it is difficult to effectively translate authority and power relationships into online behavior. Consider the case of the professor/student relationship. In the traditional classroom, the professor stands at the front of the room, decides who gets to speak and when, and commands silence and respect when he or she speaks. However, the professor's authority is surely minimized online, where students do not directly experience the professor's control over their environment. In such a situation, students will be much more likely to make comments that they never would have made in face-to-face communication with their professors.

How do we manage and deal with student online disinhibition? Establishing rapport with students is a great way of grounding students back into some semblance of an educational "reality." The author recalls an example taken from the first online course that she taught. Blissfully unaware of how the minimization of authority can unfold online, she made no attempt to establish rapport, aside from introducing herself on the online discussion board. She told the students about research interests, but did not include personal information (such as her favorite music, activities, books, etc.). She did not make any attempt to identify herself specifically, and did not provide any videos or pictures of herself. While revealing this kind of information seemed totally unnecessary, it plunged Dr. Neff into the unexpected wormhole of online disinhibition.

Toward the end of the semester, when grades were due, the instructor began to receive blunt, rude, and even disrespectful emails from a number of students. Some of these emails were direct and to the point "I NEED A BETTER GRADE PROFESSOR!!!" (original emphasis in capital letters) while others featured unnecessary overshares of detail: "I just got out of rehab for crystal meth addiction and I am having a hard time passing the course, I really need your help." At first, she was shocked and slightly disturbed by the obtuse, personal nature of these comments. During her years of classroom instruction (as both teacher and student) she had never even heard such comments made in a face-to-face setting. In the language of online disinhibition, students were emailing comments (asynchronously) that they would never say to their professor's face (minimizing authority) in part because they had no idea who their professor was, what their professor looked like or sounded like (invisibility), and partly because they knew that the professor knew nothing about them except for their name (dissociative anonymity).

The following semester, the instructor decided to actively attempt to reduce this apparent online student disinhibition by establishing rapport early on. She asked students to share their personal information on the discussion board, such as favorite bands, activities, interesting facts about themselves, life goals, and favorite areas of study. In turn, she shared the same information and participated in discussions early on. From the first class, she video recorded lectures, targeting the material specifically to that course section, and posted these materials directly to the class (for descriptions on how to do this, see chapter 4). That semester, the instructor received fewer disrespectful emails from students, even during those stressful times at the end of the semester. No more capital letters, no more comments about drug addiction, and fewer complaints.

This example illustrates how it might be possible to reduce online disinhibition by establishing rapport, and making yourself more accessible and more visible to your students. A great way to expand upon this further would be requiring each student to film their own video of themselves during the first week of class, reducing their experience of dissociative anonymity and invisibility. Note that some level of disinhibition can benefit an online course and lead to insightful, in-depth discussions of controversial or sensitive subject areas. Consider then that online courses may require some kind of balance in anonymity and invisibility: too much, and online disinhibition can occur in an extreme way; too little, and students may feel overly accountable and less likely to share or participate.

NETIQUETTE

Online disinhibition in the virtual learning environment can lead to potential behavioral difficulties and problems, such as rudeness, personal attacks, and generally inappropriate comments between students, or between student and instructor (as presented in the previous example). Shallert and colleagues (2009) discuss how the virtual classroom can sometimes become a dysfunctional space for communication, even though most students understand what types of online communication are acceptable or unacceptable. In the interest of avoiding these types of problematic interactions, consider integrating *netiquette* into your syllabus and establishment of rapport. As mentioned earlier, *netiquette* refers to regulations that dictate what should or should not occur with respect to online communication (Shea, 2004). Online instructors might find it useful and effective to include guidelines for netiquette in the course orientation or college training for new online students. Mintu-Wismatt, Kernek, and Lozada (2010) reported that a number of educational institutions already integrate netiquette policies into their code of conduct, academic honesty policies, or code of ethics. Thus, making this an explicit part of your online course appears to be the next logical step. Mintu-Wismatt and colleagues (2010, Appendix A) provide an example of types of information to include in a syllabus:

2.4 NETIQUETTE FOR YOUR SYLLABUS

Netiquette is a way of defining professionalism through network communication. Students who violate proper netiquette will be administratively dropped by Professor XXX from the course.

Here are some Student Guidelines for the class:
   Do not dominate any discussion.
   Do not use offensive language.
   Never make fun of someone's ability to read or write.
   Use simple English.
   Use correct spelling and grammar.
   Share tips with other students.
   Keep an "open-mind" and be willing to express even your
      minority opinion.
   Be aware of the university's academic honesty policy.
   Think before you push the "Send" button.
   Do not hesitate to ask for feedback.
   When in doubt, always check with your instructor for
      clarification.

Another way to reinforce netiquette would be to create examples of appropriate and inappropriate remarks to provide guidance to students. So, attacking a classmate with an insult or slur would fall into the unacceptable category, and so forth.

One of the most difficult challenges when establishing rapport and netiquette involves striking a balance between rudeness, on the one hand, and reserved politeness on the other hand. Indeed, Yang and colleagues (2006) showed that online learning is disrupted when students try too hard to be "nice" in their online communications. According to this study, students are reluctant to share a dissenting opinion that may be perceived as disrupting the harmony and cohesion of their online group. However, this is no different from students in the traditional classroom, so we must consider individual differences in personality—some students will help "stir the pot" and rile up the class, while others will happily "go with the flow." Trying to maintain a balance might be a difficult, but by no means an impossible task!

SUMMARY: MAKING IT WORK

This chapter highlights the central issues that instructors face when they embark upon the journey of creating and launching their online psychology courses. Of key importance in this chapter is that instructors adopt the "test, test, test" philosophy of ensuring that courses are properly organized prior to being launched for student consumption. The take-home message here is that a successful, fruitful online course is one that has been prepared and tested before the semester begins. Much of the chapter focused on the variety of issues pertaining to the preparation and implementation of online courses, including the choice between online and hybrid course delivery, selecting the appropriate course schedule and due dates, and determining the ideal class size. In online courses, a carefully thought out orientation is vital to ensure student success. Usually delivered during the first week of the semester, the orientation should feature information and training on the topics of access, software, policies, assignments and grading, as well as a manipulation check to ensure student retention. In many ways, the online orientation functions as the living, engaging version of the text-based course syllabus. This chapter also addresses troubleshooting for problems pertaining to implementation, including student attrition, stress, and email insanity. Lastly, this chapter began to explore how the student mind-set may shift in an online environment, including how rapport and netiquette can help to address some of the effects of online disinhibition. Bridging from this closing notion that students may perceive their online relationships and discussions to be qualitatively different from those that occur in the face-to-face environment, the following chapter will explore communication in an online learning community in greater depth.

CHAPTER 3

COMMUNICATION IS KEY

Good communication remains fundamental to teaching an engaging, satisfying online course. This chapter will feature research regarding the unique importance of communication and community to online student success, followed by advice on how to create and implement your own learning community, and troubleshooting strategies. As you proceed through this chapter, consider that the word *communication* is closely related to another word, equally important for online education: *community*. It is undeniable that individuals who utilize electronic media often create and foster feelings of community and togetherness. Just a peek at the burgeoning relevance of online social communities like Facebook indicates that many of our online psychology students may already be establishing their own virtual social groups and finding identity and meaning within them. Successful participation in your online class may potentially evoke the same types of feelings of community and engagement. After all, researchers have often defined participation as akin to belonging to a community (e.g., Jaldemark, Lindberg, & Olofsson, 2006). More specifically, imagine a cyclical form of engagement between collaboration and community, where participation enhances feelings of community, and feelings of community in turn heighten participation (Palloff & Pratt, 2005). So, how does participation in online courses evoke community and vice versa?

PURPOSE: ONLINE PARTICIPATION AND COURSE SUCCESS

In the last few years, theoretical positions have been presented arguing that online participation serves as the fundamental driving force behind online learning (Hrastinski, 2009). From this perspective, if we want to improve upon online learning, then we need to increase the intensity and quality of online participation. During the last 10 years, a formidable body of research has been accumulated in the social sciences supporting the notion that online students learn better, and are more successful, when they actively participate in their online learning community (LaPadula, 2003; McLoughlin, 2002). Typically in these studies, success is measured by student's self-reported perceived satisfaction with their course. One example is a study conducted by Veesley and colleagues (Veesley, Bloom, & Sherlock, 2007), where 85% of online students reported that being part of an online community was helpful to their learning. In a survey of nearly 1,500 State University of New York online students, Fredrickson and colleagues (Fredrickson, Pickett, Shea, Pelz, & Swan, 2000) found that the top three predictors of online learning effectiveness were (a) interaction with teachers, (b) level of participation in the online class compared with the traditional classroom, (c) interaction with classmates. Another study that utilized final course grades as the outcome measure of learning success showed that frequency of online participation and duration of participation predicted 31% of the variability in students' grades (Morris, Finnegan, & Sz-Shyan, 2005).

Generally, there appears to be a positive correlation between student sense of online community, their engagement in the course, their satisfaction with the course, and their perceived learning (Liu, Magjuka, Bonk, & Seung-Jee, 2007). Based upon the idea of participation as community, Rovai (2002) developed a scale to measure the experience of community in an online environment via four underlying components: spirit, trust, interaction, and learning. Researchers using this scale have found that involvement in an online community is positively associated with perceived learning success in online courses (Ouzts, 2006; Shea, 2006). The obvious trend here is that student participation and sense of community are both strongly associated with each other, and with successful online learning outcomes (Sadera, Roberston, Song, & Midon, 2009).

What Is an Online Learning Community (OLC)?

There are a number of definitions for an online learning community (OLC). In fact, definitions so widely abound that it can often create confusion and misunderstanding. According to Ke and Hoadley (2009), the term *online learning community* has been used to describe virtual groups, models for e-learning, online learning development, virtual environments, or virtual locations. Tu and Corry (2002) argue that when students engage in activities and interactions, an online environment develops which we call an online learning community. Others, however, have argued that the presence of an environment does not necessarily connote a community—and that for a community to emerge learners must engage and influence one another in the learning process (Kowch & Schwier, 1997). Some educators have debated whether online learning communities are created by design only (Johnson, 2001) or if they can evolve organically online (Steinkuehler, 2004). Chapman, Radmondt, and Smiley (2005) argue that online learning communities include familiarity, rapport, trust, and openness. Others (such as Veelsey et al., 2007) have proposed additional dimensions that comprise online learning communities, including respect, boundaries, shared behavior, and shared purpose. Even Wikipedia (2012a) has weighed in on the debate, defining an online learning community as a "common place on the internet that addresses the learning needs of its members through proactive and collaborative partnerships."

For our purposes as online psychology instructors, how can we define the online learning community? Obviously, it is difficult to create and foster something if we cannot define it. First, online learning communities are interactive by definition. They facilitate communication while delivering content and promoting engagement with that content. This interaction is multifaceted, occurring between learners and instructors, learners and content, and learners and other learners (Moore, 1989). Participation in online communities is not synonymous with reading and writing (Hrastinski, 2009) but rather, extends beyond these forms to include critical thinking and other higher order thought processes. While online learning communities can arise at any time, in the context of online courses, they are very much created first by an instructor using an online course management system designed to facilitate participation in the community.

Second, online learning communities require a certain level of trust between members (which could be defined as comfort, respect, or belief) regarding expectations about what will and will not occur, leading to safety and openness within the community. This trust is required so that online learners can become fully immersed in participation without fear or apprehension. Third, online learning communities are more than just the collection of technologies used to manage the course (Sadera et al., 2009). While the technologies (discussion board, email, video chat) are important for facilitating participation, the community reflects not only the modes of technology, but also the constant negotiation of attitudes and beliefs of its members.

From the authors' perspectives, online learning communities are best understood as a group of learners, unified by a common cause and empowered by a supportive virtual environment, engaging in collaborative learning within an atmosphere of trust and commitment (Engestrom, 1993 cited in Ke & Hoadley, 2009).

Now that the reader has an understanding of what is included in the online learning community, the following section identifies features of a successful online learning community. As you conceptualize setting up your online learning community, consider how the distance between you and your students is not only a physical distance. Of course the physical distance and lack of face-to-face interaction may be the first level of separation you imagine from your students, but the lack of proximity in online courses may result in a perceived emotional or psychological distance between the students themselves, and their instructor. One of the central goals of creating the online learning community should be to reduce the perceived psychological and physical distance between the students and the instructor.

What Makes a Healthy Online Learning Community?

According to Collison, Elbaum, Haavind, and Tinker (2000), a healthy online learning community contains a number of components, including the following five: Participants post regularly; the online community meets its members' needs; participant-to-participant collaboration; reasonable venting about technology and content; and participants show concern and support for their community. An updated discussion of Collison and colleagues' (2000) components, featuring new technology, is presented below.

Participants Post Regularly

While it is true that online learners are participating even at times when they are not making posts or writing emails (Wenger, 1998), one of the more effective ways of building community and gauging student interaction surrounds facilitating active communication through posting. In fully online courses, students will never meet face-to-face and thus communication via the discussion board becomes the main source of interaction and community building activities. The recommendation that posts should be made regularly is intentionally unclear so that instructors can tailor their posting requirements relative to the courses' learning objectives and goals. At some online campuses, students and instructors are required to make one post per day. In other online courses, students are required to make several posts per week that can be completed in one day, or throughout the week. In other instances, students are required to make only a few posts, but these posts must build from a previous student's comments.

In terms of building community, instructors should try to encourage discussions that are built from deeper thoughts and reflections upon other student's comments. So, writing, "I agree, good post" would not be as beneficial to the community as extending upon the idea such as "I agree, and your comment suggests that this theory could be applied," and going on to give a more detailed explanation. As mentioned earlier, a large part of building online learning communities occurs through focused engagement, collaboration, and critical thinking. Therefore, instructors looking to build community may want to consider selecting assignments and posts that emphasize these strategies (see chapter 5 on assignments).

Meeting Needs

In their initial theoretical definition of psychological sense of community, McMillan and Chavis (1986) describe how it is very important for a community to meet the needs of its members. Clearly, this same sort of reasoning can be translated to online learning communities. Generally, the most important needs surround trust, respect, and reaching important learning goals. Collison and colleagues (2000) argue that an online learning community is able to meet its learners' needs when they are comfortable providing feedback and sharing concerns with the instructor. One of the easiest ways to establish this type of comfort and trust is to invite students to ask questions or share feedback. For example, consider closing every correspondence (from the orientation video, to the syllabus, to my exam prompts, to weekly announcements) with "As always, please email me immediately with any questions or concerns. Best, Dr. Smith".

While it may be true that even the smiley face itself invites comfort and openness, students love to feel that they can be free to ask questions without being judged or penalized by the instructor. This is the same in face-to-face classroom interactions, where students sometimes preface their questions with "This is probably a stupid question" to which we may often respond, "There are no stupid questions, only stupid professors who can't answer them!" Because let's face it, when we close our eyes and imagine a "community," we usually conceptualize a place where we are freely accepted to share our ideas and give feedback without fear or shame. The opinions and attitudes of all community members should thus be treated as a valuable commodity. McMillian and Chavis (1986) conceptualized this as the "influence" component of community, understood as a reciprocal process where community members provide feedback and in turn, changes are made, which they can then provide feedback on.

Giving feedback (even when it involves a problem about the course!) is an integral part of an OLC. Consider the following email, of a type which many online professors receive each semester: "Professor, I am having a hard time studying for the quizzes. I feel like I know everything, and my mind blanks out during the quiz and I run out of time. Is there anything I can do?"

Any professor could completely ignore this email, but imagine how that would make the student feel. The student went out on a limb by sharing a problem, and, by ignoring his or her comment, the professor might have caused the student to feel excluded from the community. Generally, the student's question is a tough one and while recommended studying strategies for students are presented in chapter 6, it would be important to let this student know that (a) he or she is not alone and (b) there are strategies to engage in for active learning, including making note cards, outlines, and other study guides. The instructor's goal is to facilitate an open, engaging environment. If a student sends an email highlighting his or her concern, do not be offended. After all, the instructor must be doing something right for students to feel comfortable enough to share their honest (and perhaps, contrary) opinions!

Collaboration and Spontaneous Moderating

Instructors frequently post prompts to initiate conversation on the discussion board. These can range from direct questions ("What are the specific behaviors of a person with antisocial personality disorder?") to more free response type formats ("Discuss how personality disorders can potentially fluctuate across gender and age"). Still, much like the traditional classroom, we cannot assume that interactions between instructors and students are unidirectional. In fact, it seems that very frequently, students post their own questions on the discussion board, often directed toward their classmates as opposed to the instructor. Fear not instructors, you have not become obsolete; quite the opposite. If you have successfully developed a healthy online learning community, then you should expect students to create their own content, mediate their own discussions, and exchange new ideas based on class assignments. Collision and colleagues note that students spontaneously moderate their discussions in a variety of ways. They often ask questions directed toward their classmates that can be related to course technology, course content, the course interface, or even their own personal feelings. They can spontaneously moderate their own discussions by piping in to give words of encouragement, or responding in a supportive way to their fellow classmates.

Venting

The evidence of some venting directed at the course content, interface, and even the instructor is acceptable, and shows a level of comfort and trust associated with a healthy learning community. After all, the common goal shared by both the instructor and the students alike is to promote open communication and build education. Thus, in many ways a reasonable amount of venting shows how community members are vested in the learning experience and want their voices to be heard! It is beneficial then for the instructor to respond (within 24 to 48 hours ideally) to the aggrieved student, to ensure that they do not stew in their frustration and feel neglected.

What is reasonable venting? Well, this is rather subjective and based upon one's overall threshold for engagement. If an instructor does not mind responding to daily posts from a student who always has problems or feels confused, then it would be great to go ahead and help that student. He or she will certainly appreciate the attention and assistance. Consider posting these types of questions and answers in a public space because other students may share the problem(s). At the same time, if a student begins to take a harassing or disrespectful tone (such as those discussed toward the end of chapter 2), then it is probably time to confront the student via email and do a little bit of venting (or reprimanding?) yourself. An instructor in this situation can still be supportive by prefacing responses with comments like, "Great question" or "Good for you for expressing yourself!" so that the student does not feel like he or she is being chastised. Also, it might be beneficial to let students know during orientation that the instructor would rather they spoke up and shared their frustrations as opposed to staying quiet, making mistakes, becoming disenchanted, and having an unsatisfactory experience.

Concern and Support

The last component for a healthy online learning community is that participants show concern and give support to the community itself. According to this perspective, the community in and of itself becomes a "thing" of value and substance; it is something that its members want to foster and flourish. In order to demonstrate concern and support for the community, setting ground rules and proper netiquette (as discussed in chapter 2) becomes very important. Collison and colleagues (2000) give the example of an instructor posting materials and using capital letters meant to convey concern, while students interpret this as yelling. All these years later, it would be helpful to assume that most students equate capital letters as yelling and instructors should therefore avoid using them. Try to opt for italics, bold, or underline instead. Still the warning remains clear: irrespective of your intent, your *message may be perceived differently by your students*. What matters then is how students receive and process your messages, not how you might have wanted them to come across; so try to be clear, concise, and explicit!

EVALUATING ONLINE LEARNING COMMUNITIES: WHAT WORKS?

Because online learning communities vary so much in their definition and manifestation, it is difficult to comprehensively review exactly what methods of delivery lead to the most successful online learning communities. The situation is especially ambiguous when looking at the discipline of psychology in particular, where little to no research has been conducted on online learning communities for the teaching of psychology. Perhaps the best review of effective online learning communities published to date comes in the form of Ke and Hoadley's (2009) meta-analytic review of 42 studies that evaluated OLCs. The authors concluded that a one-size-fits-all evaluation of online learning communities was ineffective and instead recommended guidelines depending on the type and goals of OLC you are looking to evaluate. For online learning communities in psychology, a few of the recommended evaluation strategies in their taxonomy are applicable. First, the reviewers suggested that it is possible to evaluate the *"Community spirit"* of an OLC by examining the level of student *participation* (active involvement) and *sociability* (the idea that participants should interact not only academically, but socially to create and engage in their community). In general, participation and sociability in an OLC can be measured by time spent participating, the number of participants, the number and quality of interactions, help provided by participants, and the quantity of new ideas produced (Preece, 2000; Renninger & Shumar, 2002). Second, the reviewers suggested that evaluators of OLCs examine the correlation of quality of *community* (defined as participation in and sociability of the OLC) and *learning oriented achievement* (defined as the achievement of the learning goals for the course). Research already reported in this chapter (such as Rovai, 2002) found that when online learners participated in their community, they experienced greater achievements in learning. For an online psychology course, this correlation should hold true: Greater active participation in the community should result in more robust attainment of learning goals.

If we can take anything away from this comprehensive meta-analytic review of the evaluation of OLCs, it should be that they must be evaluated in light of their goals for learning and level of community created. How does this translate into instructor strategies for fostering a healthy OLC? Consider a number of practical approaches cited by the researchers. First, as already discussed, there ought to be an open, respectful forum for students to share ideas. Second, the instructor should engage in this forum to provide timely feedback to close the physical, psychological, and emotional divide. A cautionary note: instructors should try not to interrupt the flow of the forum by providing an expert or "correct" opinion. This is particularly true when students are engaging in controversial debates (such as the debate over gay marriage rights in a psychology of sexuality course). Sometimes when the professor wades in with his or her opinion, it might make students with dissenting opinions feel uncomfortable. Thus, the authors' recommendation is to give encouragement, and respond to questions, but to try to hold back from sounding like the definitive voice of reason. Fourth, summarize! It's always great when the instructor reads the entire discussion thread and then shares the key points with the class. More specific strategies for effective communication are discussed below, as we examine the changing roles of online instructors.

IMPLEMENTATION: FROM LECTURER TO MODERATOR

Online instructors are seemingly displaced from their classroom-based position leading the class from the front of the room or from behind the podium. What develops in an online learning community is often a very different modality of instruction than witnessed in the traditional classroom. This instructor displacement, in and of itself, is not problematic, but rather, it captures the essence of online education as a more learner-centered, instructor moderated dialogue. The change in the instructor's role only becomes a problem if the instructor is unwilling to let go of his or her position as class "leader" and take a slightly different approach. As mentioned earlier, instructors who constantly butt in to the discussion board, and who interrupt a flow in progress by laying down the law or reinforcing a rigid point of view, can greatly stunt student growth and confidence in their OLC. Therefore, it is very important to consider this changing role in your online psychology classes: You are moving from being the instructor or lecturer, to the role of facilitator or moderator. In other words, while as a classroom lecturer you were the disseminator of knowledge, now, you will become the facilitator of the learning process as it unfolds online (Howell, Saba, Lindsay, & Williams, 2004).

This transition from instructor to facilitator is really not that new or surprising. McKeachie's (1978) definitive volume on teaching tips identifies a number of roles taken by good instructors. According to Bender (2003), an online communications expert, many of these roles can also be applied to good online instructors, including the role of facilitator, formal authority, socializing agent, expert, and person who demonstrates compassion. For example, McKeachie (1978) discusses how instructors should work as *facilitators*, resisting a condescending, know-it-all attitude to help encourage active participation and learning through discussion. Indeed, the principle of facilitation is central to the success of online learners. Other tenets also apply, such as online educators as *formal authorities* who establish deadlines and boundaries (think orientation, netiquette, and respect in the OLC). Further, online educators also act as *socializing agents* who can set an appropriate example for online interaction, and assist students to further their professional careers. Online educators should be *experts* in their subject area, able to communicate effectively about the subject matter. And finally, online educators should serve as *people* who provide compassion, understanding, and guidance. According to this updated application of McKeachie's teaching tips then, perhaps a good online instructor is not so different from a good classroom instructor after all!

Nonetheless, the modality of course delivery differs substantially in the online classroom, and online instructors must adapt to this new environment. In their review of empirical research studies on communication in online courses, DeLaat, Lally, Lipponen, and Simons (2006) conclude that across the literature, "teacher involvement and active participation is appreciated by students ... [who] find communication with their teacher constructive and encouraging" (DeLaat et al., 2006, p. 266). In the online learning community, instructors should thus be aware that their position as a moderator who facilitates interaction and discussion is of great importance. A *moderator/facilitator* is defined as "a person charged with fostering the culture and the learning in an online dialogue or online course discussion area" (Collison et al., 2000, p. xiii). Indeed, scholars of online teaching roles have argued that moderation takes many different forms and often requires a range of activities. For example, Goodyear and colleagues (Goodyear, Salmon, Spector, Steeles, & Ticknor, 2001) distinguish between *process facilitation* (moderating the range of activities that support learning) and *content facilitation* (direct concern with fostering learner growth and understanding of course content). Likewise, others have argued that the central moderation duties of an online instructor involve: Motivation and engagement of student learning (Anderson, Rourke, Garrison, & Archer, 2001); using emotions to solve conflicts constructively (Salmon, 2003); facilitating group processes and monitoring participation (Harasim, Hiltz, Teles, & Turoff, 1997); as well as advising and counseling students (Goodyear et al., 2001)

Online learning as a whole functions akin to a process where students first engage with material, then interact with their peers surrounding this material, leading to a heightened understanding and sense of community. The participation itself seems to boost knowledge and function as an excellent form of active learning and community building. In light of the arguments for participation as learning that have been presented (such as by Hraskinski, 2009), instructors can help students by nurturing the trail where presentation of material leads to interaction and communication leads to increased learning. First and foremost, one of the central roles of an online instructor is to moderate this process and make sure it runs smoothly. Broadly speaking, as facilitator you are responsible for creating and monitoring the majority of interactive activities that your students will engage in to build knowledge.

FACILITATOR ROLES

Do not be discouraged if the number of roles and responsibilities outlined in the empirical research literature can feel quite burdensome. Many new online teachers report feeling overwhelmed by the complexity and breadth of student posts, challenged by their range of tasks, unsure how to handle criticism, and unclear about their role in general (DeLaat et al., 2006). Despite all that is required from an online moderator, the task is intuitively easier than one might think when the key components are properly organized. How can we better organize these contrasting principles and roles? Is there a simple set of guidelines that would enable good facilitation of online communication? The authors argue, yes. And to convey these guidelines, the authors use the metaphor of a theatrical play. Imagine the process of putting on a play. While it is not vital to consider every component, think broadly about what is entailed in the process and use this to help structure your approach to online facilitation.

Outline the Script

Every great play has a well-written script just as every successful online course has a well-thought-out course outline. Think of the syllabus and course orientation as the stage directions, and the course content, lectures, and assignments as the outline for the course script. Unlike a script for a theatrical play, the script for your online course is not yet written, nor is it set in stone. Rather, the online learning community and its members (akin to the actors' guild and the actors themselves) take a more hands on approach, engaging with your course material and establishing their own script, based around your stage directions and outline. This is a good thing! Much of their learning is facilitated through interaction and dialogue. If the facilitator holds students to a very rigid script, it may become frustrating when the discussion does not lead exactly in the intended direction. Further, setting rigid guidelines may put unnecessary pressure on students, who may pick up on the facilitator's frustration (in terms of negative feedback or poor grades) and become unsure about what the facilitator expects of them. To put it simply, the instructor or facilitator is not the be-all, end-all writer. Unlike a true theatrical play, the actors in an online course have some say over the direction of discussions. Perhaps then, an online course is more akin to an improvisational comedy show than to Shakespearean drama!

For an experienced instructor transitioning a face-to-face psychology course to the virtual world, first identify the elements of the traditional course that were most successful in sparking discussion, debate, and piquing student interest. Try to include these in the course content and online to enable the emergence of online discourse. For a new instructor who has never taught a certain face-to-face course before, outline the course to cover the necessary topics during the first semester, and examine which topics evoke the greatest amount of user interest and discourse. In the subsequent term, it is completely acceptable to focus a greater deal of attention on these successful, discussion-producing items. Let us not forget the research discussed earlier showing that the greater the level of participation in the online community, the greater the academic success and satisfaction.

Set the Stage Early

At the beginning of the course, facilitators are very much like directors or producers as they provide guidelines and feedback (akin to the stage directions and script outline) that set the process of online learning in motion. It is important for the facilitator to emerge as a capable, competent director/producer during the first few weeks of the course, because your actors need guidance! Online students often require early assistance and orientation to ensure their familiarity with the course (as we know from chapter 2). In the early stages of the course, facilitators need to provide direct, intense personal communication, while monitoring student awareness of the course interface (Levy, 2003). At this early stage, try to moderate course proceedings with efficiency, clarity, and detail. Just as a director looks to break in his or her actors to ensure they give a great performance, an online facilitator may benefit from ensuring that students understand what is expected of them early on so that they can succeed. If you sense a problem (such as violation of netiquette) or confusion (such as lack of clarity with a prompt), it would help to quickly respond to ensure that confusion is reduced. In terms of a facilitator's discussions and involvements during the early section of the course, it is useful to set the stage for the emergence of the online learning community by encouraging students to actively develop new ideas and perspectives. You may find that at the beginning of the course, you are heavily involved in a number of discussions and email exchanges, just as a director gives copious notes regarding early performances. As students become more familiar with the facilitator, with the interface, and with their peers, the frequency of concerns should begin to diminish.

Waiting in the Wings (or, Wind Beneath My Wings)

Once the course is launched, the instructor is responsible for facilitating the development of the online learning community throughout the semester. While instructors often take center stage at the start of the semester, they must continue to monitor and moderate from behind the scenes and provide input at the right time (Ferry, Kiggins, Hoban, & Lockyer, 2000). As already discussed, one the biggest mistakes facilitators can make is to dominate the content and direction of the discussion board. However, if you feel you would like to get involved in the discussion, try to wait until the assignment has concluded to give your students time to build knowledge and express their own ideas. Imagine a director who interrupts an actor's performance with criticism before the scene has even finished. The actor will feel frustrated and unfulfilled, unable to complete the scene and express him- or herself properly. Unlike the director of a play, a facilitator does not have to force the actors to perform the same script repeatedly. Rather, facilitators can give options and suggestions, and then sit back and allow students to flow within those guidelines.

A great way to facilitate dialogue involves choosing text from student posts that can bridge the gap towards future commentary (Collison et al., 2000). In other words, it might be very tempting to give praise ("Excellent job!") or criticism ("Your post lacks insight") but then, what motivation does the student have to continue posting on that thread? Rather, choose elements from a post that are intriguing, and frame follow-ups to encourage additional related dialogue. If a student writes a post about the right to privacy but transitions to writing about adults possessing child pornography, it would be rather tempting to jump in and steer the discussion back to the right to privacy. If possible, try to avoid this temptation (in other words, try to reject your inner director). Allowing the script to develop organically gives your students the autonomy and expression that enables their learning and sense of community to flourish. Rather than steering the discussion back to the original topic, try to bridge the discussion by bringing in another post, and tying back to the original question: "How does pornography fit into the right to privacy debate?"

Think about Barbara Streisand's *Wind Beneath My Wings*: a good facilitator will continually be raising issues, provoking discussions, while providing support and allowing students to fly with their own ideas. Giving support and encouragement becomes very important when students are new to online discussions and they are looking for a foothold. While giving help and feedback is discussed at length in the troubleshooting section, consider the following example: Often a director has to "massage the egos" of his or her A-list actors. The director tells them how beautiful or handsome they are, how talented they are, how much the audience loves them. While the authors are not suggesting that facilitators should throw out random compliments and plaudits to online students, as a good director it is part of the job to make your students feel comfortable and ready to perform at their best!

Often, emotional support is required in the realm of establishing closeness. Recall that online students are faced with the task of overcoming physical, psychological, and emotional distances, between each other and between the instructor and themselves. One of the central benefits to establishing online learning participation through *community* is that the perception of distance seemingly lessens when people share common goals, common needs, and a common outlook. So, a good facilitator can potentially conduct the morale-boosting akin to a director's ego massage, but efforts should be aimed at building closeness and community (while the director is charged with the difficult task of winning over a spoiled, surly A-lister).

How then, can a facilitator become the wind beneath their wings? There are a number of tips to follow for building community and social support. Facilitators can start on the right track by personalizing their courses, complete with unique facilitator specific photos, IM chats, and especially video lectures or conferencing. Just seeing the instructor's face and hearing his or her voice can potentially reduce the social and emotional distance. Chatting synchronously with students can also reduce the psychological distance and increase the facilitator's stake as a member of the group. Try to divide students into virtual study groups who work together, and ask each group to make a presentation at the end of the semester. When possible, encourage students to ask for help, and to post Q & A with other students to show the class how the online community is developing. Finally, facilitators can encourage students to moderate the discussions themselves, or serve as experts on a particular topic that they would then teach to the class. Peer mentoring and teaching not only enhances learning, but can deeply involve students in their learning community.

Stay off the Stage

Remember, the facilitator functions only as the director and producer of the show: A good facilitator never takes center stage!! To facilitate productive online learning, you must allow your students to be the actors, while you sit back and produce the overall show. Particularly as the class peaks and heads toward its inevitable conclusion, try to stay off the stage and create exercises that enable your students to demonstrate what they have learned. One frequently proposed distinction here is the facilitator as

Guide on the Side as opposed to *Sage on the Sage*. According to Collison and colleagues (2000), a "Sage on the Stage" lectures to students who then memorize and repeat that information, while a "Guide on the Side" shares leadership and encourages from the sidelines. Again, try to stay off the stage and remain there after you have launched the course. The "Guide on the Side" strategy can be effective by enabling students to develop their online learning community in ways that feel comfortable and organic to them. The authors who coined the term *Guide on the Side* actually equated it with being "partially invisible" (Collison et al., 2000, p. 202). Do not worry if you are used to being the "Sage on the Stage" in your traditional courses and you cannot see the results of shifting strategies right away. Sometimes evidence of a successful "Guide on the Side" can be subtle, ranging from the student using a new idea, to evidence of critical thinking, discussed later.

Cast and Crew Strike

At the end of any show, the cast and crew get together after the last performance and take down the set. They reminisce about their experiences and evaluate their performances. They talk about the highs and lows of the production, and about the working conditions. They exchange contact information, and vow to stay in touch until they are thrown together again in their next performance. A good facilitator can ensure that similar steps occur at the end of a course. Obviously, students are not required to take down the course interface. But it might be beneficial to ask them to go through the discussion boards and rate their favorite comments (or, depending upon the assignment, their favorite performances, videos, or activities). Likewise, you will want them to evaluate their director/producer: Were they satisfied with their learning conditions? Was it worth their efforts? What would they change or add to the class, if they could? It is useful to collect all of this information and apply it to improving your future courses in this discipline.

Also, consider that an online learning community does not have to disintegrate just because the course is over! Palloff and Pratt (1999) argued that the final step in creating an online community is *termination*. Given the breadth and depth of technology that can be incorporated into online classes, there might be another alternative. In other words, why let a perfectly good online community go to waste? For example, a good facilitator might want to migrate his or her course onto an invitation-only Facebook group page. Or, consider directing all former students to the same fan page, blog, or website: You might end up with hundreds, even thousands of students in one large, lasting online social group (more details on creating such a page are presented in chapter 4). Such a community page gives students a place to stay in touch, and provides you with a space to continue to disseminate relevant information. Particularly in psychology, new research is always being published, and student interest often outlasts the course itself. For example, students in the author's psychology of sexuality course debated at length over the potential differences in psychological adjustment and academic performance of children with heterosexual versus gay or lesbian parents. The overwhelming lack of empirical research stunted the discussion somewhat. Then, a few months after the end of the course, a research study was published at the University of California showing that children of lesbian couples may have fewer behavioral problems than children of heterosexual couples. The instructor immediately posted the link to that article, a page she had created for past students, and it lit up with over 10 comments in a few hours. An act that takes only a few minutes of your time can help foster the online community long after your class has finished.

Why does it matter to maintain the online learning community after the class is over? Just like an A-list director who creates new films that the fans love to see, every professor functions like an academic brand that develops a fan-base over time. Many former students may become fans and supporters, and giving them a little bit of lasting attention and support could go a long way. Students often enroll in classes because of recommendations from past students, and continuing virtual contact is a great way to remind former students to recommend your courses to their family and friends! Because geographical limitations suddenly evaporate when teaching online, members of your Facebook group might share information about your class with other Facebook friends at different institutions, who may elect to enroll in your class for transfer credit. Why deprive yourself of an excellent opportunity to promote your academic brand, your courses, and online learning in general? Considering that it only takes a few minutes to create and maintain such a page, this is surely time well spent.

FACILITATING ONLINE STUDENT COMMUNICATION

Who are our online students? How do they like to communicate? What do they expect in their communications with each other, and with their instructor? These are all important questions for facilitating communication, although they may be difficult to answer. First, let us return back to McKeachie's (1978) teaching tips and explore some important learner characteristics. According to Bender (2003), McKeachie's student qualities of *independence, authoritarianism,* and *anxiety* can also be applied to students in the online learning community. First, some online learners are highly *independent* and require little guidance or feedback from the professor. We see this often in student moderated discussions when the instructor adopts the role of guide on the side. However, should the instructor introduce an unfamiliar activity (such as asking students to create YouTube videos of themselves) more frequent facilitation and intervention may become necessary. Likewise, some students who are new to online instruction may welcome increased instructor activity and interaction, helping to make them feel less isolated. To deal with varying levels of student independence in the online learning community, try to avoid the one-size-fits-all approach and notice that some students may seek extra help, through email, chat, or other communications (see section on giving feedback later). Try to pay special attention to nurturing these students. Likewise, other students may feel that their growth and expression is stunted by constant professor interruption.

Next is student level of *authoritarianism*. According to McKeachie (1978), some students prefer a high degree of control surrounding their learning environment, while others prefer for the instructors to have control. Based upon the literature discussed in this chapter, it appears that active student engagement is the best approach for productive participation in the online learning community. Therefore, instructors are cautioned to relinquish the traditional control they might have experienced in the classroom, and allow student discussion to dictate the flow of the course. This could, of course, seem unpleasant for students who are shy, unconfident, or who are accustomed to taking a back seat in their learning. These students may struggle online where they have to be self-motivated and driven to complete their assignments. Again, one of the goals for good facilitation should be drawing these students out of their shells, and encouraging them to participate without fear of criticism or failure.

Finally, McKeachie (1978) discusses level of student *anxiety*. In an unfamiliar online environment, students may be prone to anxiety and confusion. Consider that students who experience lack of familiarity with online learning may be seeking a highly structured course environment. This is not in contrast with your interests as an online instructor. A good facilitator will no doubt want to provide accurate structuring and deadlines, ranging from due dates, to rules for discussion, to instructions for obtaining feedback. Anxiety can be reduced when students discover a structured protocol for obtaining feedback. One cautionary note: Once the course structure is put in place, it might be useful to allow for a more free exchange regarding course content. In other words, although the structure itself may feel rigid, the facilitator can make the exchange of ideas regarding content feel fluid. So, if a student asks a question about persuasion in the middle of a social psychology discussion about relationships, do not chastise that student. Rather, help the student relate the question to the discussion or at least allow the discussion to develop surrounding that topic.

COMMUNICATION TECHNOLOGY

Online instructors are blessed with a wealth of communication modalities at our fingertips, and the choice of this modality may in turn affect the flow of discussions, and more broadly, the style of the online learning community. Consider the numerous types of technology available for your utilization:

3.1 ONLINE COMMUNICATION TECHNOLOGY

Email: messages sent to users via electronic mail. Reading and reply to emails occurs asynchronously.

Discussion Board Post: Your Course Management System (CMS) should facilitate a discussion board where students can post messages and reply to them in a public, asynchronous forum.

Text-Based Chat: Real-time text synchronous conversations occurring between two individuals (Instant Messaging) or between members of a group (Chat).

Video Conference/Chat: Real-time audio/visual synchronous communication occurring between individuals or a group. Video conference requires the use of a webcam and microphone, and is sometimes integrated into the CMS (such as through Elluminate).

Podcasting: Audio-based recordings that can be asynchronously distributed to students and then listened to on computer or portable devices.

Social Networking Websites: Websites that facilitate social interaction and community, through making posts, sending emails, and chatting. Including but not limited to Facebook, MySpace, Linkedin, Twitter.

Wikis: A web collaboration tool where site content can be modified by visitors.

(Source: Edwards & Helvie-Mason, 2010; Parker & Chao, 2007).

Although the practical usage of these technologies will be discussed at length in chapter 4, consider how the type of technology you choose to communicate with can have an effect on the learning styles of your class. For example, an instructor who selects to use social networking sites to distribute information may build a comfortable social community more quickly than one who relies upon emailing PDF documents to individual users. Likewise, podcasting your lectures may have a different effect on processing and retention than video-based lectures, or PowerPoint-slide lectures. And importantly, if the instructor decides that students will communicate via discussion boards and emails only, this may result in qualitatively and quantitatively different types of communication than if live chat and video conferencing are selected. Consider that students using discussion boards only will never have a real-time interaction, whereas those using live chat will participate in discussions simultaneously.

Indeed, one of the key decisions that must be made when creating an online course is whether synchronous or asynchronous discussions will be utilized to facilitate communication. *Asynchronous* communications are those that do not occur in real-time. This includes emails, discussion posts, and other exchanges of information that are not conducted as a live feed. When a person sends an email, and that email is read at a different time, one would label this as asynchronous communication. When online communication first became commonplace in the 1990s, it was assumed that asynchronous discussion would comprise the lion's share of all online communication (Moore & Anderson, 2003). However, even in the last 5 years, technology has developed at such a fast rate that now it is very easy to interact synchronously with numerous individuals, simultaneously. *Synchronous* communication occurs live and in real-time, such as instant messaging chats, telephone conversations, or video conferencing. In order to effectively communicate synchronously, users must be logged into the course interface at the same time.

Which style of communication is better for teaching psychology, asynchronous or synchronous? Thankfully, as an instructor you are not necessarily confined to a one-or-the other type of framework. Rather, it is very probable that instructors may incorporate synchronous and asynchronous elements into the same course. The choice of synchronous or asynchronous communication depends upon the needs and goals of the students. Some students seek out synchronous communication to build community, and feel that real-time connection and interaction with their professors and classmates. Other students choose to take online courses specifically due to the lack of synchronous meetings. Asynchronous communications means that they are free to select their schedule as they choose without adhering to time constraints (Moore & Anderson, 2003). Unless your college specifies otherwise, you are not required to utilize both asynchronous and synchronous discussions. However, creating a balance between synchronous and asynchronous activities can lead to high levels of student engagement, online community building, and student satisfaction.

ASYNCHRONOUS COMMUNICATION

Online asynchronous discussions are usually the most common form of communication in online courses second to email (Kearsley, 2000), and participation in them can lead to critical thinking, knowledge construction, problem solving, and collaboration (Penny & Murphy, 2009). There are a number of benefits to allowing students to communicate asynchronously. First, students can become more deeply involved in asynchronous discussions when compared to face-to-face communication or in live text-based chat. Students who make posts on discussion boards have the benefit of extended time to research, reflect, and think critically about the subject area, as opposed to feeling pressured to generate ideas on the spot. Second, asynchronous discussions provide opportunities for communication for students who may shy away from involvement in live chat or face-to-face interaction. Indeed, asynchronous discussions present a level playing field where students have equal chances to comment and interact. For example, participants in asynchronous discussions can augment their posts by conducting outside research (such as discussed by Du, Zhang, Olinzock, & Adams, 2008) and integrating this into their discussion. This type of research integration would be difficult in a face-to-face or live discussion. In many respects then, asynchronous discussions benefit students by providing the greatest opportunity for critical thinking and reflection, and enabling students to participate more deeply than through other mediums.

According to some online educators (such as Al-Shalchi, 2009, and Rose and Smith, 2007), a strong asynchronous discussion assignment features several key procedural elements including clear directions, feedback, motivation, expectancies, and organization.

Clear Directions

Students should be aware of due dates, prompts, and requirements for each assignment long before it is due. Because some students can take a very long time to complete their asynchronous posts, be considerate and provide the assignment early on.

Feedback

Try to respond to student questions about the asynchronous assignment as soon as possible. Unlike face-to-face or synchronous communication, participant concerns are not met immediately with instructor feedback.

You should thus do your best to bridge the digital divide and help provide support in a timely fashion.

Motivation

One of the many individual differences online facilitators must contend with is that some students are highly motivated to participate, while others may avoid it altogether. This can lead to an imbalance on the discussion board, where some students might go way beyond the assignment by writing 10 high quality posts, while another makes one post comprised of two sentences. How does one deal with the student who does not want to participate? This can become a potential problem. Bender (2003) cautions against publicly humiliating or criticizing this student, and instead suggests sending a personal email to understand why he or she has not been contributing.

Further, it has been widely noted that some students only make the necessary discussion posts to satisfy the grading requirement (Bullen, 1998; Hara, Bonk, & Angeli, 2000). Discussions can therefore become stunted because students wait until the last minute, which does not allow time for a discourse to develop. Indeed, it appears that the proximity of the deadline does affect the extent and degree of participation and dialogue (Dennen, 2005). If a significant percentage of the class waits until the final half hour before the deadline to respond, then the discussion will feature comments like "I agree, good post!" instead of in-depth critical analyses or reflection. Nonetheless, combating this "lazy student" phenomenon always reflects a challenge. One suggestion by the authors involves asking students to rate each other's posts, and gives one bonus point to the most highly rated post. This will encourage students to think critically about creating a quality post, and will get them onto the board early and reading the posts of other students. When using this strategy, the authors tend to see a greater amount of participation spaced over a longer amount of time.

Expectancies

Students need to know (a) how they will be graded and (b) what types of posts are acceptable or unacceptable. First, in terms of grading, the common features of asynchronous discussion rubrics are discussed below, and sample rubrics are presented at length in chapter 6 on assessment. Second, the level of acceptability of posts should be evident because students should have been briefed on netiquette and acceptable content prior to the first discussion board. Students may want more specific guidelines as well: "Can I introduce research from outside the course material? Can I give encouragement to fellow students? Can we talk about personal issues on the discussion board?" Anticipate these questions and reduce confusion by providing answers before the board is launched.

Organization

The instructor's decisions regarding organization of the discussion board may result in different levels of communication. Sorting the board by topics and threads is one way to keep it well organized (Rose & Smith, 2007). The authors recommend creating different topics for each assignment. So, if a discussion board about cultural norms is due, this board should be completely separate (a totally new board) from one relating to social identity, for example. After creating different boards for each topic, begin to organize the threads pertaining to specific topics in the board. To start with, try to create your own threads. In this example, the cultural norms discussion asks about the influence of religion, society, and the media upon people's beliefs and behaviors. So, the best practice would be to create three threads, one related to religion, one related to society, and one related to the media. Then, the facilitator can encourage students to make posts relevant to each topic along these threads. Also, create another thread for "questions" where it is easy to disseminate and post feedback. Organizing discussion posts by thread topic is a very easy and effective way to maintain good organization throughout the semester.

What makes an asynchronous discussion post successful? While assessment will be discussed at length in chapter 6, there are some elements to consider when constructing a discussion board prompt. In their review of over 50 rubrics for grading online asynchronous discussions, Penny and Murphy (2009) identify four key components that instructors generally look for in their discussions: cognitive, mechanical, procedural, and interactive.

Cognitive components (including critical thinking, problem solving, creative thinking, knowledge of course content, and argumentation) accounted for about 40% of all grading rubrics in this review. In terms of critical thinking, the grading rubrics look to see a deep (rather than superficial understanding) of the material, and the ability to evaluate that material and apply it to real-life or personal experience. *Mechanical* components refer to assessments of language, grammar, spelling, writing style, and use of citations and references. Central here is clarity in the expression of ideas and the organization of one's post. *Procedural/managerial* elements of assessment focus on participant conduct, presence, and contribution. It is important to measure the level of persistence in student participation. Finally, *interactive* assessments refer to the level of positive interaction, and the student's contributions to building the learning community.

While it may be the most difficult to objectively measure, this component can include students who encourage others to share their reflections, or give statements that elicit responses from others or that provide responses to others. Comprehensive discussion of grading rubrics will be presented in chapter 6.

SYNCHRONOUS COMMUNICATION

The majority of synchronous discussions employ text-based live chat (such as instant messaging but between a group of people instead of one-to-one), although video and audio conferencing are becoming more frequent thanks to technological and CMS developments (Ko & Rossen, 2010). Synchronous discussions bridge the digital divide by connecting people in a real-life virtual world. Many students and professors alike already utilize this type of communication through instant messaging (e.g., Yahoo Messaging, AOL instant messenger, MSN messenger, Facebook chat, or Gmail chat) and thus, synchronous discussion feels like a familiar way to interact in an online social space. Before creating a synchronous assignment, consider a few guidelines. First, assigning a chat-based assignment at the last minute can be problematic. Live chats often require intense cognitive commitment, and students should be provided with ample time to prepare. Second, live chat can be highly immersive and cognitively draining, so try to ensure that any live chat assignment does not last longer than an hour.

Before the chat begins, advise students that their preparation should include the following: Reading the relevant course materials, brainstorming discussion questions, citing outside research, and using a certain level of decorum (read: netiquette). Of course outside sources are not necessarily required, but students should be given enough time to prepare in case they would like to conduct outside research. Is there an ideal group size for online chat? Bender (2003) argues that 5 students should be the maximum in a live chat group, to avoid confusion and missed information. However, the authors have experienced successful discussions mediated through Elluminate containing upwards of 40 students. So when designing a live chat, try to select a size between 5 and 40 students that you feel comfortable with. Is there an appropriate time limit for a live chat? Some online teachers, such as Bender (2003), suggest that a 30- to 45-minute time limit can be effective, whereas others may conduct chats longer than 1 hour. Chats can become mentally draining, so to avoid distractions or restlessness the authors recommend capping any chat at 1 hour.

Synchronous communication lends itself to a number of activities in addition to basic discussions and chats, including debating, group work, and online guest lecturers. *Debates* are frequently included in classroom activities in psychology, so why not hold these synchronously online? Using your CMS, 2 students can debate via chat-link while the rest of the class observes the performance (usually by reading the text). So, pick a pair of students and assign each of them a debate. For example, imagine a common Introduction to Psychology debate. One student (or, group of students) can debate the merits of "Psychology as History" perspective, while the others can debate in favor of "Psychology as Science" perspective. The authors recommend structuring this type of debate into a 15-minute time-frame, where each side can give a 3-minute opening statement followed by 8 minutes or so of open debate, ending with a 1-minute conclusion from each side. This time frame can be altered depending upon the number of students and the complexity of the issue being debated. For courses using Elluminate or another program that offers this option, it is possible to display the timer on the screen so that students are aware of how long they have left. Then, if you desire, the students who did not participate can vote on the winner of the debate. This is a great exercise that highlights the most engaging elements of face-to-face classrooms and enables the students to take center stage.

Another benefit to synchronous communication is that *small groups* of students can work on projects in real-time. Small-group projects provide an excellent avenue for building the online learning community and making strong connections between students. One of the benefits to this approach is that small groups can decide for themselves when to meet and chat, without requiring the presence of the entire class or the instructor. This helps to reduce the scheduling conflicts often associated with synchronous interaction, as it is much easier to find a common meeting time across three students than 30 students. One benefit to using group chat on your CMS is that the instructor should be able to read and comment on group chats even after the chats have ended, and email this feedback to the group. Group activities work well in certain situations, such as when you have a very large class and want to encourage meaningful discussions between smaller groups of students, or when you assign a group project or presentation as a course assignment.

Bender (2003) suggests that when students are assigned to a group project, they should also be assigned specific roles in their groups to reduce confusion and ensure that each student contributes to the overall learning process. For example, one student can be assigned to present the material; one can be assigned the role of researcher; one the role of editor; one the role of organizer, and so on. When it comes time to present, this should also be done synchronously, with the rest of the class watching, if possible. Otherwise, students should record their presentation (as a video file, audio file, or PDF) and disseminate it to the rest of the class so that they can comment, give ratings, and questions. This process is really very similar to group work in the traditional classroom, although due to this medium it is easier than ever for students to communicate. Instead of finding a time to meet up after class, they can log on to their CMS from home.

Finally, online learning enables facilitators to easily provide access to *online guest speakers* that students may never have the opportunity to hear otherwise! While it's true that instructors can asynchronously link students to numerous websites featuring guest lecturers (iTunes U and Open University are just a few of the many featured in chapter 4), there is something special about a live interaction with an expert. The first step is to recruit your expert. This could be a colleague from your university, or someone that you have conducted research with in the past. Perhaps it is someone you heard speaking at a conference, or someone whose research is relevant to the course on that day. If so, ask them to provide a PDF or PowerPoint of a lecture beforehand, as well as relevant articles. This way, the students can prepare questions, much as they would in a traditional lecture-based classroom. You can even assign one student, or a small group of students, to prepare and deliver the introduction for your expert as a preface to the conversation.

Your guest speakers could also be another person of interest, and they do not have to be fellow research psychologists! Guest speakers are beneficial because they can provide access to individuals your students may never otherwise meet. This is particularly true in the case of courses featuring controversial, nonnormative, or abnormal content. For example, online it may be easier to recruit speakers who are transgender, or who have had abortions, or who live in a different part of the world and understand other cultures. Online discussions might also be more comfortable for your speaker in this type of a situation, where they may not want to be publicly acknowledged as someone who is in some way nonnormative or "deviant." Other types of different people would make great guest speakers in an online course, including individuals for an abnormal psychology class who have been treated for mental illness; parents of small children for a developmental psychology class; and older adults to discuss sex and aging in a gerontology course; or a research intern for a methods course. While these individuals may not hold graduate degrees in psychology, their real-world expertise remains relevant to your courses (and exciting for your students).

Guest lecturers are not exclusive to synchronous communication—it is also possible for a guest lecturer to interact asynchronously with the class via the discussion board. While this kind of interaction may not be as exciting as a live chat with the expert, it has been argued that this approach might actually lead to a more comprehensive, critical, and reflexive discussion

(Bender, 2003). Students will have more time than just a 30-minute inter-action to craft their posts and responses, and critically evaluate those of their classmates. However, logging on to the class and reading/replying to posts does require a greater amount of time commitment from your expert. It might be easier for him or her to conduct a one-time live session. Either way, it is important that as many students as possible attend this online session. Inevitably there will be scheduling issues with a handful of students who cannot attend. If the expert interacts asynchronously, this does not pose as much of a problem as missing the synchronous meeting. However, if the meeting is synchronous, try to ensure that it is recorded and disseminated immediately after the session so that all students can access it. Further, ask your expert if he or she would mind responding to a few follow-up emails after the session from interested students and those who missed it the first time around.

Scheduling issues pose the greatest number of challenges to employing synchronous communication. Often, at the start of a semester online pro-fessors receive emails from students who are concerned or worried about a synchronous element: "Professor, do we have to log-on at the same time in order to take the course? I don't think this will be possible." Generally, making synchronous activities at only one specific time mandatory (such as, "every Friday morning we will be communicating via Elluminate") could alienate students who are not free at this time. There are a few ways for getting around this. First, make sure that students are aware of syn-chronously scheduled activities at the time of course enrollment. Post this information on your course website, CMS, and Facebook page. This may deter some students from enrolling in your course, if they are unwilling or unable to commit to a meeting at that time each week. Remember that students often live in different time zones, and that you should provide the schedule early to reduce confusion and attrition.

Alternatively, instructors can also offer a few synchronous meetings throughout the week to triangulate student availability, such as a live chat on Monday afternoon, Friday morning, and Wednesday evening. However, remember that each scheduled synchronous activity may require a facili-tator to monitor it. This means that in addition to all of your asynchro-nous work (such as emailing and commenting on discussions) you may also be required to devote weekly chunks of time to your online course. Going down this route, you may end up as a "24 hour professor," which is something you probably want to avoid! An alternative is making weekly synchronous activities "optional but encouraged" so that students do not feel pressure to adhere to a weekly schedule, but they have an opportunity to interact in real-time should they desire it. However, if the activities are optional, it means that (a) they cannot comprise a large percentage of the students' grade and (b) the instructor must find another way to cover this material for the students who miss the live session.

CREATING QUESTIONS THAT PROMOTE INTERACTION

The remainder of the implementation section deals with strategies for promoting effective interaction. What are the types of questions an instructor would ask on the discussion board, and how could these influence participation? First, consider a constructivist perspective on online learning, where the learner is actively involved in creating (or constructing) meaning from the course content. Within a constructivist framework in an online course, the best questions are higher order questions that allow students to construct knowledge from past experience/course material, and enable collaboration. So instead of asking questions like this: "What do you think about intersexed individuals?" (which may be met with a negligible reply), ask students "If you were intersexed, how would you feel? What would you do?" Online scholars have suggested that these types of *hypothetical* questions are exciting, engaging, and call upon past experience and new information to create knowledge (Bender, 2003). Likewise, avoid "yes/no" questions like: "Do you think prostitution should be legal?" and instead ask an *evaluative* question "What do you think would be better for our society—illegal prostitution or decriminalized prostitution? Why?"

Try to avoid asking questions that require extremely long responses. While the authors have read some well-crafted multiparagraph discussion posts, they hardly promote interaction and community. Encourage students to save this for a paper or other type of assignment, and post only a short summary of their lengthy thoughts on the discussion board. Sometimes students feel that quantity equals quality. They believe that by writing a very long post, they are bound to meet all of the criteria required for getting a good grade. In actuality, long posts can come across as impersonal and actually reduce the participation of other students, who may not be inclined to read and reply to so much information. When you are organizing your discussions and providing introductory information, encourage students to make shorter (paragraph-long) posts or set a word limit on their posts, as students will benefit from applying a critical eye to their posts. Rather than rambling in their responses, they should demonstrate that they can edit and crucially, that they can write for the audience of fellow students seeking to engage them in discussion.

Types of Question

There are a number of different types of questions that an online facilitator can utilize to promote discussion and engagement. After reviewing the relevant research literature, Akin and Neal (2007) proposed several types of effective questions:

Metacognitive Questions

These types of questions encourage a type of "self-questioning" where users seek to solve a problem by considering what they already know, and how it applies to their current questions. The authors cite four ways to facilitate metacognition through questioning: comprehension of the problem, making connections between former and current problems, using strategies to solve the current problem, and reflections upon the process (Mevarech & Kramanski, 2003). What does this mean for creating good questions in psychology? From an applied perspective, we are often looking to solve difficult problems based upon theory and past research. A good example is asking students to create an intervention: For example, challenge them to think of innovative ways to convince borderline alcoholics to enroll in a sober living facility. A metacognitive approach would guide students along the four pathways. First, focus on the problem. The nature of the problem is alcohol addiction. Second, what is the relationship between current and former problems? Well, alcoholism is genetic and hereditary, and many alcoholics who rehab end up drinking again. Third, how can we solve the problem? Well, we have to use a combination of persuasion and attitude change (behavioral), as well as support from friends (social), and detoxification (medical/clinical). Fourth, reflect upon the process. Do you think this approach would work? What alternatives are there? Just based upon this example, we can see how a metacognitive line of questioning leads to well thought out, deeper responses than the simple questions like: "How can you get alcoholics into treatment?"

Follow-Up Questions

These types of questions often occur after the dissemination of important course material. In a health psychology course, the assignment might feature a video documenting the experiences of women being screened for breast cancer, or a report on behavioral tactics for encouraging enrollment in breast cancer screening. Good follow-up questions should go beyond the obvious "What was this about?" to consider different perspectives, identify related outcomes, provide clarity and address importance. So for a breast cancer screening video, good questions might be "What alternative explanations are there for the decision to obtain a breast cancer screening?" or, "What do you think will happen to the women who get screened/ who do not get screened?" or, "Which theory mentioned in the report best accounts for the decision to receive a health screening?" or, "What are the life consequences for women who miss screenings?"

Evaluation and Reflection Questions

These types of questions should provide brief, 1- to 5-minute assessments of the student's experiences in the course thus far. In this short time they can reflect upon the course in general or the specific weekly topic, but their comments should be content-based (as opposed to procedural, "I don't like posting on the board" type of comments). The prompt for these questions should not be a vague "What do you think?" but rather encourage reflection, "Take a few minutes to reflect upon the course content and share your thoughts on this discussion board." There should be a varied depth and range to these responses, which should allow participants to gather their thoughts for a moment before proceeding. In a research methods course, students might make posts like "I would like to create a quasi-experimental study" to reflections like "I never realized that causation was such an important part of experimental design."

Student Created Questions

Facilitators have already been reminded to share the stage with students when possible, and this includes the formation of discussion questions. Pelz (2004) reports excellent results when students are charged with creating their own discussion questions. Not only does this encourage their activity and collaboration, it will also ensure that students read critically and effectively. They should want to pay attention to important sections of the text and ask good questions, to show the rest of the class that they care about being involved in the online learning community. These types of student created discussions should not be aimed at confusion, as in, "I don't understand the ovarian cycle, can someone explain it to me?" but should be fodder for conversation: "Which is more important for women's sexual development, the ovarian cycle or the menstrual cycle?" So, when instructing students to create their own discussion questions, remind them that these should be questions that inspire debate and engagement, as opposed to yes/no questions or their own sources of confusion.

CRITICAL THINKING THROUGH INTERACTIVITY

The closing thought for this section surrounds the relationship between participation and critical thinking. Critical thinking is often a central learning outcome for online college courses. In fact, 89% of colleges claim that critical thinking is a central educational outcome, although only 19% provide a working definition of the construct (Paul, Elder, & Bartell, 1997). The question remains, do our online discussions promote more or less critical thinking than those conducted from a face-to-face perspective?

Some researchers have argued that asynchronous online discussions are actually better at fostering critical thinking than face-to-face discussions, because students are afforded the time to master their area of learning, and give and receive feedback over a series of days and weeks, rather than during specific course meetings only (Astleitner, 2002). Further, asynchronous discussions create a higher order organization of thoughts that require additional investigation and research, as opposed to the immediate, sometimes shallow demands of a live discussion (Mandernach, Forrest, Babutzke, & Manker, 2009).

In an experimental study comparing online and face-to-face discussions to promote critical thinking, Mandernach et al. (2009) found that asynchronous discussion boards do not inherently promote a greater amount of critical thinking than face-to-face (or, live synchronous) communication. Rather, the instructor's level of interactivity and engagement seems to account for the effects upon critical thinking. In this respect the mode of discussion (asynchronous online, synchronous online, or face-to-face) is just a tool that a good instructor can use to facilitate critical thinking. Regardless of the medium of course delivery, an instructor who engages students via a critical, exciting, constructivist delivery of course materials will be the most successful at producing critical thinking achievements in his or her students. While this study presents only one finding in a proverbial sea of critical thinking research, it does have important implications.

As online instructors, we don't ever want to lose ourselves in technology, or become so enmeshed and involved in technology that we forget what we are doing and why we are doing it. It is not the technology itself that facilitates online learning, but the people behind the technology, the students and instructors. Always try to remember that an engaging professor, who provides the tools that enable the students to flourish, will be the most successful, whether in person or online. The tools of the trade might change across the digital divide, but the trade itself remains the same. Keep this in the back of your mind as we move on to chapter 4, to discuss all of the available technology and how to use it to promote student achievement.

TROUBLESHOOTING: GIVING HELP AND FEEDBACK

Giving feedback is a fundamental part of online courses and can help to breach the psychological and emotional digital divide. In any arena, a good communicator is one who can give help, just as a good online mentor is one who can attend to the needs of his or her students. Interestingly, research has shown that online psychology students are more likely than students in traditional psychology courses to seek help. For example, Kitsantas and Chow (2007) found that students in their online educational psychology courses asked for help more frequently, and were less apprehensive about seeking help, than their traditional course counterparts. Kumrow (2007) found that among graduate nursing students, those who completed a health care course fully online asked for help more frequently, and received better final grades, than those in the traditional section of the course. This is good news because students who seek help should feel more comfortable when their questions are answered, and presumably this should have some sort of impact on their academic success. However, according to Whipp and Lorenz (2010), the relationship between types of help given and academic success remains unclear. These researchers found that students who received the highest course grades in online courses also demonstrated the highest amount of help seeking behavior. Based on their exploratory research, Whipp and Lorenz (2010) offer some guidelines for effective help-giving in online instruction, including providing timing, clear and concise feedback, having a strong social presence, using first names, reaching out to nonparticipants, and asking peers to give help to one another.

There are different types of help-giving feedback that instructors can provide, and often a distinction is made between *corrective* and *motivational* feedback. Corrective feedback is usually designed to resolve or fix errors and give feedback on student performance, while motivational feedback is focused more on helping the learner to achieve her or his educational goals. In their investigation of instructor–student feedback in online courses, Pyke and Sherlock (2010) argue that an additional type of feedback, *technology* feedback, be incorporated. This type of feedback is solely directed at helping students navigate the CMS and technological applications.

In their study on types of instructor–student feedback in online learning, Pyke and Sherlock found that in a 16-person graduate online course, over 70% of all feedback provided was corrective in nature, compared with 21% motivational and 9% technological. Of the corrective feedback provided, 63% was directed toward teams, compared with 37% toward individuals. In terms of the information presented in this chapter on communication in the online learning community, this study was surprising. One would expect that in an online course, the facilitator would devote a greater amount of time to motivational feedback pertaining to student goals, learning abilities, and understanding of activities and environment. Nonetheless, the modality of communication presented was especially intriguing. Corrective feedback was most frequently disseminated via the asynchronous discussion board, written assignments and emails, while motivational feedback was provided most frequently in the form of synchronous live chat.

VIRTUAL OFFICE HOURS

A new way for online instructors to reach out to their students using live chat is through virtual office hours (VOH). Some online instructors might argue that given the amount of time spent responding to emails, the entire week can feel like a virtual office hour! However, consider selecting only a few specific times per week to respond to emails or to communicate synchronously with students via web-based chat. Interestingly, empirical research has shown that even for students in traditional lecture classes, VOH are preferable to in-class office hours (Edwards & Helvie-Mason, 2010). In that study, students in an introductory communications class preferred VOH (which featured a Yahoo-messenger chat with their instructor) to traditional office hours because of the convenience of communicating with the professor from their home or office, without having to schedule an appointment on campus. Additionally, over 70% of students who elected to use VOH responded with a favorable attitude to them. This study shows that the usage of online chat with the instructor can become integrated into a range of courses, ranging from fully online, to hybrid, and even traditional courses!

From the perspective of a fully online course, there are some considerations that should be made if selecting VOH, the first of which is scheduling. Is there a time when the majority of students would be present to chat? Usually this time will pop up on the weekend. Are you sure you want to commit each Saturday afternoon to hosting a VOH? However, if the VOH falls at an inconvenient time, it might be possible to hire a liaison or TA to conduct them for you. Second, in your class, will VOH replace or augment typical email communication? If they replace emails, it could be problematic for a student who has a question on Wednesday, but has to wait until VOH on Saturday to ensure a reply. Likewise if you employ IM chat (such as Yahoo Messenger, MSN Messenger, or Skype) then it might be worthwhile to create a separate account for chatting with students that you only access during office hours, or leave your account so that it appears "offline" when you are not responding to student messages. If you choose to conduct VOH in addition to your regular emails to students (which the authors would recommend), just ensure that you do not find yourself falling into the "24 Hour Professor Syndrome" (Edwards & Helvie-Mason, 2010). A professor who ends up available 24 hours per day is one who may feel overwhelmed, and who may fail to establish a healthy work–life balance. If you are always checking you school inbox, or always visible on IM chat to your students, you may end up burning out very quickly into the semester.

FINDING A BALANCE

Communicating and giving feedback to students is all about finding a comfortable balance. Not enough feedback and students could feel neglected or isolated. Too much feedback and you run the risk of being overbearing, and taking the stage rather than remaining backstage. Further, too much communication and you may end up feeling disillusioned and stressed. Of course, establishing a balance is different for each individual. For the instructor who already has a very high threshold of media engagement (as in, she spends every waking minute on email and Facebook anyway), then perhaps frequent emails with students are welcomed. The instructor who shies away from technology might want to hire a TA to handle communications, or post replies in a public forum in hopes that many students have the same question that can be answered simultaneously. Posting responses on the class website, YouTube page, or Facebook page in addition to the CMS announcement page is a great way to get feedback out there without requiring personal communication with each student.

The only way for an online instructor to determine his or her optimal communication balance is with practice. If you have never taught online before, you may enter into your course with the expectation that you can handle multiple daily emails with students, only to discover that these emails cause an additional workload you had not bargained for. Likewise, you may begin your class in apprehension of email overload, only to discover that it was not as troubling as you had anticipated. One should expect that during your first few courses, communications will not run as smoothly as desired. However, do not forget that communication issues are forgivable problems and not the be-all and end-all of disasters. So long as you are open, supportive, and caring toward your students they will forgive you if you have minor difficulties with emails, announcements, and chats.

GIVING EMOTIONAL SUPPORT

Many students have emotional or psychological concerns that they have to convey across the distance of the digital divide. Attending to their needs (reasonably) is one of the best ways that a facilitator can foster support, growth, and confidence in the learning community. Sometimes, attending to student needs can be difficult. In the previous chapter, an example was presented where a student wrote to the professor about his drug addiction and subsequent rehab. While this is certainly verging on inappropriate (or perhaps an "overshare"), this student is showing the professor (and perhaps the community) that he is in a difficult position in his life and looking for support. Had the student chosen to type this comment about drug rehab on the discussion board, a supportive learning community may have provided encouragement, sympathy, and perhaps links to websites or treatment centers with more information. However, since the student did not elect to make this information public, it would be highly inadvisable for the instructor to do so. In this situation, you may want to check in with the student throughout the semester, to show that you care, to try and bridge the digital divide to instill some level of humanity.

Further, consider referring students who experience and share these kinds of issues, such as sexual risk, addiction, depression, health issues, or learning problems to the student support services at your institutions. The majority of institutions offer gratis health and counseling services to students who pay their registration fees, as well as resources for individuals with learning disabilities or who speak English as a second language (ESL). In most cases, these services are not offered in a fully online format, and online students may need to attend campus to gain access to the help that they need. Online instructors can certainly help refer students to their institution's health care, counseling services, and disabilities services by posting relevant information on the course website, discussion board, and on Facebook pages or personal websites. This information can and should include the link, phone number, contact person, and building location of the various services offered by that institution. Also, consider posting links to outside services that may be relevant to your students and course material, such as free STD screening by Planned Parenthood, or a local AA meeting group. By offering information on these student services, instructors can help to ensure that online students still receive the references and assistance they would have been afforded had they been in a classroom-based course. In other words, just because a student is learning online does not mean he or she should not be entitled to the same access to support and resources as a face-to-face student.

The sheer absence of physical cues like eye contact, tone of voice, and proximity means that online students may have a greater need for emotional and psychological support than their classroom based counterparts, so you may have to go to extra lengths to ensure that their community cares about them. The lack of emotion in communication often leads to the use of *emoticons*: text-based icons designed to display different emotions. Just a glance at Wikipedia (2012b) shows that there are thousands of emoticons being used in online communication on a regular basis, and that these vary from Western to Eastern regions as well as in their complexity (from a basic :), to a 2 channel to a live-action cartoon). Many online students might already be familiar with many of these and use them in their regular online social interactions (such as emails or chat), so allowing their use in your online course should not prove overly problematic. Just ensure that all of your students are on the same page with the meaning of emoticons. Provide a list of the most popular, such as these below:

3.2 EMOTICONS FOR THE ONLINE CLASSROOM

:-) Happy.

;-) Winky.

:-(Sad.

:-> Sarcastic smiley.

>:-> User just made a really devilish remark.

%-) User has been staring at a green screen for 15 hours straight.

:-I Indifferent smiley.

(-: User is left handed.

:-D User is laughing

:-O Oops/Surprise/Yelling/Shocked.

:-o Uh oh!

:'-(User is crying.

:'-) User is so happy, s/he is crying.

:-@ Screaming/Swearing/Very Angry/About To Be Sick.

:-0 No Yelling! (Quiet Lab).

:-P Sticking Out Tongue.

:-S User just made an incoherent statement.

8-O Omigod!!

:-& User is tongue tied.

|-I User is asleep.

|-o Bored.

:-{) User has a mustache.

:-{} User wears lipstick.

::-) User wears glasses.

%-6 User is brain dead.

&-e Disappointed smiley.

:-'| Has A Cold/Flu.

:-(*) That comment made me sick.

:-/ User is skeptical.

:-\ Undecided smiley.

:-| Disgusted/Grim/No Expression.

:-~) User has a cold.

:-V Shouting smiley.

:> :@ :Q What?
:D Laughter.
:I Hmmm...
:O Yelling.
>>:-<< Mad.

While it's great to give emotional support, try to structure it into a specific space on the course, so that it does not overwhelm the students or bog you down. The authors favor the idea of a "virtual lounge" (first suggested by Bender, 2003) on the discussion board where students can talk about personal or other issues ("How 'bout them Lakers?!") without interfering with the course delivery itself. This way, students can build community from shared feelings that will strengthen their commitment to the course itself. In some courses, students often become very personal on their discussion board and continue to carry on these conversations elsewhere.

For example, imagine that students often discuss highly provocative issues in Psychology of Sexuality, ranging from their first sexual experience to coming out as bisexual. In one such instance, a student wrote about what happened when she told her parents that she was bisexual at age 16. She said they threw her out of the house and she went to live with friends. They told her that God would punish her. Clearly, this student shared this story because it was relevant, but also because she was looking for social support from her new community of online sexuality scholars. Indeed, this was exactly what she received: Numerous encouraging posts "I'm so sorry to hear what you went through but one day they will forgive you!" to posts like "My cousin was gay and as a Latino man he went through a lot of discrimination and pain, so I know how hard it must have been for you to come out." Not only do these kinds of discussions provide personal insight and voice to the course material, they also strengthen the community through this shared emotional connection (which was a component of psychological sense of community as first proposed by McMillan & Chavis, 1986). This particular discussion eventually migrated off the course assignment board to a specific discussion board based on sexual orientation, where it continued.

An alternative to the "virtual lounge" would be to set up a course social network outside of your CMS, such as on Facebook. Given that hundreds of millions of adults around the world are using Facebook, there is a good chance that your students already fall into this group! By creating this type of group page, your students will be immediately transported to the mentality of their online social network (OSN) and begin to interact socially, getting to know each other by looking at pictures, interests, and relevant links on each other's pages. Suddenly, your community has taken on a completely social angle where you students can really interact and feel support outside of the actual CMS itself. As we proceed to the next chapter, consider the ways that you can harness technology, like social networking websites, to build community and emotional connections.

Summary: Let's Talk About It!

This chapter discussed how communication and community are of central importance to a successful online teaching and learning experience. First, the notion of "learning as communication" was introduced, followed by a review of relevant research on student participation in online learning communities. The characteristics of successful online learning communities were discussed, along with recommendations for creating a healthy learning community in your future online psychology courses. In terms of implementation, this chapter presented the idea of transitioning from a lecturer to a moderator, highlighting the roles of an online facilitator using the metaphor of a theatric play. Next, the facilitation of online communication was discussed, with a focus on synchronous versus asynchronous activities and methods for inducing critical thinking through discourse. Finally, providing help and feedback for online students was covered in the troubleshooting section, including how to find an optimal balance for helping engagement, student services, virtual office hours, and giving emotional support. Overall, the take-home message from this chapter is that communication is always important in higher education, and it becomes especially necessary for learning when we transition from the classroom to the online community. In this chapter, frequent references were made to the diverse array of technologies that facilitate our online communication, including email, text-messaging, live chat, video-conferencing, and podcasting, to name a few. In this next chapter, we will explore how, when, and why to utilize these technologies to enhance student achievement in the online learning community.

CHAPTER 4

The Multimedia Bonanza

Purpose: Media Use in Today's Higher Education Classrooms

Online education undoubtedly takes advantage of the vast array of available technology to enhance and improve student learning. There is no need to feel intimidated about these advances in software and applications; rather, view this synergy between technology and education as one that can profoundly benefit students and instructors alike. This chapter is designed to familiarize online psychology instructors with how, why, and when to use the types of technology that can most enhance learning in online courses. For many students, particularly incoming undergraduates who comprise the "I" or "M" Generation, technology serves as a comfortable, expected feature of everyday life. Thus, college courses delivered online may end up competing with other screen media that regularly absorb the attention of undergraduate students, including content on phones, laptops, video games, television, and other forms of media. In the spirit of competition then, it would behoove online instructors to incorporate certain technological and multimedia elements to grasp the attention of these students. Likewise, some students may feel less comfortable with technology and may need special assistance when developing their own creative content using tools such as wikis, blogs, podcasts, or YouTube. Consider then as you proceed that it is important to (a) know your students, (b) gauge their familiarity and comfort with technology early on, and (c) strike a healthy balance between technologically advanced and basic content. The tips and tricks in this chapter should help online instructors to effectively strike that balance.

In an effort to get to know our future online students, and their familiarity with technology, the authors reviewed the Kaiser Family Foundation's 2010 report on *Generation M²* (Rideout, Foehr, & Roberts, 2010). This large scale, nationally representative survey was designed to study the media use of young people in the United States, who are quickly approaching the age for undergraduate education. According to the report, 8- to 18-year-olds in the United States devote an average of 7 hours and 38 minutes per day to using entertainment media, totaling more than 53 hours of screen media per week. These young people are multitaskers: They manage to fit over 10 hours of screen media content into just over 7 hours per day, because they often access several types of media simultaneously. Additionally, more so than any generation before, media use has been driven by mobile technology. In the last 5 years, the ownership of mobile technology among 8- to 18-year-olds has risen from 39% to 66% for cell phones, and from 18% to 76% for iPods and other music players. In this respect, future online college students are the true M² generation: mobile media multitaskers! The majority of teens also have free rein when it comes to their choices of media use, with less than one-third reporting any parental or household rules aimed toward limiting their media use. As instructors create and launch online courses in psychology, consider that incoming students will expect mobile access on-the-go from anywhere, and in the true nature of the term *multimedia*, they may be quite proficient at accessing several types of media simultaneously. Imagine then a future student who might be accessing your course management system from his or her mobile phone, while sending text messages and watching YouTube videos.

Before embarking on a journey through the types of technologies for online courses and their various implementations, let us consider the pedagogical function of incorporating technological and media elements into psychology course work. First, the term *multimedia* is often included in the discussion on the benefits of technology for student learning—*multimedia* is generally understood as the "integration of multiple forms of media" (Jonasson, 2000, p. 207). In the context of an online course, the presence of multimedia is almost a given—students will be using online and internet technology to facilitate learning as they access web-links, videos, and discussions pertaining to the course. The authors therefore believe that online education inherently features multiple media sources working simultaneously to provide students with a comprehensive learning structure. Aside from utilizing multimedia to "grab" students' attention, how can the integration of technology directly benefit learning outcomes? An emerging body of research suggests that multimedia usage can benefit online student learning outcomes through a number of different channels (Donnelli, Dailey, & Mandernach, 2009), including illustrating key concepts, creating opportunities for critical thinking, and providing insight into relevant social issues.

In an article on integrating multimedia into social science courses, Miller (2009) argues that online multimedia can benefit cognitive learning first and foremost in its "capacity to serve as representational applications for key course ideas" (Miller, 2009, p. 396). According to this perspective, multimedia (understood as any combination of video, text, picture, hyperlink, blog, wiki, etc.) can help introduce students to new concepts, and provide them with the "mental imagery necessary for conceptual understanding" (p. 396). While the benefits of multimedia should be present in a traditional classroom setting, in the online course environment these benefits should shine through. Online students in social sciences should have unlimited access to media that benefits their learning—in fact, an online course can be comprised entirely of multimedia. For example, imagine a course where students learn from a variety of sources in addition to their textbooks, including videos, asynchronous discussion board communication, synchronous chats with experts, and web-links to psychology research. As discussed in previous chapters, many of these elements are naturally included in an online course to foster communication and growth.

The presence of multimedia in social science courses can also help to induce analysis and critical thinking, skills that are often featured as learning objectives in psychology. According to Miller's (2009) review, students should be encouraged to regard media sources with skepticism, to criticize news reports, or in the case of a research methodology course, analyze an article or paper that makes inaccurate generalizations. Thus, in addition to improving subject comprehension and retention, use of media sources can also lead to higher level thinking and analysis. Additionally, multimedia can also be harnessed to introduce students to relevant social issues. Rather than broadly discussing gay rights organizations, a simple link to the Human Rights Campaign website (www.hrc.org) and their videos would serve a significantly more illustrative function. While multimedia use might require a little bit of extra effort in a face-to-face course, in an online course it is so very easy to copy and paste a link for students to view, and assign a discussion topic. In the above example, students could be asked to view the link to the Human Rights Campaign, and then discuss numerous issues surrounding the organization, such as how they view the organization's goals and mission statement. Are the findings presented by the organization based upon peer-reviewed research, interviews, or the organization's opinions? In this respect, online psychology courses enable students to quickly and effectively analyze and critique not only research articles, but also, current events and institutions related to the issues discussed in the course.

Another issue is how much multimedia and technology to include when integrating technology into online psychology courses. Too little media might be boring and uninteresting to your students who may have a very high threshold and expectation for media engagement. Likewise, too much multimedia may feel frustrating, repetitive, and even impersonal. In their review of multimedia use in higher education, Donnelli and colleagues (2009) point to Clark and Mayer's (2002) rules for media inclusion, based upon cognitive learning theories. According to this perspective, there are six rules (understood as principles) to consider when selecting the combination of multimedia elements in higher education: the multimedia principle, the contiguity principle, the modality principle, the redundancy principle, the coherence principle, and the personalization principle.

1. *Multimedia principle:* Visuals (such as pictures, outlines, slides, or videos) should be included with written text to increase learning through dual-coding.
2. *Contiguity principle:* Relevant visuals and text should be placed close to one another to ensure that working memory is utilized for learning content.
3. *Modality principle:* Using multiple sources simultaneously, such as audio to explain visuals and texts, will activate multiple sources of memory encoding.
4. *Redundancy principle:* Instead of providing audio that mimics written text and visuals, to reduce cognitive overload use audio alone to supplement and explain visuals.
5. *Coherence principle:* Avoid unnecessary information in visuals, text, or audio, which can lead to incoherence and make it more difficult to integrate information.
6. *Personalization principle:* Enhance learning via a personal tone or narrative to introduce graphics and visuals.

Taken as a whole, these principles suggest that a combination of visuals, audio, and text reflects the best overall approach to enhancing learning with multimedia. One caveat: Make sure to edit and reduce unnecessary sources of information. For example, instead of repeating written text in an audio podcast lecture, consider providing written bullet points and embellishing upon them in the audio portion. In addition, the "more is more" approach can sometimes confuse students and overload their processing. Choosing the right combination of media sources should engage students without overwhelming them (such as, a podcast paired with written slides, as opposed to a video lecture, podcast, and written slides covering the same topic). The authors recommend a "one for one" approach where one text-based medium is selected along with a complementary audiovisual medium. So, for example, when given the option of three or more modes of transmitting the same information (such as written outline, PowerPoint slide, audio podcast, and video lecture), selecting one text-based medium (such as a written outline) and one complementary audiovisual-based medium (such as an audio podcast) should provide an optimal amount of multimedia engagement for students.

Of course, skeptics might argue that incoming freshmen in the next few years will be so accustomed to media multitasking (recall cramming 10 hours of media usage into 7 hours of screen time?) that perhaps these coherence and redundancy principles will no longer apply. In other words, future online students might be training their brains from a young age to process multiple sources of information simultaneously. However, psychology instructors today are a long way off from knowing whether this will be the case in the future. It is also very important to recognize that not all online psychology students represent the media multitaskers of the "I" or "M" generation. Students who use media less frequently may be more likely to experience cognitive overload when they are faced with audio, text, and video disseminating the same information. For this reason, it is important to follow principles to ensure that students who are less accustomed to media engagement do not become overwhelmed by the required media usage in your course. The safest approach then for online psychology instructors is to assume a diversity and range of technological abilities and media usage.

When selecting the depth and breadth of multimedia tools that students will utilize in their online learning, try to focus on a combination that will appeal to more tech-savvy students but that will not be so complicated that students new to multimedia will feel alienated. The following section provides a detailed description of many of the types of multimedia and technological tools available for use in online education. Of special focus in the following section are "what," "why," and "how" questions. For each type of medium or technology, the following section will address: What is this technology/medium? Why would an instructor use this in a psychology course? How does an instructor utilize this tool? As you proceed through the following section, please do not feel pressured to utilize all of these technologies in your online psychology courses! Rather, based upon what is available to you, select a healthy balance of tools that best serves the educational goals and interests of your course and students.

IMPLEMENTATION: ONLINE COURSE TECHNOLOGY— WHAT, WHY, AND HOW?

The following section discusses the "what, why, and how" of many of the types of technology and media often associated with online learning in psychology. Some of these are omnipresent in almost all online courses (such as your CMS) while others may benefit only certain courses and certain instructors (such as wikis and podcasts). Recall that past research has shown that multimedia enhances student learning by improving concept recognition, increasing critical thinking, and enhancing memory encoding. Another important outcome of technology and multimedia use in online courses is the engagement of student creativity! Given that the many tech-savvy young adults are no longer the passive recipients of media, but rather, active creators of their own media flow through social network sites, blogging, and YouTube, online courses may benefit from channeling this user-generated creativity. The implementation section focuses on the following modalities as resources for creative technological content, with attention to the "what, why, and how" of content and creativity: Course management systems, video lectures, podcasting, wikis, blogging, and social network sites.

COURSE MANAGEMENT SYSTEMS (CMS)

What is CMS?

Recall the example of the traditional face-to-face classroom from the beginning of chapter 2. The instructor stands at the front of the room, lecturing to students who sit quietly facing the instructor, who may be using some visual cues like a projector screen with PowerPoint slides. In an online course, this physical environment evaporates, and transitions into something new. Online courses are not bound in physical space, and yet they still require some degree of hardware in order to operate. This hardware that enables the course to exist in virtual space is known as the course management system (CMS). Every online course is hosted by some kind of CMS, which is basically a computer program and database that holds all of the information contained in an online course. Using the hardware and software provided by the CMS, online instructors create virtual learning environments (VLEs) which are where students experience the online course. In this respect, the CMS is used to create the virtual classroom, which contains many of the elements that students will require for their learning, including announcements, lectures, quizzes, tests, and the discussion board. These are all part of the VLE.

Although there are a variety of CMSs used in online education, by far the two most popular in today's market are Blackboard and Moodle. The central difference between these two systems is that Blackboard's software is "closed source" meaning that it is privately owned and cannot be modified, whereas Moodle is free and "open source" meaning that anyone can modify or copy the software so long as the original license is not removed and the same license is applied to all derivative work. Blackboard is the most commonly used CMS in colleges and universities across the United States. After acquiring another CMS called WebCT, Blackboard is now estimated to account for 80 to 90% of the entire CMS market (Roach, 2006). Blackboard is licensed to over 2,200 educational institutions in more than 60 countries. It is a privately owned "closed source" system estimated to be worth upwards of $1.5 billion, according to the NASDAQ. In 2010, Blackboard launched its 9.1 update called *Blackboard Learn*. This new system offers huge advances from previous versions by integrating numerous forms of technology directly into the course interface, such as an array of course tools, YouTube, and *Elluminate—live*.

On the other hand, as noted above, Moodle (short for Modular Object-Oriented Dynamic Learning Environment) is an open source CMS. Moodle is best defined as a software package that produces internet-based courses and websites. According to their statistics tracking, as of July 2010 there are 3.8 million Moodle-based online courses being delivered to 37 million registered users in 215 countries! Some of the best known Moodle courses are derived from the Britain-based Open University (open.ac.uk), which now offers over 5,000 Moodle-based courses. As noted above, Moodle is free and it's very easy to use. As an alternative to the proprietary, closed-source approach by Blackboard, Moodle takes a social constructivist approach where course creators from across the globe come together to develop modules and software to benefit the learner.

Why Use a CMS?

Nearly all universities and colleges that offer online courses designate a certain CMS for instructors to use to create their virtual classroom. So, the most obvious answer to the "Why use a CMS?" question is, because it is required! Hosting an online course without a CMS would be extremely difficult. The CMS should provide a number of key functions at a minimum, whether an online course is being run using Blackboard, Moodle, or another system. These should include announcements about the course, basic teaching materials, links to resources, different levels of access for students and instructor, formal assessments, course statistics, student registration and tracking, discussion boards, and tools to create and post hyperlinks, docs, PDFs, and assignments. But why choose Blackboard over Moodle, or vice versa? Often the instructor has no real say in this matter. It is usually up to the college or university to make these decisions. Both Blackboard and Moodle offer very similar capabilities and functions, although Blackboard may seem more polished and offer more bells and whistles (for example, the new Blackboard offers Elluminate video conferencing built right into its interface). However, as mentioned earlier, Blackboard can be expensive, whereas Moodle is completely free to use! So, a new instructor lobbying for the creation of an online program might promote Moodle as an excellent low-risk option, whereas an instructor teaching at a more established, well-funded online program may already have access to Blackboard. Indeed as mentioned earlier, about 80 to 90% of all higher education institutions that offer online instruction use Blackboard as their CMS.

How to Use a CMS

Whether you are using Blackboard, Moodle, or another CMS, the interfaces of these programs are relatively straightforward and easy to use. How to interact with the general components of a CMS is discussed briefly in this section. Because software changes so frequently, updated step-by-step instructions can be found on the accompanying website for this book (www.TeachingPsychologyOnline.com). After logging onto a CMS, an instructor will be greeting with a variety of options on their "home" screen. On Blackboard, for example, these options include links to *My Courses* (all courses you are teaching and their availability to students), and links to *My Announcements* (all of the announcements you have sent to various courses). There will also be a *Tools* section featuring the numerous available tools for an instructor, including announcements, calendar, grade book, send email, discussion board, as well as newer options including NBC archives, playlist, and Elluminate. Likewise, when an instructor first logs on to Moodle, there will be an array of options to choose from: *Participants* (the students enrolled in the course); *Activities* (including assignments and modules); *Forums* (discussion boards); *Administration* (such as grading and assignments); and *Courses* (all of the courses the instructor is teaching). Moodle also will list the news, events, and recent activities on this page.

Usually, to access your specific class of interest in the CMS, there will be a button for *Courses*. Depending upon the institution, the course itself may be created automatically, or the instructor may have to manually create the course each semester. Consult with your institution if you are unsure about this. After clicking on the course you are interested in modifying, both Blackboard and Moodle will bring up a variety of tools that can be integrated in the course. While the specifics differ slightly across the different programs, generally instructors have the option of including tools surrounding communication (sending announcements, discussion board, sending emails, and live chat), content (including uploading lecture slides, activity modules, links) activities (quizzes, tests, papers, and other assignments) and administration (grade book, dropping students, and general performance assessment).

The good news is that both Blackboard and Moodle are relatively instructor-friendly and easy to use. The instructor is given tons of choice, in terms of how messages are displayed, how grades and feedback are dealt with, how content is disseminated, and what kinds of options are made available. Then, the online instructor has a large amount to say over the way that the course is developed and experienced by the students—even more so than in the face-to-face classroom. For example, one of the most useful parts of creating your learning environment in the CMS is that both Blackboard and Moodle are predominately WYSIWYG (What You See Is What You Get), meaning that announcements and assignments created by the instructor will appear to students exactly as the instructor types and designs them. Along with this, both Moodle and Blackboard give the instructor latitude and control about when assignments are due, how they are graded, and how student feedback is delivered. Further, instructors using Moodle and Blackboard can display their desired content in whatever way they would prefer. On Blackboard, content can be organized into folders of lecture slides, or folders of weekly topics. On Moodle, course content can be organized into a weekly format (where the course is organized weekly with a clear start and end date for each week), a topic format (where each topic section consists of activities), or a social format (where the course is organized around a specific forum). Finally, instructors have total control over the types of tools students can use, and can enable or disable tools ranging from live chat, to YouTube plugins, to shared video whiteboards. In addition to institutional training and support, for more information on using these features, readers are encouraged to visit the website portion of this book, as well as docs.moodle.org for Moodle Support and blackboard.com/support for Blackboard support.

VIDEO LECTURES: TIPS FOR SUCCESS

What Is a Video Lecture?

A video lecture, broadly defined, is any audiovisual recording of an instructor speaking about a subject area. In the context of online courses, video lectures are then uploaded to the CMS, and possibly to other websites like YouTube or Facebook, where they can be viewed by students "on-demand" (translation: students can watch these videos whenever they want!) While it might sound like a daunting task to a beginner, making video lectures is easier than one might expect. Essentially, there are two main categories of video lectures: Live recordings from actual lectures, and recordings of the instructor made specifically for the purposes of online dissemination. Before creating a video lecture, the instructor should consider which type of video he or she finds more appealing. What is involved in recording a live lecture in the classroom? To do this, the instructor would bring recording equipment to a live lecture and possibly recruit a student (or tripod) to hold the camera. These types of "live lectures" might require some production efforts, ranging from trimming to full-blown editing. Alternatively, instructors can "perform" a lecture in front of a computer web-cam and distribute it directly to online students via the web. This type of lecture can be made at home, often with minimal production efforts.

The authors have experimented with both types of lectures, and have found that shortened lectures performed directly into the web camera tend to be easier to record, and require less editing efforts. Further, it seems that these personalized videos help to increase students' familiarity and comfort with the instructor. These web camera videos also offer much greater control over production values than footage of actual live lectures, which often feature poor lighting quality, inaudible sound, and editing time. In a video lecture recorded for the direct purpose of online dissemination, it is easier to focus on a target audience, include only the information deemed to be relevant, and to manipulate the appearance of the video (lighting, sound, etc.). It may take several hours to edit material into a shortened clip for a recording of a live classroom lecture. However, if the instructor believes that students want to experience what it feels like to be sitting in the "actual" lecture, then a live lecture video may be preferred. While arriving in the classroom and videotaping one's lecture is relatively straightforward, tips for successful creation of videos specifically for online dissemination are discussed in the following section.

Why Make a Video Lecture?

Instructors and students alike can benefit from watching video lectures. Why? Students seemingly *love* having access to the professor and to lectures outside of class. Not only do these videos boost personal rapport for the instructor, but they can also assist with dual-coding learning when combined with related text. Furthermore, a video lecture gives the instructor the ability to clearly and succinctly communicate with students, an invaluable benefit to any online instructor. Interestingly, even students in face-to-face courses can benefit from being enabled to go online and view a video recording of their professor lecturing. For example, a 2008 study conducted at Harvard Medical School showed that students found video-recorded lectures to be equally or more valuable than attending class lectures, and that they stayed more focused, and learned more when they used video-recorded lecture technology (Cardall, Krupat, & Ulrich, 2008).

How to Make a Video Lecture

The first step for an online instructor who wants to make a video lecture is to determine the purpose of the lecture. Is the video lecture going to be used for orientation, to provide information about a specific topic, or to give a review for a quiz? Of crucial importance when making a video for online consumption is the creation of a *script* to guide you, the speaker, through the topics you want to address to ensure you reach your goals. Rather than writing a formal lecture and reading it directly into the camera, this is an opportunity to convey your style and personality, and make a connection with your online students. If you make jokes or share stories in your live lectures, include these in your video lecture. Of course, there is no doubt that *this process takes practice!* It is unusual for even the most seasoned expert video creator to nail it the first time. Once you have created your script or outline, take a practice run and time yourself. The authors have found that videos in the range of 10 to 15 minutes appear to be the most effective. First, this is the length that many hosting websites (such as YouTube) will permit for upload. Second, in 10 to 15 minutes it is possible to convey a substantial amount of information about a very specific topic, or give a general overview of a broad topic. It can be useful to create a 10-minute lecture on a general topic (such as sexual orientation) and then create a supplemental video speaking in detail about an especially relevant issue within that topic (such as the constitutionality of gay marriage in California).

One of the more important tenets to remember, which coincides with most teaching philosophies, is that a video lecture *does not have to be perfect!* If an instructor attempts to make a video aimed at too high a standard, there may be countless takes of the instructor saying the same sentence, which can become a very time consuming process. It is important to accept that mistakes, flubs, distractions, are a natural part of lecturing and that online video lectures should be no different. When your pet jumps onto your desk and interrupts you, introduce him or her to your class. If a police car drives by with blaring sirens, just continue as normal. It is important to convey a semblance of reality and authenticity to online students. If anything, it is the imperfections that should ingratiate you to your students and make these lectures feel more natural and enjoyable. All in all, just be yourself rather than trying to create a fake or embellished persona. Try to wear the same type of clothing, style, accessories, and makeup as you would in daily work life. In terms of setting, a desk in an office is completely acceptable, and there is no need to go too overboard with flashy artistic backgrounds and design. Remember, the content and its relevance to the course should shine through. Definitely scrap it and start again if you lose your train of thought badly, or if you swear, curse, or get angry. Always try to maintain the supportive, kind, and enthusiastic tone of a successful instructor.

Once the script is ready, and the stage is set, it is time to start recording. While any number of video recording software can be used, the authors recommend Apple QuickTime (free download at www.apple.com/quicktime). If your computer has a built-in microphone as most of them do these days, then a separate microphone is not required. Simply select "New Recording" and hit the red button when you are ready to start. When it comes time to press Record, be natural. Smile. Stare directly into the camera and imagine that you are speaking to your students. It can feel very strange at first to find yourself looking into a tiny ocular opening and delivering the same kind of warm, engaging tone that might be reserved for students or people in a face-to-face environment. But with practice, even the most camera-shy person can master this technique. Always speak slowly and annunciate clearly, as sometimes technology can mute or blur syllables. Stay with it, even if you feel ridiculous. If you make a mistake, try to recover and soldier on. When you have finished, watch the video and imagine you are taking a student's perspective. Ask the following questions: Is this lecture sufficiently informative? Is it engaging? Does it portray accurate detail about the topic provided? Is it clear? Would students have trouble understanding this? It is okay to be a critic of your own work, but just try not to be too critical of yourself, as this benefits no one.

How to Disseminate a Video Lecture

After you have created your video lecture, it is time to share it with the world! One important decision surrounds whether the video will be uploaded to the course CMS only, or also to the web via video hosting websites like YouTube and Facebook. If the video is uploaded to the course CMS only, it will ensure that only students in that course during that specific semester see it. If there are two sections of a course, then the instructor will have to upload the video twice, once to each section, and so on. Realistically, once a video lecture is created, it is probably in the instructor's best interest to disseminate this to the greatest number of individuals via YouTube. Not only will all students in all sections be able to view it without constant reuploading, but people all across the globe could stumble upon the work. Prospective students can examine the videos and determine if they want to take the class. Usually, students would rather enroll in an online class where the instructor posts her or his own lectures, than one in which the instructor does not use videos. In many ways, having customized lectures posted online is a deal-maker for students who are on the fence about your class. You might be contacted by students from all across the world. Further, other instructors at different institutions might also show your videos in their classes. If you decide to create your own YouTube channel complete with lecture videos, this becomes a further extension of your online community, of your resume, and ultimately, of your brand!

YouTube is extremely easy to use and is constantly being updated with newer versions. For detailed technical information on creating a YouTube video and channel, check for the most up-to-date information on the website that accompanies the present work. Once you have a free YouTube account, you can select My Channel to design your channel. Having a channel is beneficial because it enables you to provide information about yourself, upload your videos to one place, communicate with students, and even have students subscribe to "follow" your videos (they will receive a notification each time you post a new video). A glimpse of Dr. Neff's channel is available on YouTube (see URL below). From your channel, you will also be able to moderate comments on and ratings of your videos. Because people can sometimes leave extremely inappropriate comments and you want to remain professional, it is recommended to allow comments with approval only so that this way lewd or unpleasant remarks are not displayed below your videos without your consent. From here, it is also possible to add "annotations" (text-based comments that "pop-up" during your video) to clarify and expand upon important points. Finally, if you are curious about who is watching your videos, you can view "insights" to determine the number and locations of video views by visitors (see Dr. Neff's updated YouTube Channel: http://www.YouTube.com/ProfessorNeff).

PODCASTING: TIPS FOR SUCCESS

What Is a Podcast?

The word *podcast* is a portmanteau of the words *pod* (taken from the name of Apple's portable audioplayer, the iPod) and *cast*, taken from the word *broadcast*. Although originally derived for use with Apple iPods, podcasts are playable on any Mp3 player as well as computers, laptops, and smart phones. Essentially, a podcast is comprised of either an audio or visual file that is available for download and syndication. Currently, there are free podcasts available for download on a multitude of topics, from the *New York Times Front Page* to *Grape Radio* (about drinking wine!), to numerous university resources such as the lectures provided by the Open University. From an educational perspective, podcasts enable instructors to deliver supplemental materials directly to students' phones, media players, and computers.

Why Use Podcasts?

In face-to-face courses, students can use podcasts to make up classes that they missed, or to obtain additional information on their course materials. In the online course context, podcasts can help the instructor to disseminate portable class materials that online students can download and listen to while they are on the go; for example, in the car, at the gym, or while at work. Creating your own downloadable podcast is an excellent way to personalize the course and to provide students with easy access to your lectures and materials. You can podcast supplemental course information, interviews with experts, or weekly summaries, depending on the type of material you wish to convey. According to Leppien-Christensen (2010), an experienced podcaster who has delivered numerous instructional presentations to psychology professors, podcasting has a multitude of benefits for the instructor, including: Podcasts are one of the simplest forms of media to produce, they are easy to edit, they add another modality for students, they allow students to review concepts and study, they are accessible to students anytime, anywhere via their media players (and at least 80% of students have an iPod or equivalent), they increase the perceived contact with the instructor, and finally, students simply love learning through the use of technology (Rosen, 2010).

Research has also supported the notion that podcast usage can potentially benefit student learning. In their article on the use of podcasting in the classroom, McLean and White (2009) conclude that instructor-created podcasts "are beneficial to the students and to the instructor in terms of delivering additional course information" (p. 345). Just remember that not all students will download your podcast right away, unless you make this a course requirement. Williams and Bearman (2008) estimated that as many as two-thirds of students did not download the instructor's podcast. But whatever happens, don't be discouraged! Research has shown that podcasts are most useful for students when they are studying for exams. In fact, one study showed that students who downloaded podcasts scored higher on their final exams than students who did not (Bond, Wells, & Holland, 2008). One podcasting professor reports that 89% of podcasts were downloaded during the week of the corresponding exam—wow! (White, 2009).

If you do not feel compelled to create and develop your own series of podcasts, consider that numerous existing podcasts in psychology are already available to supplement your students' learning, free to subscribe and download through iTunes U. Here is just a brief selection of these "PSYC-Casts" from the iTunes U page at the time of going to press (the number and availability are only going to increase over time!):

4.1 Free Psychology Podcasts

- Yale University School of Medicine: Psychology
- PsychOUT: Where We Explore Psychology Outside the Classrooom
- Great Ideas in Psychology
- Oakland University: Cognitive Psychology
- MIT Open Course Ware: Introduction to Psychology
- Open University: Exploring Psychology

How to Create a Podcast

While the resources listed above are certainly useful, remember that it is worthwhile, and relatively simple, to create your own downloadable podcasts. To get started, Leppien-Christensen (2010) recommends first taking "baby steps," including recording shorter clips and finding your comfort zone. He also warns strongly against perfectionism, so the same rules that apply to your video lectures can also apply to your podcast! Students do not mind a few mistakes or sounds of sirens coming from outside your door. In fact, one study showed that students actually felt that "low fidelity" podcasts (with imperfections) gave a greater sense of realism and instructor presence than highly produced podcasts (Brown et al., 2009). Assuming you have a computer, you are already on your way to gathering the necessary technological components for podcasting. Additionally, podcasting requires an external microphone, a digital audio recording device, as well as audio editing software to produce the podcast. Because technology evolves at such a rapid pace, the accompanying website for this book features up-to-date recommendations for podcasting. Once you acquire the necessary tools, consider how you are going to distribute your podcast. There are a number of services that will allow you to upload your podcast for student subscription and download, including Gabcast, uStream, Justin.tv, and now, iTunes U (which already hosts a number of psychology related podcasts). Once you have decided on distribution, it is time to create your podcast! Vogele and Townsend Gard (2006) suggest the following five steps for use with your podcast:

1. *Create a Script:* This is an outline based on your lecture notes—use this to prompt your podcast. Remember, let yourself flow and don't be a perfectionist!

2. *Record the Content:* Use your microphone and audio recording device to record your content. You are probably better off recording "in the studio" (at your home computer specifically for the podcast) rather than trying to podcast a live lecture which might have background noise issues. Leppien-Christensen (2010) recommends the closet as an excellent recording studio!

3. *Edit the Content:* This is when you use your editing software to pull the podcast together. You might want to remove a section where you went off on a tangent, or you might want to add an introduction with voiceover or even insert music. Again, make sure the podcast is professional but don't overproduce it. This just leads to extra work that your students may not even appreciate!

4. *Upload the Audio File:* This is when you use a hosting website, such as iTunes U, GabCast, UStream, or Justin.Tv to upload your file. Given that iTunes U is becoming the major hub for psychology podcasts, consider using this to host your podcast. For an updated list of hosting websites, please visit this book's website.

5. *Publish the RSS Feed:* This is when you let your students know that your podcast is available for download, and that they should subscribe! Once your podcast is available, students can download via iTunes or another hosting service. Then each time a new podcast is available, the RSS feed (Really Simple Syndication) will update them. If you are looking for more information or additional technical support, visit this book's website, along with these other websites, to get started:

4.2 ONLINE PODCASTING RESOURCES

www.how-to-podcast-tutorial.com
www.freesound.org
music.podshow.com
www.podcastalley.com
www.soundclick.com
ccmixter.org
wiki.creativecommons.org/Podcasting_Legal_Guide
www.ubercaster.com

WIKIS: TIPS FOR SUCCESS

What are Wikis?

Wikis enable multiple users to review and modify the contents of web pages, both synchronously and asynchronously (Sandars, 2007). Perhaps the largest and most recognizable wiki is *Wikipedia,* the free encyclopedia, which features user-generated content and definitions for a multitude of constructs. Wikis promote collective knowledge construction where users can access a page, and update it based upon their own knowledge, which is then modified by other users, and so on.

Why Use Wikis?

As online psychology instructors we are constantly seeking to enhance student collaboration and communication. Huang (2010) discusses how, unlike other forms of social media technology, wikis are particularly useful for promoting collaboration and interactivity:

1. Wikis are organized by topic of interest rather than chronological postings (such as on blogs, discussed later).
2. Wikis allow users to modify the progress of document (how it has evolved through user contributions) using a time and date stamp.
3. Anyone can be a creator of a wiki, and start their own wiki by posting a basic idea which is then modified by other users.
4. Due to peer review, inappropriate or inaccurate comments can be removed as the entire editing process is archived.
5. Wikis provide "learner-centered" environments where users can construct a knowledge base, give instant feedback, and collaboratively solve problems (Baird & Fisher, 2005).

Research shows that wiki use positively enhances online student learning, whether undergraduate, graduate, or professional training levels. For example, one study on first-year undergraduates showed that while they initially felt apprehensive about wiki use, after engaging with the technology they felt that it had positively enhanced their learning (O'Shea, Baker, Allen, Curry-Corcoran, & Allen, 2006). Other studies of graduate student learning have showed that users believe that wikis help to facilitate their learning (Coutinho & Bottentuit, 2007), especially when the learning pertained to group work (Carpenter & Roberts, 2007). Additionally, wikis are also effective at promoting group communication and collaboration at the professional development level (Foley & Chang, 2006). Wikis are even effective at promoting interaction and knowledge building among K-12 students (Deters, Cuthrell, & Stapleton, 2010).

How to Use Wikis?

How then, do we integrate wiki use into our online psychology courses? Wikis are easy to use and create, and depending upon your course management system, they may already be built into your online course! At the time of going to press, for example, Blackboard already provides all of the tools necessary create a wiki. If you do not have a CMS that supports wikis, Huang (2010) recommends PBworks (www.Pbworks.com) as the best wiki-hosting software for educational and professional purposes. For the most updated information on wiki creation, please consult this book's website.

In practice, wikis look similar to online discussion boards, except that users directly modify content. As opposed to a series of posts by different users, wikis feature one post or paragraph modified repeatedly by numerous users. It is possible for the instructor to track and view the history of changes made to a wiki, which makes it especially useful for charting the creation and synthesis of knowledge in online activities. For more information on wikis, including sample wikis, visit: http://www.wikipedia.org/wiki/Wiki.

Are there certain activities or assignments that would benefit from wiki usage? Wikis make great assignments any time that collaboration is involved, especially if group work is involved. However, there is no specific set of activities in psychology that are appropriate for wiki use. Rather, the instructor has discretion here. If one is transitioning from a face-to-face to a fully online course, think of the types of group work and collaborative in-class exercises that were effective, and consider translating these into a wiki. If students are required to conduct a group research project, why not use a wiki that they can modify to present their work? One of the greatest complaints about student group work is that it's impossible to tell who does what, but using a wiki, the instructor can view exactly how much time and effort each student contributed to a project. Any time the instructor seeks to engage in knowledge construction or ask students to give feedback, a wiki-based assignment can be effective. Research cited above shows that wikis are effective group work and knowledge building tools for all ages and difficulty levels, ranging from K-12, to undergraduate, graduate, and professional programs. Specific activities in online psychology and how to implement them are discussed at length in the following chapter.

BLOGS: TIPS FOR SUCCESS

What is a Blog?

A *blog* (combination of the words *web* and *log*) is a type of website, or part of a website, usually managed by an individual who makes regular updates, comments, or entries that are reported in chronological order (Wikipedia,

2012c). Blogs can take on a number of different functions, from social commentary, to personal diaries, to updated news on a specific topic. Blogs are also interactive, as users can leave comments and give feedback (although unlike wikis, users cannot modify the blog itself, only the original blogger can do this). So many blogs have sprung up that Wikipedia (2012c) suggests characterizing them in terms of various categories, including personal blogs (an ongoing diary or commentary by an individual), corporate and organizational blogs (such as those aimed toward marketing, branding, and consumer culture), and by genre (such as political blogs, fashion blogs, legal blogs, and parenting blogs).

Why Use Blogs?

Blogs can fit into the online classroom because they can be created and modified by both students and instructors. Furthermore, other people's blogs can be utilized as web resources. Instructors can benefit from creating a blog for students to follow. Long after the course is over, students may continue check in and see what you're up to, which helps to solidify your brand as an online instructor. Blogs can be fun and rewarding to create! For example, your blog does not have to be exclusively focused upon your course—it can be about your experiences with teaching (like a personal diary), or about a particular subject matter of interest. Try to make your blog as engaging as possible by choosing a topic that your students will be drawn to and enjoy. Usually, professor blogs seem most successful when they are focused on a topic of interest, and do not delve too deeply into the professor's personal life. Often, blogging requires practice and a bit of trial-and-error as your choose your direction. Note that there is no set rule here and that the blog can focus on any topic of interest, from research reports in a psychological area, to critiques or news media, to your own random weird thoughts.

Student blogs also provide a potential area for assignments in online psychology courses. While this might sound labor intensive at first, today's students relish the opportunity to create and distribute their own media. In fact, they might even work harder and better knowing that their content will be available for perusal not only by their professor and classmates, but also the entire world via the web! Your students may value this opportunity to broadcast their ideas to the public and to receive feedback on them. Some activities are particularly well suited to blogs, such as diaries (e.g., a report of a naturalistic observation of research over one week, or a self-study of abnormal behaviors) as well as attention to current events (e.g., psychological topics of interest and how the news media chooses to cover them). When it comes to the dissemination of online content, anything is possible. One of your students might end up creating a highly successful, well-read blog! If you are looking to encourage independent thought and creativity, this is an excellent route to take.

Finally, existing blogs can also be utilized to supplement course offerings. While the activity of creating a blog is more interactive, there are also a number of psychology blogs that provide a wealth of insightful information about the discipline. Just remember that blogs are not peer reviewed, and that one cannot always guarantee the accuracy of all of the information conveyed in a blog. Existing blogs can be assigned for students to follow during an entire semester, or specific postings can be shared with your class. Some of the best psychology based blogs include:

4.3 Notable Psychology Blogs

PsyBlog: (http://www.spring.org.uk/). An applied perspective on the most recent psychological research, with an emphasis on technology use.

We're Only Human: (http://www.psychologicalscience.org/index.php/news/were-only-human). Commentary on how psychological findings shed light on our true nature.

Mind Hacks: (http://mindhacks.com/). A fusion of psychology, psychiatry, and neuroscience.

Not Exactly Rocket Science (http://blogs.discovermagazine.com/notrocketscience/). A science-based blog featuring interdisciplinary research reports.

NeuroCritic (http://neurocritic.blogspot.com/). Deconstructing the most sensationalistic recent findings in human brain imaging, cognitive neuroscience, and psychopharmacology.

BPS Research Digest Blog (http://bps-research-digest.blogspot.com/). Reports on latest psychology research from the British Psychological Society.

Psychology Today: The Essential Read (http://www.psychologytoday.com/blog/essentials). Focus on the most relevant topics in psychology with frequent updates.

The Last Psychiatrist: (http://thelastpsychiatrist.com/). Thoughtful and insightful commentary from a practicing psychiatrist.

Channel N (http://blogs.psychcentral.com/channeln/). Neuropsychology video and information source.

The Situationist (http://thesituationist.wordpress.com/). Social psychology articles, videos, and commentary.

How to Blog

There are a number of ways to create your own blog. The authors have found that Blogger (also known as BlogSpot) is one of the easiest free blog software packages available at the time of press. (Please consult the text website for updated information on blog creating software and tips.) It takes three simple steps to sign up for Blogger—choose a user name and password, sign up for your blog, name your blog, and choose your template, layout, and design. In terms of design, Blogspot provides colorful templates, custom colors and fonts, a WYSIWYG text editor, picture posting, and drag-and-drop page elements (so that the user can decide exactly where everything goes before approving the finished product). Blogs can be easily accessible, including the ability to edit via one's mobile phone. The creator of the blog also has the option to decide who posts comments on the blog, as well as who can read and write on the blog. The best part about blogging is that there is no specific one way of creating and moderating a blog—rather, the author has total control over content, layout, flow, and direction.

ONLINE SOCIAL NETWORKS: TIPS FOR SUCCESS

What Is an Online Social Network?

Broadly defined, an online social network is "any online service, platform, or site that focuses on building and reflecting social relations among people, who share interests and/or activities" (Wikipedia, 2012d). Interestingly, online courses also fit within this definition. In an online psychology course, a platform (the CMS) builds social relationships (through communication on discussion boards, email or synchronous chat) for people who have a common interest (studying psychology). Perhaps the fundamental difference here is that the relationship building is not the sole intended purpose of online courses, but rather, a bonus biproduct. Indeed, as discussed in the previous chapter, the sense of community created in online courses (which could also be understood as a network of relationships) helps to facilitate investment in online learning and student success.

Unlike online courses, there are numerous online services and platforms whose sole goal is the creation and maintenance of online social relationships. Users of these platforms and websites usually create a personal profile featuring their information and interests, which is then viewable by their online network, often labeled their "friends," "fans," or "followers." Of these numerous services, the most commonly utilized website at the time of going to press is Facebook, which currently boasts a worldwide membership of over 600 million users (Carlson, 2011). Facebook's mission is "to give people the power to share and make the world more open and connected" and they have certainly attained huge levels of success in this endeavor. Millions of people across the world access Facebook each day via the web or mobile devices to communicate and share information, links, photos, and videos with their "friends" and their "fans." Other online social networks readers may be familiar with include Twitter, MySpace, LinkedIn, and Bebo.

At the time of going to press, Twitter is the second most popular and fastest growing online social networking platform, with over 100 million active users worldwide, and 230 million new tweets each day (Taylor, 2011). Twitter is different from Facebook, describing itself as a "real-time information network powered by people all around the world that lets you share and discover what's happening now." Whereas users on Facebook can create and share lengthy status updates and notes with their friends and fans, Twitter users make *tweets*: Posts that are 140 characters or less and are viewed by one's *followers*, or, users who subscribe to your tweets. The central difference between the two, then, is that Twitter users amass followers who view their succinct updates, comments, or messages, whereas Facebook users amass friends or "fans" who view potentially longer, more detailed updates or comments. In other words, the function provided by both sites appears increasingly similar.

Why Use Online Social Networks?

The easiest answer to this question is, why not? Why not harness some of this online social capital for the purposes of online education? As mentioned in previous chapters, an instructor's social network page can continue to facilitate a sense of community between students long after the online course has ended. While research on the use of social networking sites in education is limited at best, some studies have shown that students who use Facebook as a supportive tool in their education experience affective communication as a result that includes encouragement, group reinforcement, and support (such as English & Duncan-Howell, 2008). Thus, consider that the use of social networking sites can enhance a sense of community created during the course, and maintain these connections and closeness even after the course ends.

In our current context where online education can be accessed from anywhere, at any time, students (whether they are prospective, current, or former) may expect that same level of access to their instructor. The creation of a social networking page to exclusively serve this purpose should enhance student closeness and fulfill the expectation that instructors are accessible at any time via the web. By maintaining an online presence on a social networking website, the instructor can give students the perception of accessibility, friendliness, and closeness while engaging in only a minimal amount of effort. In addition to promoting community and maintaining an online presence, social networking websites offer instructors an additional outlet for disseminating important course information such as reminders for upcoming due dates, announcements regarding course policies, and links to relevant sources or news events.

How to Use Social Networking Sites

Unique to social networking websites is the notion that the instructor must create and maintain an online "identity" for use when interacting with students. Fear not if you are concerned that participation in this type of website may open up unsatisfactory or uncomfortable relationships between instructor and students. It is absolutely possible to create a professional presence on these websites that does not bridge into "discomfort" territory. Possibly the best way of doing this is to ensure that your "personal" account does not bleed into your "professional" account. The protocol may differ depending upon the type of social networking website you are using, but the underlying idea is the same: Have one page (or identity) that reflects your personal and private relationships with family and friends, and create another separate page (or identity) that can be used in professional life to engage with colleagues, research participants, and your students.

Why is this level of separation between personal and professional so important when using online social networks? Indeed, there are some instructors who make friends with all of their students, as well as their families, colleagues, and actual friends, all on the same page or same profile. A separation of personal and professional is probably a wise choice, however, in the interest of minimizing potential risks and maintaining focus. For example, imagine the statistics professor who uses the same Facebook identity to provide information to his students, friends, and family. Inevitably, a friend from college who hasn't been heard from for 15 years reconnects via Facebook, and begins posting pictures on said professor's website of Spring Break in Cancun, 1994. While his statistics students were undoubtedly amused by photos of their inebriated professor wearing a speedo, this type of event amounts to career suicide when trying to establish a professional presence online. Creating a separate page for professional activities greatly reduces the likelihood of potential humiliation or fallout from a friend or acquaintance posting personal documents or information online.

At the time of going to press, creating a "fan" page on Facebook, or amassing "followers" on Twitter is probably the safest way to ensure a professional online presence without this bleeding into your personal life, and vice versa. On Facebook, it is possible to create a "personality" page that your students can choose to "like," thereby becoming your "fans." From this page, students will see only the information that you decide to make public, and they can make posts and interact with each other on this page. As the administrator, you can decide who sees your content, and you can quickly remove or hide any information that is not appropriate to your professional life. "Fans" do not have access to the "friend" areas of your profile, such as personal pictures, wall-posts, or information. However, you can still communicate with students and build community in this way. Alternatively, by agreeing to "follow" you on Twitter, students will see only the 140 character posts that you make, which they can in turn subscribe to. As with Facebook fans, Twitter followers do not see your personal information, pictures, or anything unless you decide to make that information public. Because these software platforms are constantly evolving, please check the book website for further information on creating and maintaining professional online pages.

Troubleshooting: Important Issues in Technology Support

Student Technical Support

It is inevitable that at some stage during your online course, students may have technical issues with the various software and multimedia applications that you decide to use. While there is no fail-safe way of avoiding this, there are a number of procedures you can put into place to make the technical support process as easy as possible.

Technological Orientation

As mentioned in chapter 2, a comprehensive orientation is highly beneficial when students join online courses. If you plan to ask students to create media (such as videos, wikis, and blogs), then you might want to include a specific training session focused upon this technology. This will raise student awareness about what is expected of them from the very beginning and prompt them to seek help early-on if they have questions or issues. Even basic technology training on the functions of your CMS could be very helpful. Check with your institution about the type of CMS used and training associated with it. For example, both Blackboard and Moodle offer extensive help videos and FAQs on their websites.

Student-Mediated Support

Consider creating a discussion board dedicated to student technical issues, and ask students to make posts and reply to posts in this forum. Some of your students who are technologically savvy will take pleasure in assisting other students in their learning community. This also saves the instructor from sending individual emails to students when a reply can be posted directly on a forum accessible to all students. Consider also how to use student created technology, such as blogs and online social networks, to disseminate student help. For example, posting a question to your Facebook or Twitter page might result in quick and accessible assistance for students. If you have "fans" or "followers" who subscribe to your page and took your course during the previous semester, they may have already experienced the problem and found a solution. Encouraging users on online social networking sites to communicate about the course is a great way to help students help each other!

Technology TA

Depending upon the institutional resources available, it might possible to hire a technology TA to be in charge of giving technical support and training to students. Often, this might be a former student who was successful in your course, or a graduate student looking for training. Consider proposing this to your institution if the service is not currently being offered. Graduate students in particular take up many of these roles in psychology departments, working as statistics consultants, research consultants, or giving help with grant writing or dissertations. Thus, it is hardly a stretch to ask for a technology savvy graduate student to assist with online course creation and maintenance. Purely in terms of a cost-benefit analysis, the salary for this student certainly justifies the tuition gained by enrolling numerous students in your online course. Depending upon an instructor's technology abilities, the TA may just be on hand to provide student technical support, or the TA may assist in the creation and implementation of the entire course.

Institutional Resources

Any college, university, or institution that offers online courses should also provide a technical support center where instructors can refer students with questions. Often, technical support is required for issues that the professor does not deal with directly, such as logging in to the CMS, registration, and gaining access to schedules. Usually, the registrar or admissions and records provide a good starting point when it comes to helping a student with log-in or registration problems. Sometimes, students will have questions regarding the setup for their WiFi, which might be directed toward student services. Likewise, sometimes students may have an issue that the professor cannot answer, such as "Why is this video not working on my computer?" These can be frustrating problems sometimes, especially when the video seems to work for everyone else. Often, the institution cannot help with this. Troubleshooting these types of issues will probably involve taking the following steps: (a) making sure software is up-to-date, (b) using the right web browser for the CMS, and (c) making sure the internet connection is strong enough. Generally, if it is not possible to help a student, and the institution cannot provide additional insight, try to give that student a summary of the video (or ask another student to summarize) and then, move on.

If your academic institution offers instructional support to students, then you are very fortunate and can direct students to this support center should they experience any type of problem. To get the most out of your institution's technical support, be sure to post their website and contact information in as many places as possible: the CMS, syllabus, your blog, your website, your Facebook page. If live support chat is offered, this is even better. From here, students can communicate directly with a support professional who can troubleshoot their issues. Not all institutions that offer online courses provide such comprehensive technical support, but many of them do, and the number is constantly increasing. If your institution does not offer satisfactory support for online students, try to petition them to do so. After all, the cost for an online support center is minimal when considering the sheer number of students who can be taught online. It is in the best interest of the institution, instructor, and students to offer the highest quality support possible.

Outside Assistance

If institutional technical support cannot solve student problems, or there is no institutional support and the instructor remains unclear, begin to refer students to outside websites that may help. Often, software is not up-to-date, which can make it difficult to obtain the right security settings for accessing all of the CMS content. As mentioned earlier, the instructor might want to direct a student with software problems to Microsoft's technical support (http://support.microsoft.com/) or Apple's technical support (http://www.apple.com/support), depending on their computer and operating system. If a specific outside application such as YouTube is causing them problems, then certainly provide the link to their support (http://www.google.com/support/youtube/). These outside websites are constantly being updated and tend to provide highly efficient, user-friendly information. Please check the textbook website for the most up-to-date online support websites.

INTELLECTUAL PROPERTY

One of the most frequently asked questions of online professors is, "Who owns my course materials if I put them online?" At a recent presentation, the authors were asked the same question, to which an online professor in the audience answered, "Are you kidding, we can't give this stuff away for free!" All humor aside, there is a disconnect between wanting students, employers, and the general world out there on the web to be able to access your course materials, and the desire to keep ownership of what you have created. What do you do if another professor at another university is using your lectures, or copying your lecture script? Can other instructors show your videos to their classes?

To address the issue of ownership of online course materials, the authors consulted a 2010 article by Masson published in the *Journal of Online Teaching and Learning*, titled "Online Highway Robbery: Is your Intellectual Property Up for Grabs in the Online Classroom?" Based upon this review of the literature, it seems that the answer lies in the rules of your institution and your employment contract. Surprisingly, the rules regarding intellectual property online vary tremendously, even within different universities associated with the same institution in the same geographic area!

First, let us begin with basics. Copyright is defined as "the exclusive legal right to reproduce, publish, sell or distribute the matter and form of something (as a literary, musical or artistic work)" (Merriam-Webster, 2012). In an academic setting, copyrightable work can be extended to include PowerPoint slides, Adobe PDFs, handouts, syllabi, web-based videos, tests, and assignments, and any other course materials (Kromrey et al., 2005).

So, does a professor have ownership over his or her online course offerings? According to Masson (2010), "until recently, many generally believed that universities owned anything and everything an instructor generated as part of a traditional or online course because the work was done as part of the duties of the job, a 'work for hire' situation." (p. 257). According to the U.S. Copyright Law of 1976, any course-related materials (there is a scope of employment requirement) created by teachers when they are employed by a college or university are owned by their employer, because the materials were created on a work for hire basis. This means, according to Masson and the experts cited, unless you agree in writing with your institution that you have ownership over your course materials, your employer owns them, not you.

Still, legal precedent does suggest that the professor holds copyright over his or her work, even as work for hire. One example cited by Masson is Douglas Kranch's (2008) report of a UCLA professor who sued for copyright infringement and won when an outsider published his lecture notes, even though the defense argued that UCLA should hold the rights to the materials, not the professor. Normally, an employer cannot do a whole lot with a syllabus and a bunch of PowerPoint slides. But when the information is nicely packaged into an online course that can be used again and again, it becomes much easier for the institution to reuse it without the instructor's consent, if they choose (Dahl, 2005). Indeed, Masson (2010) provides a compelling argument put forward by Carol Twigg (n.d.), the executive director of the Center for Academic Transformation, who argues that online "courses are being 'commoditized' and sought as commercial products by online distance learning companies, for-profit universities, and publishers" (Twigg, n.d., quoted in Masson, 2010, p. 257). Suddenly, when you create an online course, your university could use your course shell without your consent, or worse, sell it to a third party.

But do universities actually take ownership of your materials? While researchers are lacking a comprehensive dataset on this topic, Masson (2010) cites the most detailed research to date, presented by Kromrey and colleagues (2005), a study of intellectual property regulations at 42 public and private doctoral extensive research universities. This study found that 100% of private and 93% of public institutions did claim ownership of at least some faculty-created property. However, around half of these institutions also "ceded control" to instructors of various course-specific materials such as lectures, notes, and syllabi (Masson, 2010, p. 258). Also, around 20% of institutions claimed some kind of joint ownership of these works. While it appears that the amount of faculty control over course material has been increasing, it nonetheless seems that many faculty members do not have ownership of their online course materials.

How do you know if you have ownership over your material? First and foremost, read your employment contract! If you see the words *work for hire* in your contract, you can assume that you will not retain ownership of your course materials. If you are looking for a job, make sure that you address the intellectual property policy as part of your search. Masson (2010) suggests that in the future, ownership of online courses might become the deal breaker for the hiring choices of highly desirable instructors, or experts in a particular field. In other words, institutions that offer academic freedom for instructors will, in the long term, become more desirable places to work. Masson also offers some steps for faculty members who have unsatisfactory contracts or find themselves in situations where they are frustrated over their lack of ownership: (a) Join a teacher's union, and get involved in the American Association of University Professors (www.aaup.org); and (b) Let your voice be heard! Work with your academic senate and other instructors to push for policies that enable ownership over online course materials.

Additionally, there are steps you can undergo to protect your course materials, according to Ko and Rossen (2010). First, there are technological methods of protecting your work, including a (obvious) password protection on your course website, CMS, or Facebook page. Using a program like Adobe Acrobat can also help protect your work because it is possible save a .PDF file in such a way that unauthorized editing and revision is not possible. To turn any document (Word, PowerPoint, etc.) into an Adobe PDF, go to "print" and then choose "PDF." From there, you can make the document password protected, limit the reprint of photos and slides, and even restrict printing. Then, if another instructor obtains your document, it will be virtually useless to them. You can also protect your media by making it "streaming" so that users cannot physically download your file. YouTube is an example of streaming media—your video is viewable on the web, but not downloadable for editing.

USE OF COPYRIGHTED MATERIAL

Copyright of outside material also requires very important consideration when teaching online. Just as you do not want other instructors using your materials without your permission, generators of original content do not want you using it in your courses without permission! Copyright law can be confusing and subjective, because you are allowed to use other people's materials so long as you do not go beyond the "fair use" of that material and make that material openly accessible. "Fair Use" as outlined by the U.S. Copyright Law of 1976 is not a legal rule, but an open-ended standard, meaning that it gives courts guidance when making decisions, but also allows a lot of room for maneuvering. Basically, it is very difficult to predict whether your use of the copyrighted work would be allowed under the "Fair Use" defense, because fair use is rarely applied in a consistent fashion. One thing you can keep in mind, however, is that almost *all* professors use copyrighted work in their classes and they seldom get sued. The fair use standard according to U.S. copyright law is discussed below. The authors strongly advise you to ask permission from the copyright owner before using their work, which can usually be done through your institution's library or administration (for information on copyright law see http://www.copyright.gov/fls/fl102.html).

Purpose and Character

What is the *character* of use? In terms of character, you must consider whether the work is not for profit and whether it is transformative. First, are you using this for commercial or noncommercial purposes? As a professor, you are most likely using the work (such as showing your class a DVD or YouTube video) for nonprofit educational purposes. If you are assembling materials for sale (such as a textbook or educational video), then this could be a potential violation of copyright. Second, is the work transformational (meaning you used the original work to create something new) or nontransformational (as in, a mechanical reproduction)? If the work is transformational (such as video clips taken and then combined into a montage or lecture), then this cuts in favor of fair use. Further, what is the proprietary nature of the conduct? The courts usually only consider this if you are using the work in a negative or reprehensible fashion (and only in some jurisdictions). As an educator, this should not (one hopes) apply to you!

The Nature of Copyrighted Work

What is the *nature* of the work used? Some works are in the *public domain*, meaning that they were never copyrighted, or are older than copyright law (examples include the English language, Shakespeare's works, and Newtonian physics formulas). If a work is in the public domain, then copyright law is not a problem. If the work is not in the public domain, then the need for permissions depends upon the nature of the work. Is it factual data or original creative content? Factual or data oriented works are more likely to get fair use safe-haven in the courts because the justifications of copyright cut toward disseminating factual work. If you are taking directly from an original, creative, or fictional piece then err on the side of caution and seek permission.

Amount and Substantiality of the Portion Used

How much of the work will you use? First, in terms of quantity, how long was the clip that was taken? Was it small in relationship to the copyrighted work as a whole? If so, that cuts in favor of a finding of fair use. Or did you take the majority of the work? In this case, you will probably need to obtain permission. Second, how substantial was the clip taken—was it the heart of the work? Was it just an introduction or was it a major plot twist? If you take the heart of the work, it cuts against a finding of fair use and you should seek permissions.

The Effect of the Use on the Potential Market

What effect would use have on the *market* for the original work? This provision is particularly important for *online* educators, according to Ko and Rossen (2010). If you make your course materials available to everyone across the web, and these materials contain copyrighted content, then this could be a big problem. Essentially, you could be damaging the market value by making this content available for free to a multitude of users. On the flipside, if your course is password protected and hosted by a CMS such as Blackboard or Moodle, then you are only making the information available to a select few individuals and are probably not damaging the market value of the work. Still this provision remains highly subjective. If you are showing a video clip only a few seconds long that might be copyrighted, would there be a relevant effect on the market? The answer is unclear. If a license for the work is available, try to acquire one through your institution.

There are certain additional guidelines in place for educators, according to the *Fair Use Guidelines for Educational Multimedia* (n.d.). Such guidelines provide educators with the assurance that they will not be sued if they abide by certain rules. However, these guidelines are extremely subjective and by no means reflect the extensive copyright law of the United States. *Please* consider that these guidelines do *not* have force of law and are only designed to help educators wade through what are still murky waters. When in doubt, always look into licensing and securing permission for outside sources and materials. Usually your institution will have someone in the library or administration to consult regarding copyright and securing permissions. After figuring out if you need permission, find out what the cost will be for that material—the cost can range from inexpensive to extremely pricey. Decide: Is the price worth the material's impact upon your students? Sometimes if the price of the work is very expensive, you will simply not be able to obtain it under your institutional guidelines. If your institution does not have a permission form or recommended letter of permission, consider writing to the owner of the work and asking for permission. Explain that you are an educator and would like to use the work in your classroom. When in doubt, always ask for permission!

Copyright Resources

For more detailed, up-to-date information on copyright rules and obtaining permissions, please visit the following websites:

4.4 Additional Copyright Resources

1. The "TEACH" Act (Technology, Education and Copyright Harmonization Act) of 2002:
   http://www.ala.org/ala/issuesadvocacy/copyright/teachact/faq.cfm;
   http://www.copyright.com/Services/copyrightoncampus/basics/teach.html

2. CENDI Task Force: Frequently Asked Questions about Copyright:
   http://www.cendi.gov/publications/04-8copyright.html

3. Copyright Management's Fair Use Checklist:
   http://www.copyright.com/Services/copyrightoncampus/basics/fairuse_list.html

4. Reproduction of copyrighted works by educators and librarians:
   http://www.copyright.gov/circs/circ21.pdf

5. University of Maryland Center for Intellectual Property Primer:
   http://www-apps.umuc.edu/primer/enter.php

Summary: Making Technology Work for You

This chapter covers the numerous ways in which technology and multimedia can be harnessed to benefit students in online psychology courses. First, we must consider that while many online students favor tech-heavy learning, it is vital to strike a delicate balance to ensure that your course can appeal to everyone, both technophiles and technophobes, so to speak. After reviewing relevant literature on the "M" generation making their way into higher education, this chapter focused at length on the what, why, and how questions surrounding course management systems, video lectures, podcasts, wikis, blogs, and social networking sites. Then, the focus switched toward two central areas for technology troubleshooting: student technical support, and issues over intellectual property and copyright. Now that the multimedia bonanza has been laid bare, how can online psychology instructors create excellent, high quality assignments that integrate these technologies? Tune in to the next chapter to find out.

CHAPTER 5

ONLINE ACTIVITIES

HIGHER ORDER THINKING THROUGH DISCOURSE

Engaging, enlightening activities are central to any successful online psychology course. Without activities, the online course would resemble a self-taught tutorial where students read the text and repeat back to the instructor what they have learned. Activities bring the course to life; activities facilitate discourse and community building; activities build and develop higher order skills; and perhaps most importantly of all, the activities are often what students *really* remember, and what they take with them long after leaving the course. Consider a general psychology course: Often, students who are asked to participate in simulations of classic studies, or who engage in debates, group projects, or other interactive activities, tend to reflect with great enjoyment upon these experiences. Online psychology courses should be no different: The introduction of a computer screen and a physical distance between course members should in no way hinder student ability to interact, to work together, to develop new ideas, and to arrive at innovative conclusions. If anything, the nature of the online classroom (from the incorporation of handy new technologies, to the energetic flow of the discussion boards) lends itself *especially* well to creating and implementing worthwhile, exciting activities. Thus, the goal of this chapter is to provide psychology instructors with the background knowledge and expertise to integrate valuable activities into their online courses.

The "Purpose" section that begins this chapter discusses how and why activities are so important to the study of psychology online. This portion of the chapter seeks to apply relevant research and theory on teaching and learning to the online education context. Of particular interest here is Bloom's taxonomy, and its relevance to creating online assignments for psychology. Next, the "Implementation" section of chapter discusses the types of online activities that are especially valuable and applicable to psychology courses, including online discussions, group projects, simulations, virtual worlds, and social bookmarking. Finally, the "Troubleshooting" section features a wealth of online resources for psychology activities that instructors can utilize if they ever get stuck when trying to design a successful activity. The authors personally researched hundreds of websites to arrive at an annotated selection of the most useful ones for online psychology instructors.

Purpose: Enhancing Critical Thinking

Online activities are central to the success of any online course, and arguably, these activities become even *more* important than ever when we transition to the online learning environment. Activities breathe life into the course, they encourage discussion and discourse, they broaden minds, and of course, they can build critical thinking. In addition, activities are vital to establishing an online presence between instructor and student, as well as between students themselves. In terms of an instructor–student discourse, without regular, effortful instructor–student interaction, it can be very difficult to ascertain a student's level of commitment to the course. This lack of proximity and immediate contact can be one of the challenging areas of the digital divide to conquer for instructors who are new to online teaching. Instructors therefore need to feel confident that students will adhere to the *administrative* component of their activities (completing them on time and following instructions) as well as to the *content* components (to ensure that they are learning what they should be learning).

The student-mediated dialogue that emerges from online activities is perhaps even more valuable to the learning experience than the instructor–student interaction. Recall from previous chapters the positive association between communication and successful online student outcomes. Unlike the traditional classroom, the online learning environment affords multiple venues for activities that promote communication and discourse, including but not limited to: asynchronous discussion board posts, synchronous chat, wikis, social networking sites, social bookmarking, and virtual worlds. The education and psychology literatures tend to support the notion that active learning activities (through interaction or discourse) lead to better student outcomes than passive learning activities (such as learning through memorization for a quiz). For example,

Weimer (2002) argues for the benefits of a *learner-centered* approach where "teachers do less telling, students do more discovering" and where "faculty work to create climates for learning and do more with feedback" (pp. 83, 90). According to this perspective, students learn best when they are free to construct knowledge based upon the information provided to them, and utilize their skills for critical thinking and problem solving to arrive at their own conclusions. In this approach, the focus shifts from grades to learning, affording students the opportunity to participate in activities that foster their own growth and development. Applied to an online learning context, these activities could include discussion boards, group research projects, wikis, participation in simulations, and even interacting in virtual worlds.

Can theories of teaching and learning inform the creation of assignments for online courses? In their book *Assessing the Online Learner,* Palloff and Pratt (2009) argue that prominent theories of learning can be applied to the context of online activities. For example, they highlight Kolitch and Dean's (1999) dichotomy between the *transmission* model of teaching (where the instructor literally transmits information to students) and the *engaged critical model* (where learning happens as part of a dialogue between teachers and students and amongst students themselves). This dichotomy is reminiscent of the "Sage on the Stage" versus "Guide on the Side" discussed in chapter 3. Palloff and Pratt (2009) argue that while traditional learning and assignments tend to mimic the transmission model, "the forms of instruction that happen online, however, are more in line with the engaged critical model" (p. 18). This assertion implies that online activities give instructors a unique opportunity to boost student learning through activities engagement and critical thinking. Palloff and Pratt (2009) label these kinds of activities as *authentic assessments*, including activities that promote practicing by doing and teaching others.

In addition, theories of education tend to suggest that the type of activity students engage in should be commensurate with the goals for student learning outcomes. While learning outcomes for the online environment will be discussed in detail in chapter 6, consider how Bloom's taxonomy of educational objectives (Bloom & Krathwohl, 1956) can be applied to the creation, selection, or implementation of online activities. Bloom's taxonomy demonstrates how learning outcomes can be scaffolded, ranging from lower order skills to higher order skills. The six steps of Bloom's taxonomy each correspond to a major area of cognition, with categories ordered from simple to complex and from concrete to abstract, using action verbs associated with student abilities at each step (Krathwohl, 2002). In order, these six steps are: Knowledge, Comprehension, Application, Analysis,

Synthesis, and Evaluation. Each step corresponds to activities that can help the learner to reach the objectives highlighted by each step. Based upon suggestions from Paloff and Pratt (2009), the authors provide types of online activities that can meet the criteria for each of the six steps for students studying psychology online.

KNOWLEDGE

The first and most simple step in the taxonomy deals with recall, knowledge, and the familiarity with basic concepts. In terms of the study of psychology, this could include definitions of important constructs, or the memorization of theories, dates, and authors. This phase is best described by action verbs including define, list, memorize, recall, recognize, and recite. Potential activities related to this phase include quizzes and tests that focus on recall, as well as listening to lectures via podcast or video and answering follow-up questions. Further, student discussions that address definitions or the creation of definitions (who, what, where, when, why?) could be useful, whether conducted via an asynchronous discussion board, or on a group wiki page.

COMPREHENSION

The next step deals with the ability to explain, interpret, and understand the material, as well as to describe the implications of any data or content presented. For the study of psychology, this phase often involves understanding the meaning of theories (such as the relationships between variables) as well as being able to read and interpret charts, graphs, and other statistical output. The verbs associated with this phase include discuss, classify, describe, summarize, identify, explain, locate, recognize, and paraphrase. Activities related to this phase could include student presentations (either text-based, audio, or full-video), or conducting and summarizing literature searches via the internet (such as Jstor, PsychInfo, EsbscoHost, or Google Scholar). Group work where students must view charts or graphs and then explain their meanings to the rest of the class via discussion board could also be very useful here.

APPLICATION

In this step, we begin to see higher order thoughts, like critical thinking skills, emerge, including problem solving, extending information to new situations, finding the best answers, and applying theories to practical situations. In the study of psychology, the application step becomes very important as we look for students to apply their knowledge of theory and research to actual behavior and situations. The verbs associated with this step include demonstrate, employ, solve, use, interpret, draw, provide, operate, report, and implement. At this step, the *authentic assessments* alluded to earlier also become especially relevant, including student participation in case studies or simulations that apply psychological theory to actual real-life situations. In addition, at this stage research projects (either conducted solo or in conjunction with a small group) can be very beneficial, along with discussion activities aimed toward answering questions like this: "How are A and B related? Why is this significant?"

ANALYSIS

The analysis phase deals primarily with comparing and contrasting important elements, identifying components of knowledge, and understanding structure and composition. In psychology, this phase is particularly important for understanding theory, including theory generation, testing, and critique of theory. Learners at this phase should also be able to distinguish between fact and conjecture, essential for examining and analyzing the methodological underpinnings of psychological research. Verbs associated with this step include differentiate, illustrate, compare, contrast, categorize, calculate, criticize, examine, infer, prove, test, and relate. Central to online psychology assignments for this step would be debates about the merits of certain theories or research programs, which could be conducted via synchronous chat, video chat, or via asynchronous discussion board activities. If the course maintains a research focus, this might be a good time to assign a group research proposal or project, or group wiki for the purpose of comparing and contrasting certain key concepts. Alternatively, student papers, or blogs, that express higher levels of analysis would also be effective here.

SYNTHESIS

Central to this step is the higher order ability to creatively combine, extend, and apply knowledge to new areas. In terms of the study of psychology, many features of synthesis can serve as required course elements, including the ability to create a new hypothesis or propose a research design, or to explore new connections between variables. Also relevant here is the ability to make convincing arguments based upon the combination of multiple complex ideas. The action verbs associated with synthesis include categorize, negotiate, reconstruct, revise, organize, propose, plans, integrate, assemble, and manage. Often, activities that deal with synthesis involve questions about making predictions based upon a certain theory or behavior, which can be central when studying psychology. For activities in this realm, small-group projects or group activities like wikis can help students to work together to combine and apply their ideas to solve important problems.

EVALUATION

The final and most complex step in Bloom's taxonomy deals with the ability to assess the value, quality, and viability of material presented. When studying psychology, evaluation of specific programs, outcomes, or research proposals can be of the highest importance. The verbs associated with this step include appraise, defend, interpret, choose, value, score, argue, justify, and select. Online education affords a number of different opportunities for constructing activities surrounding student evaluation abilities. Group debates (synchronous or asynchronous) covering the rationale for a certain program, or the viability of a research project, would be very useful, along with small-group projects where students review each other's proposals or arguments. Activities that facilitate students working together to devise their own evaluation, or to critique a preexisting one, would be especially useful.

This examination of Bloom's taxonomy helps to elucidate how one of the most preeminent psychological classifications of learning helps to advise the types of assignments selected for the online teaching of psychology. Clearly, all of the levels of the taxonomy are important for student learning in psychology, particularly for higher level courses in research methods, program evaluation, as well as more applied courses like health psychology, clinical psychology, or social policy. Notice that the recommended online activities, particularly at the upper levels, are often focused on interaction, critique, application, and debate, all forms of discourse that are enhanced in the online learning environment. In fact, simple testing and quizzes seem most relevant to the lowest order skills, knowledge, and comprehension. As we move into the higher order areas including application, analysis, synthesis, and evaluation, we begin to reach skills that are highly relevant in the psychological sciences. As these higher order skills become the focus of the course, online activities that feature learner centered interaction such as synchronous debate, group projects, wikis, asynchronous discussion boards, and simulations become increasingly more prominent. Keep in mind how online interaction corresponds to higher order cognition and we move into the following chapter on the implementation of online assignments.

INSIGHT FROM THE REVISED BLOOM'S TAXONOMY

In 2002, Bloom's taxonomy was revised to highlight two separate dimensions that were combined in the original model: knowledge and cognitive processing (Krathwohl, 2002). One of the key criticisms from the original model was the unique duality of the *knowledge* dimension (in that it functioned both as a noun and verb) whereas the other dimensions operated as verbs only. Thus, in addition to incorporating factual, conceptual, and procedural knowledge from the previous model, the knowledge dimension was revised to function only as a noun, and was broadened to include *metacognitive* knowledge (knowledge about cognition in general and one's own cognitions). In terms of cognitive processing, six categories remain but they were renamed or rearranged. First, *knowledge* as a noun became its own dimension (as stated above) while knowledge as a verb was changed to *remember*. Second, because the word *comprehend* can apply to so many different levels of thinking, it was changed to *understand*. *Application, analysis,* and *evaluation* remained unchanged, but were labeled in verb form: *apply, analyze, evaluate*. Finally, *synthesis* was changed to *create*, and swapped places with *evaluate*. Graphically, the entire revised taxonomy can be represented as a table, with the knowledge dimension on one axis (factual, conceptual, procedural, metacognitive) and the cognitive processing dimension on the other (remember, understand, apply, analyze, evaluate, create).

While these revisions are relatively minor, and the crux of the message remains the same, they do offer insight for online activities in psychology. First, the addition of metacognition as a key knowledge concept suggests that we encourage students to think more critically about how cognition can influence behavior, and how their own cognitions are shaping their lives and affecting their educations. Second, the separation into two distinct dimensions enables instructors to delineate both the type of knowledge as well as the type of cognitive process sought by any particular activity. This offers a level of specificity and accuracy previously unavailable in the prior model, and maps nicely onto the creation of learning objectives. Third, the dimensions in the revised taxonomy remain hierarchically ordered, but not as rigidly as in the original, suggesting more flow and overlap between categories. It is possible then to have an activity or assignment that addresses several types of knowledge or cognitive processes simultaneously, as is often the case in psychology activities such as group research projects. Finally, *create* now sits at the top of the pyramid, as the highest level dimension of cognitive processing. Thus, in order to create, students may need to master the other dimensions first (remember, understand, apply, analyze, evaluate), implying that cognitive processing and knowledge both comprise important parts of the creative process. Many activities for online psychology involve creation, including research projects, original thought papers, group work, debates, blogs, and video creation. Consider how these types of assignments can be incorporated to develop higher order thinking skills.

IMPLEMENTATION: FROM DISCUSSION BOARDS TO 3D VIRTUAL WORLDS (AND EVERYWHERE IN BETWEEN!)

This section of the chapter deals primarily with the creation and implementation of successful psychology related online activities. Based upon the literature reviewed in the previous section, the authors argue that online education is especially suited to the delivery of discourse-based assignments that can help students to develop higher order thinking and skills. As alluded to throughout this book, numerous activities are available to online psychology instructors aiming to foster both a sense of community and critical thinking skills—think *application, analysis, synthesis,* and *evaluation* as derived from Bloom's taxonomy. The technological background required to facilitate many of these activities has already been discussed in the previous chapter on the uses of technology and multimedia. In this section, the most applicable and beneficial types of online activities are discussed, along with best practices for developing these activities specifically for online psychology courses. This section focuses on central areas of interactive online activities, including discussion board questions, group projects, online simulations, virtual worlds, and social bookmarking.

DISCUSSION ACTIVITIES FOR PSYCHOLOGY

By now, readers should be familiar with the idea that the discussion board forms the heart and soul of the online classroom. Not only does the discussion board foster community building, but it also helps students to build critical thinking skills, and yields high levels of student learning and success. The implementation of discussion activities is relatively simple: The instructor selects an activity or topic (such as a particular theory, a research article, a case study, or other element to start a discussion) and then creates a discussion forum that poses a series of questions for the class. Students are then required to respond to a certain number of questions, or respond a certain number of times to other students, usually before a deadline after which the discussion board would become unavailable. The number of student responses required (such as one post each day, or one post in response to another student's post) can be decided at the instructor's discretion, depending upon the course schedule and course goals. All of these posts (whether they are answers to questions, or more questions, or something else) are made asynchronously, meaning that conversations do not occur in real-time, but instead, students can reply in their own time so long as they meet the requirements before the deadline. After the time for the assignment has elapsed, the instructor then assigns grades to these posts, using a series of grading criteria usually described and provided to students ahead of time as a grading rubric. For more on the grading of discussion assignments, please see chapter 6 on assessment.

Asynchronous online discussions should be particularly effective when instructors choose the right kinds of questions. How do psychology instructors build discussion board activities that serve their goals? How do they know which questions to select for which kind of topics? Currently, the authors have been unable to locate any published literature addressing the creation and implementation of online discussion activities specifically for the field of psychology. To address these questions, then, the following section examines relevant recommendations from prominent educators in the field of online teaching, and applies them to the discipline of online psychology.

A Socratic Approach

Boettcher and Conrad (2010) recommend in *The Online Teaching Survival Guide* that online instructors should first and foremost try to construct discussion questions that will lead to open-ended, exploratory responses. This can be understood as a *Socratic* approach to questioning, where students are asked to learn by "knowing" and providing information (whether it is data, theory, or some other support) that lends credence to their arguments. In other words, students should "inquire within" about their knowledge and beliefs and make arguments or provide evidence to support their point of view (Boettcher & Conrad, 2010, p. 88). In the field of psychology, these kinds of exploratory questions can be very useful. Students across the discipline are often asked to share various personal experiences and apply them to a particular theory, empirical approach, or line of research. Often, being able to explain something important in their own life through the lens of what they have learned in their course is very exciting for psychology students. Remember that many students choose to study psychology because they have fundamental, unanswered questions about their own and others behavior. The online discussion board provides a perfect forum for students to make these types of applications, and to compare and contrast how their experiences are interpreted via different theories and perspectives. According to Boettcher and Conrad (2010), discussion activities that take on this type of questioning approach tend to broaden the student role from learner to "questioner, summarizer and encourager" (p. 90).

Consider the practical value of an exploratory, open-ended approach to discussion activities. If a question asks for a factual or objective answer, such as a definition, date, and place, or name of a theory or theorizer, what will other students have left to contribute after someone answers the question correctly? Most likely, they will have very little to add, leading to a stunted discussion that does not help to foster student development and learning. To return to Bloom's taxonomy, these factual type questions might help to boost knowledge and comprehension, but exploratory, open-ended questions can help students to build skills pertaining to application, analysis, synthesis, and evaluation. This is not to say that discussions cannot be utilized as fact checkers (as opposed to quizzes or other pop-up assignments), but take note that discussion activities pertaining to facts will test and build a different set of skills than exploratory, open-ended ones. Nonetheless, Boettcher and Conrad (2010) still remind educators that the facts about the topic (in psychology these could include the name of a theory, its date, previous research, related studies) should be presented in the question dialogue to help ground students to the core ideas for that section of the course.

The first key message about creating discussion activities for psychology therefore involves leaving questions open, and giving students the opportunity to develop and interact with one another using their higher level critical thinking skills. Particularly in psychology, the importance of relating course topics to explaining real-life experience or behavior remains heightened. For online discussion activities then, the authors suggest that instructors focus on question prompts that contain action verbs like *examine, interpret, illustrate, compare, contrast, integrate, criticize, assess*, and *evaluate*, as opposed to verbs like *summarize, identify, repeat, recall, order,* or *define*. In an application to the field of psychology, the line of questioning might look something like what is offered below. Often, it helps for students to read a case study, research project, or other published article as an assignment before answering these questions.

5.1 SOCRATIC QUESTIONS

- What is the main issue associated with this theory?
- How does this theory relate to our previous discussion of behavior (insert: abnormal, developmental, clinical social, health, etc.)?
- What is your main argument and how does research support your perspective?
- Compare and contrast these two theoretical perspectives—which one is better illustrative of (insert type of) behavior and why?
- Is your view supported by research, what you have read, other theories, or your own life experience?
- Do other students agree with your perspective?

A PROBLEM-SOLVING APPROACH

Socratic-type questions are extremely useful for building critical thinking and community for online students, and this should be especially true for those studying the psychological sciences. One of the other most useful types of discussion questions for psychology are *problem-solving* questions, where students apply their knowledge and skills to creating solutions to real-world problems. In the field of psychology, such problem-solving questions provide the outlet that many students and instructors are seeking, as many programs shift to a more "applied psychology" focus. Within this realm, courses that address social policy, health psychology, clinical or counseling psychology, program evaluation, i/o psychology, abnormal psychology, positive psychology, and social policy studies (to name a few) seek to apply research and theory to improving people's lives through delivering treatment, implementing interventions, evaluating the effectiveness of programs, and lobbying for social changes. Thus it would be very useful for students in these types of programs to begin discussing these issues early on. In addition to wanting to learn about their own and others behavior, many students also pursue studies in psychology because they want to make a difference in people's lives, or make important contributions to society. Thus, integrating problem-solving questions into discussion activities should not only help students learn the material, but also encourage them to develop the skills they will need to succeed in applied fields. Some sample problem-solving questions are provided below.

5.2 PROBLEM-SOLVING QUESTIONS

- What are the implications of this study on lesbian parenting for gay couples' right to adopt?
- How would terror management theory help to predict the behavior of the survivors of Hurricane Katrina?
- Based upon your readings for this week, how would you intervene to help reduce adolescent risk behavior?
- How would you evaluate Head Start's ability to deliver education to needy children?

A CORE APPROACH

So far, we have discovered how *Socratic* questions can help students integrate course content by applying it to their own and each other's life experiences, and how *problem-solving* questions can encourage students to analyze how course content can be extended to finding solutions to real-life problems and issues. The final type of question well suited to online activities in psychology is *Core* questions, which are designed to "map directly back to the general and personal performance goals and learning outcomes of a course" (Boettcher & Conrad, 2010, p. 91). Often, Socratic questions and problem-solving questions have elements of the core course components, featuring applications to different scenarios, experiences, and issues. Core questions themselves should address the central learning outcomes of the course. For example, students in social psychology should be able to distinguish between, and understand the chain of causation that connects attitudes and norms with behavior. In addition to defining each of these, students should be able to relate how theories (such as the theory of reasoned action or cognitive dissonance) connect each of these ideas and explain how they would in turn predict behavior. A core concept discussion might ask students to explain a particular scenario using this theory, while identifying the specific attitudes, norms, and behaviors present. Then, this core concept might extend into a Socratic or problem-solving question where students will be asked to relate this chain of events to their own lives, or extend it to solving a certain problem.

Synthesis: Socratic, Problem-Solving, and Core Discussions

In summary, three types of discussion questions seem best suited for online activities in psychology: Socratic, problem solving, and core. However, achieving some kind of balance with these three formats might seem challenging or unclear to the new psychology instructor. While there is no right or wrong combination of these discussion types, consider beginning with discussion activities that address core concepts, and then branching out into Socratic or problem-solving applications of these questions. Many topics in psychology lend themselves to multiple applications and multiple levels of knowledge. In the previous example on the theory of reasoned action, once students can compare and contrast the core concepts (such as comparing an attitude with a norm), they then can be afforded follow-up questions, or follow-up activities that address either their own exploratory knowledge ("How have attitudes and norms related to or predicted an experience in your life?) as well as real-life applications ("Based upon what you have read, how could this theory be used to help to reduce adolescent drug use?"). In other words, the advice here is not to imagine these three types of questions in isolation, but rather, to look at the bigger picture and examine how each topic area that you teach (whether it is subdiscipline, research program, or important theory) can be assessed as a core concept, a Socratic exploration, and a problem to be solved. This approach is seemingly in line with Bloom's taxonomy, which suggests that students build their critical thinking by engaging first in knowledge and comprehension, and then in applications, analysis, synthesis, and evaluation.

The Four-Question Technique

In the past few years, there has been burgeoning support in the educational research literature for the notion that multiple forms of discussion questioning result in enhanced critical thinking for psychology students. For example, Dietz-Uhler and Lanter (2009) found that multiple forms of questioning led to higher student achievement in psychology. In this study, students in an introductory psychology course participated in a web-based series of interactive activities, and then answered these four questions, or did not answer these four questions, before they took a quiz. Students who responded to these four questions scored higher on the quiz than those who did not answer the questions:

1. *Analyzing:* "Identify one important concept, research finding, theory, or idea in psychology that you learned while completing this activity."
2. *Reflecting:* "Why do you believe that this concept, research finding, theory, or idea in psychology is important?"
3. *Relating:* "Apply what you have learned from this activity to some aspect of your life."

4. *Questioning:* "What question(s) has the activity raised for you? What are you still wondering about?"

That students scored better on a quiz after responding to these four questions suggests that multiple discussion questions may lead to enhanced knowledge retention and student performance. Also, it should be noted that these four questions are not at odds with the previous discussion on Socratic, problem-solving, and core questions. Rather, these approaches seem quite complementary. Question 1 (analyzing) is reminiscent of a core concept question, while question 2 (reflecting) implies a potential for application and problem solving, as does question 4 (questioning). Question 3 (relating) suggests a level of Socratic-based inquiry. Based upon the research, it seems that the four questions technique is more effective when students are prompted to engage in an activity before answering the questions, such as viewing a video, reading an article, learning about a theory, or making a presentation.

Alexander, Commander, Greenberg, and Ward (2010) extended Dietz-Uhler and Lanter's (2009) four-question approach to promote critical thinking in the online learning environment. In their study, online psychology graduate students participated in three online discussion forums after reading case studies about behaviorism, social cognitive theory, and metacognition. Before they engaged in the second discussion board only (on social cognitive theory), students were prompted with the "four questions" worded as follows: (a) Identify and describe one important concept, research finding, or idea about social cognitive theory that you have learned. (b) Why do you believe social cognitive theory is important? (c) Apply what you have learned about social cognitive theory to some aspect of your life. (d) What questions has the reading raised for you? After students made their posts, the researchers rated the level of critical thinking in each forum by using the Washington State University Critical and Integrative Thinking Scale. The results showed that students met a significantly higher number of critical thinking criteria when they answered the second discussion board that prompted them with the four questions, when compared with their responses to the first and third discussion boards that did not feature the four questions. They also found that there were no effects of previous experience in online discussion boards, or age, on critical thinking, suggesting that the four questions technique appears to be effective in building critical thinking skills for online students at any age and at any level of experience. However, more research needs to be conducted on the relationship between the four questions technique and critical thinking, because this study had a very small sample size, and did not randomly assign participants to conditions.

AUTHOR RECOMMENDATIONS FOR DISCUSSION ACTIVITIES

Even in spite of the limitations, it is promising that the four questions can be harnessed to build critical thinking abilities in online psychology students, and even more promising that educators are beginning to pursue research in this area. Based upon the available research literature and suggestions by the experts, the authors recommend the following approach to creating successful discussion activities for online psychology courses:

1. *Aim High*: In terms of Bloom's taxonomy, that is. Save the knowledge and comprehension objectives for multiple choice or true/false quizzes and tests. For discussion activities, select lines of questioning that address application, analysis, synthesis, and evaluation. Discussions are one of the best ways of enacting those higher order thinking skills.

2. *Multiple Methods*: Why settle for just one type of question or activity when asking many questions about the same topic can greatly extend student knowledge and success? For each core topic, there can be questions aimed specifically at understanding the phenomenon, as well as Socratic attempts toward application to one's life, and problem-solving applications to real-life situations. Recall that the core-Socratic-problem-solving approach can be easily mapped onto the four question technique and its application to online learning, where questions are analyzing, reflecting, relating, and questioning. Requiring students to respond to all of these types of questions should enhance their knowledge base, critical thinking skills, and their overall course performance.

3. *Respond to Something Meaningful*: If students are asked to discuss a dry, uninspiring topic, they may be less likely to stay engaged in their discussion. In other words, a big part of active, student-centered learning is student involvement and commitment, which will be heightened when the assignment feels relevant and important. When students are asked to respond to discussion questions surrounding a particular topic, activity or assignment, ensure that the core concept is being represented in an accurate and engaging way. Instead of just posting the definition of a theory and asking students to respond, try posting a case study describing how an individual would behave according to that theory, or post a research article that describes how the theory predicts real-life behavior. Or, post a debate that other psychologists have had about that particular theory, or ask students to critique a YouTube video of the media coverage of that theory and its applications. Students should respond with greater depth and excitement when they become inspired and engaged by

the topic. By boosting student involvement in this way, application to real-life issues, as well as to problem solving, should feel like the appropriate, natural transition for students.

4. *Group Activities and Projects:* While similar to discussion board assignments due to their interactivity, group activities nonetheless require an increased amount of student collaboration and focus. Unlike discussion boards, which usually involve the entire class making posts and commenting upon one another's posts, students who engage in group activities are frequently broken up into much smaller sections that are then supervised in some way by the instructor. This next section deals with issues pertaining to instructor roles in groups, dividing students into groups, moderating their efforts, and finally, troubleshooting when problems arise.

Instructor Roles in Group Assignments

First and foremost, it is important to be aware of the instructor's fluctuating role in student group work. One recommendation is to remain flexible in the role of group facilitator, since the duties of the instructor may fluctuate depending upon the type of group assignment. For example, if students in small groups are asked to engage in a debate, the instructor will probably end up moderating the debate and may take a more active role than if the instructor was only observing comments during a group discussion. Likewise, in the case of group research project, the instructor may need to check-in more frequently to ensure that all students are staying on-top of the work. While there is no perfect formula to determine the right amount of instructor involvement in group activities, always trust your instincts and try to make comments and direct interjections only when they are deemed necessary, or in response to a student question or concern. Remember the "Guide on the Side" perspective? In the case of group work, the instructor should try to remain out of the frame and observe as much as possible. Usually when assigning group activities, the instructor has universal access to all student comments and discussions, and can read and assess student work during activities. However, experts have warned that it is important to play down the "Big Brother is Watching You" feeling by explaining to students that you are observing their group work not to be oppressive or controlling, but to ensure that everyone is contributing fairly to the process (Bender, 2003).

Best Practices for Dividing Students into Groups

Is there an ideal method for dividing online students into small groups? This is one of the more common questions that online instructors ask when they begin to devise small-group assignments. While there is no right or wrong method for creating small groups, several experts in the field of online education have weighed in on this debate with their opinions based upon their past online teaching experiences. Both Bender (2003) and Ko and Rossen (2010) agree that it is probably best for the instructor to create and assign the groups, rather than allowing students to choose the groups themselves, which could be time consuming and confusing for students. In traditional classrooms, one of the biggest constraints to group work is scheduling, specifically for students to find times where they can work together outside of class. In the online learning environment, the problem disappears, particularly when students are able to interact asynchronously and leave messages or comments for each other when it is convenient for them.

There are a number of different ways to divide students into groups, including randomly, based upon alphabetical order, on the basis of information you have already gathered about their interests or abilities, or on the basis of their grades. If the instructor divides students based upon mixing levels of abilities and skills, this might help students learn from each other and grow through the collaboration. Others, however, have warned that when students of varying abilities are integrated into the same group, the more high achieving students may feel saddled with the brunt of the work. A good recommendation from Bender (2003) is to place students with similar abilities in the same group, making the workload and contributions more equitable. Assigning a group with high-achieving students to present their project first will help the other groups to determine what is expected of them, and give them a high target to aim for.

Ko and Rossen (2010) argue in their book *Teaching Online* that it might be useful to integrate some level of student volition into the group work process, particularly in three scenarios. First, in some situations, instructors would like students to choose a topic or group that really interests them. Going back to the Socratic and problem-solving approaches to discussion in the previous section, sometimes students might create a better proposal, or engage more openly in debate, when they are heavily vested or interested in the topic. For example, some students in a health psychology class may really want to research or study how women cope with breast cancer, while others might want to study minority health disparities, risky sexual behaviors, or alcohol abuse. In this instance, it would greatly behoove students to be able to explore the topic that has resonance and meaning for them. Second, sometimes online courses already have "natural" groupings of students who seem to be a good choice to work together, such as a group of students who all have a specialization in developmental psychology, or a group of students who are all mothers. The authors also warn that sometimes it might be beneficial to divide these groups so that other students may benefit from their knowledge or experience, while ensuring that their individual contributions shine through. Finally, in a blended or hybrid course, students may already know each other or have friends in the course that they would like to work with.

Based on this review of the online teaching literature, what are the best practices for dividing online psychology students into groups? Well, this depends in part on the type of activity and the goals of that activity. First, it is fairly clear that groups should be small enough to enable active communication and student roles. Generally, when assigning groups for small-group projects select about five or six students per group (Bender, 2003), and consider that groups any larger than this may face problems with communication, delegation, and organization. Second, it is also recommended that once a group is created, it is maintained for the rest of the course rather than switching students to different groups in the middle of the semester (Ko & Rossen, 2010). However, if a student is unhappy and requests to transfer to a different group, it might worth honoring this request. After all, as Bender (2003) states, "feelings within group work are real" (p. 121) and feelings of exclusion and isolation from the online learning community may lead to reduce student learning and performance. Third, assigning students to groups should be conducted on a task-by-task basis. If it is important to the task to have students feel vested, interested, and motivated by a particular topic (such as the health psychology example above) then survey student interests or opinions and divide accordingly. If it is more important to have a diversity of students in the same group (such as debating the merits of gay marriage in a social policy class), then it would behoove the instructor to mix students into groups accordingly. If the task does not require vested interests, such as a program evaluation or a theoretical analysis, then the authors tend to side with previous researchers who recommend assigning students to groups based roughly around their grades in the course. This will ensure that one student does not "carry" the group, a complaint often echoed by students engaging in group work in higher education. Fortunately, online instructors have the opportunity to view the conversation and determine exactly how frequently each student participates. If this becomes part of the grading criteria, then all students should be involved, regardless of their grades, skills, or abilities. Regardless as to the task and the method that is chosen, overall, the authors recommend that the instructor controls the assignment to groups, rather than the students themselves.

Another consideration is the roles that students take on within their groups. Should the instructor assign these roles, or allow them to form organically? It is fairly clear that students in groups should be given direction and roles to ensure that they are not confused, bored, or noncontributing. The students may want to select these for themselves based upon criteria provided by the instructor, or the instructor may prefer to assign these roles for them. Depending upon the type of assignment (such as a case-study analysis, debate, or research project), these roles might include: a Summarizer, who records the group's conclusions; a Discussion leader, who presents the arguments or findings to the class; an Organizer, who makes sure the group keeps to a schedule and stays on topic; a Researcher; who finds relevant studies, websites, and other sources; and an Editor, who produces the final document for submission (especially in the case of a research project or proposal). Ko and Rossen (2010) also discuss the possibility of rotating student roles during the semester, to ensure "true sharing and cooperation" between the students (p. 178). However, do not rotate roles too frequently, otherwise students may become confused. Rather, keep students in certain roles for the duration of each assignment or project, rotating when applicable.

Moderating Group Activities

Once the task has been set and students begin to work with their groups, the online instructor should check in frequently to ensure that students are adhering to their assigned roles within the group, and that they are having a positive, interactive learning experience. The amount and frequency of instructor interaction depends upon the type of assignment. If the assignment is based upon a case study (such as, "Read the 'John/Joan case' and explain what the implications are for our scientific understanding of gender?"), the instructor may not have to hold students quite so rigidly to their roles, and may check in less frequently. It might be that this type of assignment will not require a particularly long duration for completion, and that each group will present after one week of work on the topic. If students are assigned a research proposal or project, then this undoubtedly will last for several weeks and require a heightened level of student–instructor engagement, in order to troubleshoot, answer questions, and help to direct the flow. Anyone who has taught or been a teaching assistant in a research methods course knows that students develop many questions when asked to conduct their own psychological inquiries, and often, the discussion forum is the best place to help to address those questions. Even though instructors should play "Guide on the Side" when it comes to group projects, they should also be on hand to provide support, encouragement, and help answer questions when they arise.

Troubleshooting Group Issues

As with traditional courses, problems with groups in online courses are bound to arise to some level. In planning for this inevitability, it would be useful to have a protocol in place for instructors to follow. Indeed, Boettcher and Conrad (2010) suggest that students be given a forum where they can address their concerns and issues with group work as they arise. Derived from *Building Blocks for Teams* (from the Teaching and Learning Technology Group at Penn State, 2001–2005), Boettcher and Conrad (2010) suggest that online students working in groups are most frequently concerned with the following types of questions, and some potentially effective answers:

1. How can we work together without wasting time?
   a. Place reasonable limits on planning or brainstorming, such as 30-minutes at any one time, or set a goal that by x day, we will have our protocol in place.
   b. Make sure that students stick to their assigned roles, and decide on the tasks associated with each of these.
   c. Keep a list of the tasks that everyone has completed, as well as the tasks that still need to be done. Cross them off as you go.
2. How can we deal with group conflict?
   a. Be professional and respectful first of all. Students should use supportive, not derogatory language, and should not make personally insulting comments (direct students to netiquette training from the course orientation).
   b. Be democratic in your decision-making, and let the majority rule. If you find yourself on the losing side of the vote, go with the group and move on. Being disruptive will only make everyone's tasks harder, including your own.
3. What do we do if a group member is not contributing?
   a. Speak to that group member first, either through chat or email. Let them know that you are not trying to be critical, but that you are concerned because you want to see them succeed and contribute. Remind them that the instructor is able to review everyone's logs and knows exactly how much each individual is participating.
   b. If the problem persists, just make sure that everyone takes turns in their presentations, notes, or updates. This will make it even more clear to the instructor who is and who is not participating.
4. What happens if we don't get along?
   a. First of all, not everyone gets along with everyone that they work with. It is very important to remain civil and respectful, even

when you don't get along, just as you would in a professional office environment.

b. Do not let the disagreement escalate. Sometimes, the tiniest problem can become a big issue when people do not communicate about it and express their ideas respectfully. If there is a disagreement, refer back to the topic of democratic rule and allow the group to decide and move forward. Remember, this is only one project in one class, and even if it doesn't go exactly how you wanted it, you can still make it a successful and rewarding endeavor.

The authors advise that the instructor creates a forum like this for students in each group to use when they become frustrated or experience these issues. There, they will see the questions and answers, and be able to post encouraging comments to each other when they feel confused or frustrated. In the very worst case scenario, students who will be aggrieved can call the instructor who can then try to diffuse the conflict, but ultimately, your students are adults and it is in everyone's best interests for them to solve their internal conflicts on their own (working with each other is certainly an important skill to develop during the educational process). If, however, the instructor sees rude personal remarks, disrespect, or insults, he or she should step in and let the entire class know that those kinds of words will not be accepted.

ONLINE SIMULATIONS

Role-playing and simulations are often utilized in higher education as a means of providing an enhanced immersive experience to students. Often, simulations appear in disciplines like business studies, economics, and history, as well as in the social sciences including health studies, human resources, and other disciplines within psychology. Just as role-playing and simulations can provide an interactive, in-depth learning experience in the traditional classroom, they can be harnessed to provide similar levels of engagement in the online classroom. Online role playing and simulations become particularly useful in the social sciences when they surround questions of research methodology and data collection, a point highlighted by Ko and Rossen (2010). The authors cite comments by Taylor (n.d.), an online nursing studies instructor, who utilizes online simulations to educate students on the uses of data collection tools for a particular group of employees. In this exercise, students are assigned certain roles: One group of students may serve as the data collectors, while another group serves as the participants, and a third group serves as administrators who can answer questions and provide assistance to the collectors. Taylor notes that "this type of activity is very effective in connecting the classroom with actual application in the real world" (Taylor, n.d., cited in Ko & Rossen, 2010, p. 188). As the psychological sciences evolve to focus on greater levels of application, particularly in fields such as clinical psychology, research methods, health psychology, positive psychology, and developmental psychology, online simulations can enable students to utilize their knowledge to achieve many of the skills in Bloom's taxonomy, including synthesis, analysis, and evaluation to draw connection to real-world applications. Taylor further argues that in addition to application, online simulations "improve students' ability to ask meaningful questions related to a problem" (Taylor, n.d., cited in Ko & Rossen, 2010, p. 188). In addition to enhanced synthesis and application then, online simulations in the social sciences have the power to enhance critical thinking, knowledge development, and student communication.

At the time of going to press, it is somewhat challenging to locate empirical research aimed toward evaluating the effectiveness of simulations in online education. In fact, an exhaustive literature review conducted by the authors revealed only a handful of articles written about simulations in online education, with the highlight being Jenner, Zhao, and Foote's (2010) analysis of team performance in online simulations for business management. The authors compared data collected from thousands of students who played a "Business Strategy Game" (BSG) simulation in both online and traditional classroom environments, and examined a number of related variables including overall class size, the frequency of class meetings, team size, and discussion time for the specific project. The outcome measure of interest was the overall student performance in the BSG. In their analyses, the authors found that an increased class size was negatively associated with BSG performance in the on-campus classes, but not in online classes. In other words, adding additional students to the course led to negative performance in the simulation when students were on-campus, but had *no* negative effects on the online section. Likewise, a smaller team size was associated with reduced performance in on-campus settings, but had no effect in the online environment. These findings suggest that unlike simulations in traditional classrooms, simulations conducted in online courses are not hampered by restrictions surrounding the size of the overall class, or the size of the group or team participating in the simulation. Given that online courses often vary in size and composition, this is a promising finding in support of using simulations as a learning tool in online courses.

Facilitating Successful Simulations in Psychology

While the creation and facilitation of simulations in the psychological sciences is not something that is typically discussed, the authors have conceived of a series of steps that instructors can follow to maximize their results. These steps are as follows: Assign small groups, information delivery, preparation time, activity unfolding, and postactivity reflection. Following these steps will ensure that both the facilitator of the simulation and the participants will be appropriately prepared to learn and succeed in their role-playing experiences.

Assign Small Groups and Roles

The protocol for assigning students to groups is discussed in the previous section (see "Best Practices for Dividing Students into Groups"). Depending upon the simulation you have selected, it might be useful to group students together with similar knowledge bases or interests. For example, if students are assigned the roles of therapists and patients with certain psychiatric conditions, then students who have already expressed an interest in, or conducted research or training practicums on a certain disorder (such as bipolar disorder) might be assigned to therapists or patients in that group, while those with experience studying eating disorders might be placed in a different group. Alternatively, if there is no specialized knowledge or previous work experience involved, it might behoove the instructor to assign groups randomly, alphabetically, or based upon previous grades in the course.

An additional element to consider when assigning students to role-playing groups is varying student roles throughout the semester. In the above example, the student who plays the role of the therapist will be asking questions and engaging in the lion's share of the critical thinking and analysis, while the student who plays the patient will be relying more on memory recall and their knowledge of the particular illness or disorder in question. This is not a problematic dynamic unless that student who plays the role of the patient never gets the opportunity to play the therapist, and vice versa. In other words, students can benefit from playing varied roles in their simulations throughout the semester. Being involved with multiple perspectives, whether it is therapist and patient, or researcher and participant, or team leader and organizers, can help to enhance knowledge and critical thinking. Therefore, instructors can benefit from being mindful of this and facilitating at least two different simulations through the semester to ensure that students can experience many sides of the coin, so to speak. If multiple simulations are not possible due to time or other constraints, consider switching in the middle, or running simulations back-to-back, where one student begins in the role of therapist and then switches to patient, while the other does the opposite. In simulations where students work in teams and a variety of roles are assigned, try to ensure that each student is able to experience the leadership role at least once in the semester.

Finally, when it comes to student roles, who should select them, the instructor or the students themselves? On the one hand, students who choose their own roles and are pleased with this process may be especially vested in the production of a successful performance. On the other hand, allowing students to select their own roles might lead to levels of dissatisfaction and conflict if two students want the same role. This is all compounded by the absence of a face-to-face sit down between all students. In the case of online courses, the student who emails the teacher first, or who posts in the simulation forum first, might obtain their preferred role, perhaps to the chagrin of other students who were not able to access the course right away. Generally then, it seems applicable in the online realm for the instructor to assign roles to reduce any potential confusion or conflict that might arise from students selecting their own roles. However, if a student is particularly adamant or sends a special request with an adequate justification, it might be worthwhile for the instructor to accommodate this student. Just as you would in the classroom then, trust your judgment in these situations.

Information Delivery

After the small groups and student roles have been assigned, the next step is to provide the information necessary for students to succeed in the simulation. Information, broadly defined here, can take a number of different forms, including scripts, articles, or other relevant research materials. In the above example of the therapist and the patient, information might include one or all of these: A script of the types of questions the therapists should be asking the patient; articles on the condition itself; as well as links to research materials that provide more in-depth information. In other cases, the simulation might be an actual replication of past research, such as an online replication of Zimbardo's (1971) infamous Stanford prison studies. In this case, the prisoners, guards, and the prison warden would be required to research the previous study and create their own script that accurately reflects their understanding of the events that transpired. While the instructor probably does not want to overwhelm the students with a ton of material, more information is generally better when it comes to a simulation. Unlike traditional discussions or debate, a simulation might go in an unexpected, unique, or provocative direction, and students with depth and breadth of preparatory materials can help to enable the simulation to progress in interesting directions. In addition, students who are provided with too little information may become frustrated and end up with "one-dimensional" roles, unable to flesh out their character or their part in the script. Thus, the instructor would benefit from providing enough materials to students that they can really "sink their teeth" into their role, and also provide links and directions where students can engage in additional research should it be deemed necessary.

Preparation Time

Ensuring that students have adequate time to prepare for their participation in a simulation activity is of crucial importance. In fact, preparation by students has been described as "one key to success of role-playing simulations" (Ko & Rossen, 2010, p. 190). Consider that the cognitive demands upon students who participate in simulations can become greater than almost any other activity. Not only do these students require some level of knowledge mastery, they must also engage in application, analysis, and synthesis, all the while staying in character. This is part of what makes simulations such great learning activities! However, it also means that students might require greater participation time for simulations than for other assignments and activities. In addition to understanding their roles and the materials they are provided with, students also need be familiar at this stage with the instructor's expectations, including guidelines or instructions for participation and any potential grading rubrics. As noted throughout this book, it is imperative that online students remain clear about the instructor's intentions and expectations, especially because they are not present in the physical classroom to raise their hand and ask questions. Therefore, it might even be useful for instructors to conduct a brief Q & A in the simulation forum before it begins, so that the instructions and grading details are perfectly clear.

What then, constitutes adequate preparation time? Depending upon the pace and schedule of the online course, this could vary tremendously. Consider the usual due dates for the assignments in that class. When are students required to submit their work, after a few days of being given the assignment, one week, or one month? Perhaps a better heuristic, instead of focusing arbitrarily upon the appropriate amount of time, is to first consider the level of work required for the assignment, the intensity and engagement of the assignment, and the percentage of the grade that it constitutes. As each of these three (work, intensity, and grade percentage) increases, so too should the amount of preparation time required. The authors recommend notifying students about their upcoming simulation, and assigning roles and groups, a few weeks before the assignment actually occurs, or if the simulation is especially intensive, even assigning these at the beginning of the semester. One useful strategy is to compile the necessary resources (scripts, articles, other research materials, or links) into a folder or file, and place this file in a prominent place in the virtual learning environment, such as in a course documents folder. This way, students will have access to their simulation materials from the beginning of the semester and can prepare ahead of the due date in their own time. However, even if the materials are placed in the course from the beginning, it is still crucial to email students and remind them a few weeks ahead of time to access those materials, and search the research for other relevant information.

Activity Unfolding

When the simulation actually occurs, it is important for the instructor to be especially tuned-in to its facilitation and progress. The instructor has a number of choices here, including whether the simulation will occur synchronously or asynchronously, the medium of the communication itself, and whether there will be the inclusion of changing situations. First, in terms of the level of interaction itself, will students involved in the role-play be required to communicate synchronously or will communication unfold via asynchronous means? The simulation can work either way, this is at the discretion of the instructor and depends upon the comfort levels of your students. If the entire small group involved can find a common time to sign in to the course, then synchronous communication enables the instructor to view the simulation as it progresses in real-time chat. Returning to the example of the therapist and the patient, a synchronous simulation will enable the therapist to ask questions that receive an immediate or near-immediate response, just as they would in real-life. In this case, the generalizability and application of the simulation is higher when conducted synchronously. However, this type of simulation also places greater cognitive demand upon students than simulations that evolve asynchronously, giving the students more time to think, plan, write, synthesize, and organize information. The therapist and patient simulation could still unfold via asynchronous communication, most likely through posts on a discussion board or forum. In this example, the therapist would post a question, or series of questions, and the patient would then post a response, and so on. In order for this type of simulation to be successful, it is recommended that the instructor limit the delay between postings, or require that the entire simulation be completed over the course of one day, or a few days. This way, the immediacy factor that mimics real life is still prevalent, but there is a greater delay between communications.

The medium of a simulation itself is also something that the instructor ought to consider. Granted, it is almost inevitable that text-based communication of some kind will be present, and will comprise a large part of the interaction between students working together on this task. However, as technology becomes increasingly sophisticated and easy to use, it might be worthwhile to encourage students to think creatively about other ways to communicate during their simulation. In addition to communicating via web-based chat and discussion forums, students may also communicate via social networking websites like Facebook, or text messages/ phone calls, or video chat via Skype, Elluminate, or YouTube. For example, the therapist and patient might discuss their problems and solutions via text-based chat, and after asking enough questions, the therapist might make a video of his or her diagnosis and recommendations for treatment, and disseminate this video to the class. In turn, the patient might make a response video for the course, confirming (or denying) the diagnosis and discussing how and why the recommended treatment might be effective (or ineffective). Not only will the video provide an entertaining and insightful summary for the rest of the class, but students will experience heightened engagement and immersion as they literally perform their role for the camera and the rest of the class.

A final consideration surrounds whether the instructor will interrupt a simulation to insert changes or modifications to the situation. The notion of making changes to situations is derived mostly from the more common role-playing activities featured in business, economics, and political science. In these types of simulations, news of a political event is inserted that may change the landscape for certain players, or news of a business deal or financial meltdown is announced and the players must learn to adapt. While perhaps less common in the education literature, changes to a situation can also be made during simulations in the social sciences, particularly psychology. For example, in the therapist–patient example, the instructor might interrupt and provide additional information about the patient, such as details of a family trauma, which may then alter the diagnosis. Likewise, if students are simulating a famous previously conducted study in psychology, such as the Stanford prison studies, Milgram's (1963) study on obedience, or Tajfel and Turner's (1979) minimal group paradigm, the instructor can induce hypothetical changes to protocol which students will have to adjust for. In the Zimbardo example, "A prisoner is escaping! What would you do as a guard? As a fellow prisoner?" Further, changes can also be made to protocol or even the assignment itself in the middle, to determine whether students have an adequate grasp of the concepts to be able to apply them to a new arena. For example, students who are working in roles as researchers and participants might be given additional measures to create on the spot, or told to apply their research tools to a new population. Making changes to situations is not required by psychology instructors who are facilitating simulations, but it may be useful in measuring the adaptability, flexibility, and application skills of the students involved.

Postactivity Reflection

As with many activities in higher education, reflecting upon what one has learned and integrating the experience into the context of the course is also of crucial importance. This reflection can feature many components, including detailing the personal experience of playing a certain role, highlighting any pitfalls or difficulties, and finally, discussing how participating in the simulation has helped build a deeper understanding, a more critical perspective, or a more applied definition of key constructs. The medium for delivery of this reflective component is not set in stone, although typically these reflections feature some kind of written component. However, it is up to the instructor to determine whether students should write a paper, a journal article, a forum post, or create a video or film to describe their experiences. When devising these types of reflective activities, it is important for instructors to decide at the outset whether student participation in the simulation itself will be graded, or whether a final assignment based upon the experience will be graded, or both. The authors recommend that instructors evaluate all components of the simulation: Student preparation, the participation in the activity itself, as well as the student's reflection and ability to integrate their new knowledge into the course.

Computer-Based Simulations

Online simulations and role-playing activities can enhance student learning through engagement, application, and immersion, in ways that are unique from other assignments. One key caveat here is that online role-playing simulations, where students are assigned roles that they act out in a variety of ways, are fundamentally different (and not to be confused with) computer-based simulations, which "attempt to recreate an actual process or activity, or, on a broader scale, model complex real-life circumstances" (Ko & Rossen, 2010, p. 191). Often, computer-based simulations feature some level of immersive graphics, animations, and other visual cues to guide student learning. While all online instructors can devise, create, facilitate, and grade student participation and achievement in role-playing simulations, most online instructors will not have the computing skills to literally create their own computer-based simulations for students to participate in. But fear not! Even if you cannot create a computer-based simulation, you can still utilize preexisting ones found on the internet, in catalogues such as MERLOT (web resources are discussed in the following section). In some cases, the college or university might provide instructors with computer-based simulations or resources for obtaining them. These simulations can feature graphical representations (such as an animated dialogue about the process behind auditory perception) or text (such as asking research methods students to choose between studies that reflect correlation or causation). In many cases, the simulation can respond to the student's input and highlight correct or incorrect answers. For examples of computer-based simulations for psychology and where to find them, see the section on "Resources," below.

Activities in Virtual Worlds

The computer-based simulations described above are also different from *virtual worlds* such as Second Life (www.secondlife.com), where participants become immersed in a 3-D online "reality" and where they engage with other participants from around the world using a cartoon avatar of their choosing. Interestingly, many colleges and universities have already claimed their place in the virtual world of Second Life, and some institutions have trained staff specifically to function within this space. The majority of educational institutions featured within Second Life are housed on their own "private islands," with top destinations including Harvard Law School, Hong Kong Polytechnic University, and Oxford University. Within Second Life, students can attend lectures, tutorials, and seminars, and view 3D recreations of a variety of life events, including historical phenomena and current events. For example, in Second Life, a student's avatar dressed as a flying squirrel-man with yellow sneakers can visit the 3D Sistine Chapel while listening to a lecture from an actual Cambridge history professor. Within Second Life, instructors can build giant molecules, stage massive trials or debates, or recreate crime scenes. However, all of these benefits do come at a cost—the property itself (such as a university department) in Second Life costs an actual monetary subscription fee!

What are the benefits of using Second Life to host activities in online courses? First, it is clear that in a virtual world, the impossible becomes possible, which can be an exciting experience for many students. Online teaching experts have argued that virtual worlds like Second Life provide a "coolness factor" as well as an "injection of fun" and the opportunity to engage in "complex simulations which involve danger or would incur prohibitive expense in the real world" (Ko & Rossen, 2010 p. 171). Imagine a 3D virtual world where students could log-in and replicate the landmark studies in social psychology that are ethically less viable today, such as the Kitty Genovese case, that inspired Latane and Darley's (1964) Bystander

Intervention study, or Milgram's (1963) famous studies on obedience, or Zimbardo's Stanford prison study (1971).

Second, interaction between student avatars in a 3D environment might actually help to boost online communication more broadly, it being one of the central features of online education. While research in this area is quite limited, Jones, Warren, and Robertson (2009) measured the contribution of a 3D online learning environment for 250 graduate students in computer education taking either blended or fully online courses. Their analyses revealed that the introduction of a 3D online learning environment led to significant increases in student-to-student discourse, particularly in fully online courses. Specifically, online students who engaged with the 3D learning environment experienced early creation discourse in the first few weeks of the semester, higher levels of discourse during the semester, sustained discourse throughout the semester, and more use of rapport descriptors in their text-based exchanges when compared to students in the same courses who were not exposed to the 3D learning environment (Jones et al., 2009). The authors argue that rapport was built so quickly by "extending beyond the current text-based paradigm via feedback mechanisms such as hand gestures, facial expressions similar to those experienced in real life, and other visual cues expressed by the digital avatars that represented the students" (Jones et al., 2009, p. 288). These findings certainly imply that the integration of virtual worlds like Second Life into online courses may benefit our students by boosting both their communication and sense of community.

Despite the potential benefits, instructor ability to integrate 3D virtual worlds into the online classroom may be hampered by overall lack of familiarity and experience with this technology. While millions of people around the world currently maintain avatars on Second Life, as online instructors we simply cannot assume that our students have experience using this virtual world. First-time users may find the format complicated and difficult, resulting in additional orientation and technology training on top of the standard technology orientation that online students should receive. In addition, instructors who use virtual worlds like Second Life must be prepared to practice their own skills, and may literally need to create the environment where they choose to teach. Ko and Rossen (2010) suggest that new instructors spend at least 5 hours using Second Life to ensure they are sufficiently familiar with the environment. They also argue that conducting activities and simulations can be very time consuming and might "require considerably more planning, training and preparation on the part of the instructor and students, even if the instructor is not building a new area in the virtual world" (Ko & Rossen, 2010, p. 193). Then come institutional issues, specifically, does the college or university already own "property" in Second Life? If so, the instructor might already have a space in the virtual world to conduct simulations and activities. If the academic institution does not host its own property on Second Life, it might be very costly for the instructor to create a classroom. With all of these constraints, many online instructors are asking, are virtual worlds worth the effort? Given the potential for student discourse and immersion into activities, integrating virtual worlds into the online classroom might be a worthwhile and fun endeavor! If this is something that you might want to explore, consult with your institution and begin researching on the Second Life website (www.secondlife.com).

SOCIAL BOOKMARKING ACTIVITIES

Social bookmarking, like virtual worlds, reflects a new technology that is slowly making its way into the online classroom. Very simply, social bookmarking is "a method for internet users to organize, store, manage and search for bookmarks of online websites" (Wikipedia, 2012e). Individuals can then share their bookmark reference list with others, either by making their lists completely public, or sharing their lists with only specific groups or individuals. What makes social bookmarking unique is the way that users can "tag" the information in those bookmarks, ranging from text-based descriptions of the content of the bookmark, ratings about the bookmark's quality, or actual keyword tags describing the bookmark's content. In many ways, social bookmarking can be understood in terms of the analogy of an online, peer-rated, annotated reference list of websites and web resources. Various social bookmarking tools like Delicious (www.delicious.com) enable users to tag and rate websites, and these comments can then be shared with other users. Unlike a reference list compiled on a home computer, these software tools enable users to log-in and view their bookmarks from anywhere, enabling quick and efficient access to a limitless number of website bookmarks.

How could social bookmarking become integrated into assignments in online psychology courses? Consider first how the social bookmarking process functions similarly to the research process in psychology, where web resources are shared and tagged by other members of one's group. The introduction of the collaborative, social element here is key for online courses, particularly when group projects or debates are assigned in a course. In such a case, online students involved in a group research project could benefit significantly from sharing all of their web sources via social bookmarking, as opposed to each student generating their own website list. Group research projects, debates, and other research-related activities are heavily featured in the online learning of psychology, not only in research methods courses themselves, but also in social psychology, developmental psychology, clinical psychology, health psychology, positive psychology, and evaluation. There is potential here to enhance student collaboration and group integration by incorporating social bookmarking into the group research activity process.

Social bookmarking might also present a novel way for instructors to deliver their course materials. While research in this area is relatively new, studies indicate that social bookmarking can benefit online students by enabling them to more easily explore relevant course materials (Olaniran, 2009), while being able to rate and comment upon the materials on the spot, therefore giving feedback to the instructor and their classmates. Farwell and Waters (2010) conducted online focus groups with 53 students enrolled in a social media and public relations class who were assigned course materials listed in the instructor's social bookmarking account, in addition to their traditional printed coursepacks. While only three students had heard of social bookmarking prior to their use of it in their course, "the vast majority felt that it was a worthwhile experience afterwards" (Farwell & Walter, 2010, p. 403). In fact, students actually preferred social bookmarking to their printed coursepacks, library e-reserve account, and even to web resources posted on their course management system. According to these focus groups, the low cost was the most important factor dictating student preference of social bookmarking, followed by relevant and up-to-date information, ease of use of the technology, and broad range of materials to enhance student learning.

Given the increasing costs of higher education for students across programs and colleges, replacing or supplementing coursepacks or textbooks with social bookmarking might provide a welcome financial relief for many students in online courses. In addition to the reduction of costly printed materials, social bookmarking offers the added benefits of collaboration, ease of use, depth and breadth, and up-to-date information. How then, do online psychology instructors go about incorporating social bookmarking into their course materials? Grosseck (2008) makes several recommendations for instructors, the central one being that the instructor should create a social bookmarking account for the entire class, using a shared name and password. This way, all students can log in and view the same bookmarks, and make tags, ratings, or other comments. Then, if the instructor intends to assign group activities, Grosseck (2008) suggests that students are divided into small groups, and each week, a different group be required to find and add their own social bookmarks to the class bookmarking account, to reflect their unique contributions and outside research. The instructor can also add links during this time, or comment upon the links added by the students. Using social bookmarking in this way helps students develop their small groups into learning communities more quickly, as students become active participants in the creation of their own educational discourse, rather than passive readers of documents (Grosseck, 2008). Students who must not only find resources, but tag, rate, and comment upon them for their classmates and instructor, should be more engaged in their learning communities.

TROUBLESHOOTING: I'M STUCK! RESOURCES FOR ONLINE ACTIVITIES IN PSYCHOLOGY

Sometimes, no matter how hard an instructor tries, it can be challenging to design and implement the perfect course activity. While this is undoubtedly true in the physical classroom, getting stuck is even more of a concern in the online classroom, when activities often must be planned out weeks in advance to ensure adequate preparation time for group assignments. No matter how creative an instructor is, it can always be helpful to attain extra guidance, either from ideas that have worked for other instructors, or from a large database. Sometimes, an online instructor will have a great idea for an activity, but feel unsure about how to best harness their available technology in order to successfully implement their activity. The authors conducted an exhaustive search through hundreds of websites featuring online psychology activities, simulations, and resources that could benefit instructors. The best websites and their descriptions are presented in the following section, including psychology tutorials, online labs, statistical guidance pages, and computer-based simulations. But we begin our discussion with the first stop when searching for online psychology activities: MERLOT.

WHAT IS MERLOT?

If you teach online or have attended a teaching conference in the last 5 years, you have probably heard a presenter or colleague mention MERLOT, the *Multimedia Educational Resource for Learning and Online Teaching*. MERLOT houses a plethora of peer-reviewed online teaching and learning materials across humanities, education, science and technology, mathematics and statistics, and social sciences. Just as users of social bookmarking rate the quality of the resources they find, so too do MERLOT users rate the quality of the learning materials on the site. While MERLOT is constantly being updated, the best way to search materials is through keywords specific to the area of interest. For example, at the time of going to press, typing in "Developmental Psychology" into a keyword search provides 12 web resources, listed in order of the most favorable peer reviews and comments. These include videos on developmental psychology, a website on theories of learning, and a series of psychological tutorials and demonstrations. Searching MERLOT is very straightforward: If a resource looks interesting, clicking it will bring the user to a website describing that resource, with a link to the material itself. While readers are always encouraged to check MERLOT regularly for updated links, sites, and information, the authors have already done the hard work and searched the MERLOT database as well as the web for the most useful links for psychology-based activities and resources, presented below. For the most up-to-date information on these websites, please consult this book's accompanying website.

PSYCHOLOGY-SPECIFIC ONLINE ACTIVITIES AND RESOURCES

Psychological Tutorials and Demonstrations:
http://psych.hanover.edu/Krantz/tutor.html

Hosted by the Hanover College psychology department, this page features a wide variety of tutorials and demonstrations spanning across subdisciplines in psychology, including cognitive psychology, biopsychology, social psychology, research methods, and a particularly strong section on sensation and perception. These tutorials and demonstrations can be integrated into online course activities and group work, by assigning a certain group to participate and report back to the class.

Memory and Cognition Experiments (U DENVER):
http://www.du.edu/psychology/methods/experiments/index.html)

This website hosted by University of Denver Professor Jan Keenan features a link to a downloadable software package on the topic of memory and cognition. Specifically, students can learn about the research design of classic experiments in this area and participate as virtual subjects. The package includes experiments on levels of processing, encoding specificity, semantic memory and constructive processes. Student data can then be uploaded and shared with the rest of the class. In courses that involve memory and cognition, this software could serve as a group activity where the data could be collected and analyzed.

ePsych: *http://epsych.msstate.edu/Contents.html*

This website created by Gary L. Bradshaw features an interactive, virtual textbook that offers tutorials, demonstrations, and videos. Of particular focus here are biological psychology, learning, personality, sensation and perception, and cognition. Students who visit the site will have the opportunity to participate in experiments, such as a virtual rat run through a maze. These types of activities can enhance student learning, particularly when one student (or group of students) reports back to the class about what happened in the experiment, and what he or she has learned.

Internet Psychology Lab: http://www.ipsych.com/index.html

This website, originally created by the University of Illinois, features one of the best available collections of online simulations and demonstrations in these four areas: Visual Perception, Cognition, Auditory Perception, and Memory & Learning. After highlighting the area of interest, Cognition for example, the user is then directed to a screen featuring the different demonstrations: Visual cognition, basic reaction time, symmetric faces, stroop effect, or choice reaction time. These activities require JAVA and also provide instructions on how to adjust one's web browser for maximum viewing effectiveness. These activities can be integrated into course activities and group work in the relevant topic areas.

Visualizing Statistical Concepts: http://www.du.edu/psychology/methods/concepts/

This website offers links to simulations and demonstrations of key statistical concepts, ranging from probability, to univariate distributions, power, sample size, and statistical inference. Clicking on the link redirects users to the tool, which may be located at a different website.

The Stanford Prison Experiment: http://www.prisonexp.org/

This nonprofit website, hosted by Philip Zimbardo, is an excellent resource for students who are working on debates, simulations, or other activities surrounding the Stanford Prison Experiment. Here, students will find a slide-show presentation of the stages of the actual experiment, along with authentic photos and videos of the experiment, a selection of discussion questions and thought activities, as well as FAQs and related links and resources.

All PSYC online the Virtual Psychology Classroom: http://allpsych.com/

This comprehensive website features a variety of resources for the teaching of psychology, including online texts, online tests and quizzes, a psychology references section, resources, detailed descriptions of psychiatric disorders, and links to current online research projects in psychology. This website can be integrated into course activities for a number of different disciplines; for example, by asking students to access the website and analyze the definitions provided for various psychological constructs. Clinical, health, or counseling students can also benefit from free access to the All-Psych online journal on mental health.

PORT: Psychology Online Research Tutorial: http://www.library.gsu.edu/tutorials/port/

This website, created by the Georgia State University, is designed to help students navigate the research process in psychology. Students who are assigned either individual or group research projects across disciplines can benefit from being asked to utilize this tutorial before they engage in research. Student modules in this text-based tutorial that students must complete include: Brainstorming a Research Project, Scholarly v. Popular Journals, PSYC INFO help, and interpreting a citation.

The Basics of APA Style: http://flash1r.apa.org/apastyle/basics/index.htm

When students are assigned research projects in psychology, APA style often serves as an important component of their grade. While many research methods books and introductory psychology texts feature guidelines for APA style, these are nonetheless constantly being updated and modified by APA. One of the most useful ways to ensure that students are familiar with all aspects of APA style is through their online tutorials, which students can access and review at any time. These tutorials are video-based and offer the central guidelines regarding basic APA style, manuscript structure and format, headings, reducing bias in language, citing references, and the reference list.

School Psychology Resources Online: http://www.schoolpsychology.net/

This website serves as a resource for individuals studying school psychology, developmental psychology, and clinical psychology. In addition to links to a plethora of information on specific conditions, disorders, and disabilities (such as eating disorders, anxiety disorders, and autism), it also provides links to assessments and evaluations, and a variety of links to relevant organizations and associations. This site could be a beneficial resource for students who are assigned group projects in this area, or who are participating in simulations surrounding adolescent psychology or counseling.

Psychology Demonstrations, Tutorials, and Other Neat Stuff:
http://www.uni.edu/walsh/tutor.html

This website hosted by Linda Walsh in the Department of Psychology of Northern Iowa University features a variety of links to simulations and activities that online students can engage in on the web. These are divided into subdisciplines such as biopsychology, visual sensation/perception, learning/memory/cognition, personality and social psychology, and research methods, writing, and presentation in psychology. Also offered are additional resources for psychology instructors, and links to online research projects that students can participate in.

The Society for the Teaching of Psychology: http://teachpsych.org/

The website for APA Division 2 features some information that online psychological instructors might find useful in their course preparation, such as teaching resources, links, and access to Teaching of Psychology journal articles.

Centre for Psychology Learning Resources:
http://psych.athabascau.ca/centre2/resources/#psychology

The Athabasca University Centre for Psychology offers sample interactive online tutorials aimed to enhance student knowledge of certain key concepts. Currently offered are tutorials pertaining to positive reinforcement, biological psychology, direct instruction, internal validity, and precision teaching. Of particular utility here are the biological psychology tutorials, which feature over 20 detailed tutorials with matching and multiple choice self-tests. Groups could be assigned to participate in these tutorials and compare their scores.

Queendom: The Land of Tests: http://www.queendom.com/

This is a fun website that features a plethora of psychological tests for students to engage in. Tests are divided into categories: IQ tests, personality tests, relationship tests, health tests, and attitude and lifestyle tests. These provide a fun and engaging way for students to become familiar with psychometric testing, and give the opportunity for students to critically analyze the validity of these measures. In addition, students working in groups can measure how they fall on certain constructs relative to the rest of their classmates. The site also offers some psychological resources to users, including a directory of therapists and a health professionals' dictionary.

Statistical Home Page:
http://www.uvm.edu/~dhowell/StatPages/StatHomePage.html

Hosted by David C. Howell, this website serves as an excellent resource for students who are studying statistics for psychology. In addition to a detailed glossary and lecture notes for a variety of topics in psychology, this website also features useful guidelines and software for students who are looking to use randomization in their data collection. Additionally, links to internet sites feature links to datasets, major statistical software, and statistics calculators which can be used to for a variety of statistical tests.

Activities for Teaching Clinical Psychology:
http://www-usr.rider.edu/~suler/inclassex.html

Hosted by John Suler from Rider University, this website features a variety of activities that can be utilized in the teaching of clinical psychology. These activities were originally conceived of as "in class" activities, but many of them translate nicely to online course work, especially on discussion boards or group activities. Activities are broken down into subheadings of psychotherapy and counseling, self-insight, abnormality and health, group dynamics, general techniques.

CROW: Course Resources on the Web:
http://jfmueller.faculty.noctrl.edu/crow/

This site, which is updated regularly, features a wealth of information pertaining specifically to the teaching of social psychology, including class assignments, activities, and exercises, online studies and scales, examples of concepts, and student resources. The "activities and exercises" contains materials pertaining to aggression, attitudes and behavior, attraction and relationships, conformity, group influence, gender, persuasion, prejudice, social beliefs, and the self. Examples that could easily translate to online group activities or discussion boards include critical thinking exercises, ice-breakers, and even Facebook games and "intergroup monopoly."

International Association for Cross-Cultural Psychology:
http://www.iaccp.org

This site offers information and resources for cross-cultural psychology across the globe, including conferences, publications, member activities, eBooks, online resources, teaching support and online readings in psychology and culture. Through online resources, users can access the

Google Book version of all three volumes of the *Handbook of Cross-Cultural Psychology*.

Psych Central: http://psychcentral.com/

This site offers a comprehensive web resource aimed toward psychological health and treatment with an emphasis on clinical issues and diagnosis. This website features a multitude of discussion forums that students could participate in, or alternatively, the topics of these forums could be integrated into activities within the online CMS. In addition, the most popular current links and news stories in health psychology are offered, which could be integrated into course materials or social bookmarking.

Online Social Psychology Studies: http://www.socialpsychology.org/expts.htm

This page, hosted by the Social Psychology Network, offers links to a variety of online studies in which students can participate. These include professional research on topics such as social perception, beliefs and attitudes, judgment and decision making, as well as student research and a list of web experiment resources for instructors. This page is a useful tool for both instructors and students in methods or social psychology who are looking to create their own online studies, featuring how-to guides, data collection services, and links to software for experimentation.

This link is part of a larger website, the Social Psychology Network, which features links, resources, career guidance, and up-to-date news in the field of social psychology. Managed by Scott Plous, this site is an excellent resource for both students and instructors in this field.

Mental Help: http://www.MentalHelp.net

This clinical psychology website and blog features a variety of resources for clinical, counseling and health psychology instructors and students. This page features information on relevant clinical topics and disorders, up-to-date news, as well as a discussion forum that students could access and comment upon. In addition, the website offers a series of videos and podcasts that could serve as weekly assignments for students.

Pavlov's Dog: http://nobelprize.org/educational/medicine/pavlov/index.html

Hosted by the official website of the Nobel Prize, this page offers a simulation of the Pavlov's Nobel-winning 1904 conditioning study. In this simulation, students play an interactive game where they must make their dog drool on command using the tools provided (bell, drum, horn, bananas, meat, and sausage) in the correct order. This is a great activity for online studies in Introductory Psychology.

Psychology Teaching Resources: Digital Images:
http://psych.wisc.edu/henriques/resources/Images.html

A fun database of digital photos of famous psychologists arranged by discipline, great for enhancing presentations, discussion boards, and course areas that need a little bit of refreshing.

Society for Personality and Social Psychology: Teaching Resources:
http://www.spsp.org/student/teachintro.htm

This website from the Society for Personality and Social Psychology offers links to demonstrations, assignments, and resources in social and personality psychology. These include demonstrations of self-monitoring, functioning with psychological disorders, and the matching phenomena.

Social-Personality Psychology Questionnaire Instrument Compendium
(QIC): http://www.webpages.ttu.edu/areifman/qic.htm

Hosted by Alan Reifman of Texas Tech University, this website serves as a valuable resource for students who are assigned group research projects in their online psychology courses. This website offers links to full instruments, which were put on the web by the person who created the instrument. All instruments are ordered alphabetically and can be accessed by the clicking the link. Students in groups (or working individually) who are in general psychology, social psychology, or research methods courses may find this site very useful as they search for the correct measures for their constructs of interest.

PsychBites: http://www.psychbytes.com/

This website by Jean Mandernach offers "bites" of information for psychology instructors, including PowerPoint presentations spanning across general psychology, psychometrics, human development, and social influence and persuasion. In addition, a number of psychological tests are offered as self-grading quizzes that students can take themselves, and use in their research studies.

Cognition Laboratory Experiments:
http://psych.hanover.edu/JavaTest/CLE/Cognition/Cognition.html

This website from John Krantz of Hanover College features a variety of experiments for cognitive psychology students, including those related to attention, automaticity, mental imagery, language, perception, decision making, and statistical concepts. To access each experiment, students and instructor can click each link and will be taken to a page with an animation or JAVA applet where they can view the simulation unfold. This is a great resource for students in cognitive psychology, as well as those in general psychology, statistics, or research methods who are seeking an interactive, graphic representation of the key concepts.

Faculty List-Servs and Learning Communities

As the popularity of online education continues to grow, a new crop of faculty list-servs and faculty learning communities have arisen for online educators to provide support and share strategies for success. One such list-serv belongs to APA Division 2 for Teaching Psychology (subscribe at: http://teachpsych.org/news/psychteacher.php), which calls itself a "focused discussion list on any topic that addresses issues specific to the teaching of psychology." For individuals looking to incorporate diversity and international perspectives into their teaching, consider joining the Division 2 Diversity list-serv (http://teachpsych.org/news/diversityteach. php). The Teacher.net mailrings site (http://teachers.net/mailrings/) allows users to become connected to thousands of other teachers asking similar questions or seeking information on topics ranging from teaching methods, careers, technology, and specific subject matter. A variety of academic institutions also offer online teaching and learning list-servs. For example, the Center for Technology and Learning at the University for Southern Maine also offers a list-serv for faculty who teach online or anyone interested in online courses (subscribe at: https://lists.usm.maine.edu/cgi-bin/ wa.exe?SUBED1=online-fac&A=1). Check with your academic institution to determine if it has a list-serv for its online teachers. If not, why not create one?

For additional guidance and resources on faculty learning communities (FLCs), visit the website for Developing Professional Learning Communities (http://www.units.muohio.edu/flc/), which even offers a list of communities and consortiums for faculty members to join across the country (http://www.units.muohio.edu/flc/consortium/participating.php). If your institution is not mentioned, speak to members of your division or department about creating your own faculty learning community.

Textbook Publisher Resources

If you are still stuck for resources or activities, consider that many text-book publishers are keen to help provide activities and resources for their online instructors. In some instances, a rep from the company can provide a "course cartridge," feature quizzes, reviews, and PowerPoint slides that can be directly inserted into that instructor's course management system. Alternatively, many publishers, such as *McGraw-Hill, Houghton-Mifflin,* or *Cengage* offer instructor CDs with their texts, or maintain websites that feature additional resources, including video clips and student discussion questions. Many of these can be integrated into the online learning environment as activities for students.

Summary: Keep on Talking and Thinking!

We hope that this chapter has elucidated the vast wealth of materials available to assist online psychology instructors to devise and implement the perfect blend of activities. In line with the "choose your own adventure" approach promoted in this book, use the resources and tips provided in this chapter to select the combination of activities that are most appealing to you, your students, and your course learning goals or outcomes, discussed in the following chapter. Just remember to aim for activities that promote discourse, insight, and critical thinking. Through the right combination of activities, you can ensure that your students will continue talking about and thinking about your course even after it ends and they proceed into other psychology courses. The next chapter continues in the vein of this one, but directs the reader's attention to assignments and assessments, and how to ensure that we are accurately measuring student comprehension and success in our online psychology courses.

CHAPTER 6

ONLINE ASSESSMENT AND LEARNING OUTCOMES IN PSYCHOLOGY

Assessment can seem like one of the greatest challenges facing online psychology instructors today. In the absence of direct, face-to-face communication, is it really possible to accurately ascertain whether students have retained the course material? The authors assert that while online assessment may unfold in a different context, via a different medium, using different tools, adequate, accurate assessment is absolutely possible. In fact, the following chapter should help elucidate how the nature of the online classroom, in particular the depth and breadth of student communication and technology usage, may actually yield *better* tools for assessment than offered in the traditional classroom! To explore online assessment for psychology, this chapter begins by examining the transition from traditional assessment to online assessment, with a focus on learning outcomes. Then, the ins and outs of online assessment will be presented, including issues pertaining to the creation and grading of assessments including tests, quizzes, and discussion boards. The Troubleshooting section addresses the many questions that online instructors have regarding assessment: How do we know students are who they say they are? How can we safeguard against plagiarism by online students? These issues and more will be presented here.

PURPOSE: BEST PRACTICES FOR THE TRANSITION TO ONLINE ASSESSMENT

Online assessment undoubtedly reflects a transition from the tools and evaluations utilized in the traditional classroom, to those that function for optimal success in the virtual learning environment. In order to understand this transition, let us consider the some of the relevant background theories that underlie assessment in higher education, including the incorporation of learning objectives, summative versus formative assignments, and the learner centered approach to assessment. This section discusses best practices for online assessment based upon these theoretical perspectives.

Learning Outcomes, Objectives, and Units

Across traditional and online courses, well-constructed assessments ought to reflect the overall goals of the course, and more broadly of the psychology program. Palloff and Pratt (2009) suggest that good online assessments should take into account program competencies, learning outcomes, and course unit objectives. *Learning outcomes* is a term often present in the educational psychological literature, which generally is used to reflect institutional goals for what students will *know,* and what they will be able to *do* by the end of a course. Learning outcomes are typically set forth by each institution's psychology department to reflect overall *program competencies*, which are best understood as the expected knowledge and skillset that students should develop by the time they complete their overall psychology degree program.

Unit objectives reflect the smallest level of analysis: A course is typically broken down into units and each unit has an objective to transmit a certain level of knowledge or understanding. Psychology courses in particular are often broken down into units that reflect topics of relevance and importance, such as an introductory psychology course being broken down into topics relating to cognition, sensation and perception, learning, and social behavior. Likewise, a social psychology course may be broken down into units of persistence of attitudes, persuasion, social cognition, identity, and so forth. In a psychology of sexuality course, the breakdown might consist of topics on anatomy, sex research, gender, sexual orientation, development, sexual behavior, and such. Although there is some flexibility here, each "unit" of an online course can easily be designated for a 1 week interval that includes a combination of reading assignments, weblinks, discussions, quizzes, tests, or papers pertaining to that particular unit. For online assessment to be effective, it would be ideal to ensure that each assessment corresponds with a course unit. For example, if sexuality students who complete the "gender identity" unit are expected to be able to distinguish between biological sex and gender, then this objective can be assessed using a multiple choice quiz, a discussion board, or an essay test, and so forth.

But on a broader level, how do learning outcomes advise assessment along with unit objectives? Palloff and Pratt (2009) argue that in a good online course, "every course activity (with the exception of reading assignments) should have an assessment linked to it that demonstrates mastery of concepts within the unit, and also links to the demonstration of mastery of course outcomes" (p. 12). In this respect, units should be divided in such a way that the objectives of each unit can be assessed, along with overall learning outcomes which should be measurable, realistic, and clear. According to Palloff and Pratt (2009), learning outcomes should have three components that reflect goals for student learning by the end of a course: *Condition* (the condition under which students should be able to perform), *Behavior* (describing the outcome in terms of the required performance), and *Criterion* (performance criteria to be judged as accurate) (p. 11). In a social psychology course, the *condition* might be that given a case study, the student will be able to distinguish between attitudes, beliefs, and behaviors. If this is the case, then the *behavior* will be that students will answer a series of questions pertaining to attitudes and behaviors after reading the case study. The *criterion* here reflects the grading criteria, such as that students will answer at least 80% of the questions correctly.

Alternatively, in their paper "Online Assessment Strategies: A Primer," Sewell, Frith, and Colvin (2010) discuss how many online instructors develop learning outcomes based upon Bloom's taxonomy, focusing on the cognitive domain (what learners should know), the psychomotor domain (what skills they should be able to complete), and the affective domain (how the learners feel or modifies attitudes) (p. 297). In the previous example from the social psychology course, the cognitive domain refers to knowing the difference between attitude, belief, and behavior; the psychomotor domain refers to students' ability to correctly answer questions regarding the differences between attitudes, beliefs, and behaviors; and the affective domain refers to how their understanding of human cognition has been broadened or enhanced.

It appears that these two approaches to online learning outcomes are complementary, with the first approach (presented by Palloff & Pratt, 2009) being more focused on how objectives translate to assessment, and the second (based upon Bloom's taxonomy) more concerned with how the learning process unfolds. Perhaps the most ideal synthesis would involve an added "affective" component to the first approach, along with behavior, condition, and criterion. Nonetheless, both approaches are useful for instructors who are seeking to determine the learning outcomes and appropriate assessments for their courses. Consider as well that an increasing number of institutions already offer predetermined learning objectives for core courses. In other circumstances, the institution may ask instructors to provide their own learning outcomes for departmental review.

Good online assessment should arise as a natural and logical part of the course fundamentally connected to learning objectives. In their book, *Assessing Open and Distance Learners,* Morgan and O'Reilly (1999) argue that when assessments are clearly in line with learning outcomes, they should naturally fit with the flow of an online course. Sewell and colleagues (2010) support this perspective, arguing that "learning activities and assessment are connected very closely in well-designed online courses" (p. 297). In this respect, the activities that students engage in (think discussions, group projects, or other activities, discussed in chapter 5) should be closely linked with their own assessment. This helps to ensure that assessments fit naturally into the course, that students can become deeply involved in the assessments in which they are participating, and that they can give and receive relevant feedback.

THE LEARNER-CENTERED ASSESSMENT PROCESS

Indeed, student involvement and feedback are deeply important to creating assessments that reflect a *Learner-Centered Approach,* which according to Palloff and Pratt (2009), falls nicely in line with the "philosophy of learning (through) community based online teaching" (p. 24). As mentioned in the previous chapter, in the learner-centered approach, knowledge is constructed by students through critical thinking and communication about the information presented (Huba & Freed, 2000). When assessment takes a learner-centered approach, it not only lends itself to measuring learning outcomes, but it can be utilized to promote further learning, and determine student problems. Indeed, feedback is crucial to the assessment process in a learner-centered paradigm, and it has been argued that student feedback can help to improve the student learning process (Huba & Freed, 2000). As discussed in chapter 5, several activities offered as core parts of online learning, including discussions, peer review, reflective activities, and group work, inherently seem to promote a learner-centered approach featuring integration of knowledge, critical thinking, and feedback across students and instructors.

One of the key distinctions in the theoretical study of online assessment is between summative and formative assessment. It can be easy to assume that all assessments are conducted for the purposes of grading and evaluating students. However, some assessments that promote feedback and meeting learning objectives can also be qualitatively valuable for online learners. McAlpine and Higgison (2001) define *summative* assessment as assessment used for grading, such as passing or failing students, grading or ranking students, and clearly communicating to students what they have achieved. In terms of a practical extension to online teaching, summative assessments usually feature in the final grade, and include papers, quizzes, tests, and discussion projects that feature a grading rubric (Sewell et al., 2010). Alternatively, *formative* assessment is the type of assessment that helps to promote learning by giving feedback to the learner that can be used to improve future performances (McAlpine & Higgison, 2001). The central distinction here is that summative assessments deal primarily with grading, while formative assessments deal primarily with giving feedback and helping students to reach learning objectives.

Sewell and colleagues (2010) recommend a number of potential online activities that can help promote formative assessment, including reflections and self-assessments, case studies, class opinion polls, self-confidence, or efficacy surveys. Reflections and self-assessments can include a "one minute paper" asking students to summarize the most important elements of what they learned during that week, or a "muddiest point assessment" (derived from Angelo & Cross, 1993) where students write about what remains unclear to them after their weekly course materials (p. 301). Both of these types of self-reflection enable the instructor to give vital feedback to students, and to ensure that their learning objectives are being met. Case studies can help students to practice their critical thinking skills, and to apply their knowledge to a real-world context. Application often serves as a central learning objective in psychology, and case studies enable the instructor to determine if students are able to make extensions and generalizations based upon what they have learned. In addition to graded summative quizzes and tests, online learners can also benefit from self-tests that may not directly apply to that learner's course grade, but may help both learner and instructor determine whether the information has been retained. By examining the scores on this self-test, the instructor can help to find gaps in the students' knowledge and make comments surrounding areas that the student should review. If the instructor wants to assess how the learner responds to the course material, and how comfortable the learner feels with the course, this is when student feedback is used as a formative assessment. Specifically, this feedback can take the form of anonymous discussion board posts, emails from students to instructor, the completion of feedback forms, of the submission of a competency survey.

Whether assessments are summative or formative, online instructors should strive to ensure that they are *exemplary*, meaning that they are motivational, meaningful, engaging, and guide the learning process (Huba & Freed, 2000; Sewell et al., 2010). Huba and Freed (2000) suggest eight criteria for exemplary assessments, and encourage instructors to consider these when creating assessments. Exemplary assessments should be *authentic*, meaning that they can reflect or apply to real life experiences; *challenging,* in that they stimulate the learner to apply knowledge; *coherent,* because they should help the students to achieve learning goals; *engaging,* to attract the learner's interest; *respectful,* in that they should be sensitive and not offensive to the learner's beliefs and values; *responsive,* by including some sort of feedback mechanisms to help students in the learning process; *rigorous,* in that they require applied understanding to research a successful outcome; and finally, *valid,* because they should provide information useful for meeting course objectives and learning outcomes. As you design and continue to modify your course online course assessments, consider how these rules for exemplary assessment can be integrated into your psychology courses.

Managing the Transition to Online Assessment

Many instructors and students are familiar with a series of common assessments in the traditional classroom, including but not limited to exams, quizzes, papers, essays, group projects, and research papers. With a little tweaking, some assessment techniques may translate relatively easily between the traditional and online classroom, while other techniques derived from the traditional classroom may be less successful when implemented in the online environment. Consider the following examples that help to elucidate a difference between class activities in the traditional versus online classroom. First, imagine a reflective essay, where each student creates his or her own composition and submits it for the instructor's review. Most likely, the instructor has provided students with some kind of grading criteria, which are used to assess each paper to arrive at a letter grade, numerical grade, or pass/fail grade, depending upon the course. In the online classroom, this type of reflective essay would appear quite similar to the same essay submitted in the traditional classroom, barring the fact that in the online classroom, some kind of antiplagiarism software would probably be utilized to screen the paper for copied text or improper citations. In this example, the type of assessment translates easily and fluidly between the two educational contexts.

Other types of assessment do not translate so easily across the traditional and online contexts. Now consider an instructor in a traditional classroom who often assigns the class pop quizzes to ensure that students are staying on track with their readings. This type of "keep 'em on their toes!" philosophy might not sit so well with online students because they often schedule their course time around work, family, or other life concerns. Imagine the same instructor, now in an online version of the course, announcing a pop-quiz via email or on the CMS and requiring that students attend to it on short notice. This type of assignment may be construed as highly demanding, and may trigger unanticipated levels of stress for online students, who presumably have already arranged their schedules with the assignments on the syllabus in mind. Further, students who are unable to complete the surprise assignment and cannot "drop everything" to attend to the quiz may end up withdrawing from the course. In light of the way that many online students develop expectations about their assignments based upon the syllabus, random or unanticipated assignments are probably not the best method for gauging student knowledge and retention. In fact, while this type of quiz is sometimes expected and accepted in the traditional classroom, it could have disastrous consequences for student expectations and confidence in the online classroom.

This example helps to highlight a core difference between assignments in the traditional and online learning environments. Namely, assignments in the online classroom *must* be scheduled and agreed upon at the beginning of the semester, to ensure that online learners will be able to manage their schedules and provide time to complete their coursework. While the same is usually true in the traditional classroom, consider for a moment the individual nature of online education. Online students must remain regimented and self-motivated to succeed, arguably more so than students who attend traditional classes. Unlike the traditional student who might come to class with the goal of "winging it," an online student who engages in this type of approach will be just as likely, if not more likely, to fail. In this respect, online courses can serve as more challenging to students who tend to avoid homework, but easier for students who work hard and have high levels of self-motivation and discipline.

One of the other key differences between assessing the traditional and online learner is that the online environment offers a wider depth and breadth of opportunity to assess learners and provide feedback. Palloff and Pratt (2009) highlight a number of ways that the online classroom can be used for assessment *advantage*, including: Computer generated scores and quizzes, internet-based research projects, peer review technologies, internet-based case studies, synchronous and asynchronous technologies to facilitate communication, and antiplagiarism software.

Computer-Generated Scores and Quizzes

Online testing offers a variety of functions not commonly available in tests and quizzes delivered in the traditional environment. First, many CMS interfaces automatically score all tests, enabling students to receive instant feedback on their performances. When a quiz or test is created, it is possible for the instructor to fill in the "correct" and "incorrect" feedback so that students will receive feedback for each question that they answer. So, rather than waiting until the next class for the midterm exam to be returned as happens in the traditional classroom, online students will receive their midterm exam results instantly. This can be very gratifying for students who are seeking feedback. Additionally, this means that self-quizzes to gauge knowledge and progress (think about the formative assessments discussed in this section) can also be set to give instant feedback to both students and the instructor on the student's progress. Additionally, online testing enables the use of randomly selected test questions from a test bank, ensuring that all students do not have the same test in the same order. Some instructors might recall an unpleasant situation where the midterm or final exam was copied by a student, leading to students in other sections receiving the questions ahead of time. This type of cheating is all but eliminated when randomly selected questions from a test bank come into play.

Internet-Based Research Projects

Online courses offer infinite opportunities for accessing sources of data and information on the web. While many traditional classrooms are integrating computing technology and encouraging students to conduct internet based research, online students have the advantage of already being in front of their computer with the research materials at their fingertips. Thanks to technology, students can immediately post their findings on a discussion board to share with the test of the course, or integrate social bookmarking to share their sources directly. According to Palloff and Pratt (2009), this type of shared internet research enables online students to become excellent critical thinkers, as they evaluating the postings made by their peers.

Peer Review

Often, it is beneficial for instructors to ask students to grade each other's work. In traditional classrooms, students will sometimes switch papers or tests, and grade their classmates' work as they review material with the rest of the class. In the online classroom, peer review takes a much more complex and sophisticated approach. Software is often integrated into the CMS that automatically enables peer review, by allowing students to electronically exchange documents and give comments via mark-ups or other methods of integrating electronic feedback into the document. This type of sophisticated peer review is an excellent summative and formative experience that enables students to practice their critical thinking skills and give and receive feedback together, thereby boosting their sense of community and collaboration.

Internet-Based Case Studies

Particularly in the field of psychology, case studies provide an excellent source of activities and assessments as students are able to apply their knowledge to actual real-life situations. Often, case studies are crucial for instruction in disciplines like clinical psychology, counseling psychology, and school psychology. While case studies can be presented in the traditional classroom by way of textbook or supplemental materials, they become even easier to access and study in the online classroom. Online psychology students can simultaneously view case studies and share their thoughts with each other and the instructor through emails, discussion posts, and social bookmarking.

Synchronous and Asynchronous Communication

The online classroom offers numerous innovative technologies that promote communication, collaboration, and assessment. These tools, which have been discussed at length throughout this book, include, wikis, blogs, social network sites, as well as CMS features that enable virtual chat. Unlike the traditional classroom, these forms of communication in online courses are all easily documented and viewable for assessment purposes. Students have the opportunity to review past communication and make changes, embellishments, or comments. In addition, such forms of communication tools can be harnessed for summative as well as formative assessment.

Antiplagiarism Software

The authors contend that the inclusion of antiplagiarism software into the majority of online course CMSs adds another enormous benefit to online assessment. While issues with online cheating and plagiarism continue to provoke debate and discussion (see the "Troubleshooting" section of this chapter), it is undeniable that antiplagiarism software such as Turn-it-In (www.turnitin.com; which scans documents for any plagiarized or improperly cited text), serves as a huge benefit to online learners and instructors alike. The authors recall speaking to a colleague around 5 years ago who claimed to scan his traditional students' papers through Google Search to determine if content had been plagiarized. Now, in online courses, all content written for submission is automatically scanned, greatly reducing the likelihood of plagiarism, and making assessment a clearer, more accurate process online.

An additional caveat here surrounds how, if at all, the transition to online assessment can affect faculty workload. In other words, do certain online assignments disproportionately act as drains on an online faculty members' time and focus? Research in this area has not been forthcoming, but it would make sense that the many online assignments that grade themselves (such as quizzes and tests) would help to alleviate faculty workload concerns, whereas assignments that require a heavy cognitive focus (such as grading research papers) would remain relatively time consuming. The question of how new technology and new styles of assignments might affect workload seemingly comes down to the faculty member in question and his or her background and training. A faculty member who selects an unfamiliar assessment strategy, or who neglects to receive training for that assessment prior to the start of the course, might experience an increased workload due to general lack of understanding and teething problems. So if the faculty member selects to use a student-reviewed and edited wiki assignment, but has never used a wiki before, that instructor might experience heightened workload pressures and concerns during that first semester. Likewise, an instructor who frequently reviews and edits wikis should encounter minimal difficulty with grading this assessment, and in fact, might even have a lower workload than if using traditional methods to teach.

Based upon this discussion, it is undeniable that the tools afforded by the online classroom can become a huge advantage for online instructors who are seeking to create high quality assessments. Granted that assessment occurs in a different context and modality online from the traditional classroom, certain vital considerations must be afforded by online instructors pertaining specifically to heightening clarity and communication. For example, Morgan and O'Reily (1999) argue that online assessments should feature several key elements, including that assessments must be sufficient and timely in their delivery. Due to the absence of "face time," it is more important than ever that online assessments are delivered with clarity and that the expectations for assignments are explicitly defined. Managing student expectations is discussed in the following section of this chapter. Meanwhile, other experts in online instruction have put forth the case for a stronger integration with communication and assessment. Gaytan (2005) argues that communication and feedback should function as an ongoing part of the assessment process, and that assessments should focus in particular on "dynamic" activities that feature a high degree of student to student interaction, including group projects, peer review, and discussion activities. It appears then that the online learning environment calls for assessments with explicitly clear instructions that promote collaboration and feedback. The next section explores these types of assessments and how to create and implement them.

IMPLEMENTATION: THE INS AND OUTS OF ONLINE ASSESSMENT

At first glance, online assessment can feel like one of the more challenging areas for some burgeoning online psychology instructors. For many instructors, our understanding of assessment can be firmly grounded in activities that we can directly observe and implement in an in-person context, such as exams, quizzes, and discussions. As highlighted by the previous section, however, all of these (and many more) can be executed with similar levels of satisfaction and success in the online environment, so long as we can make adjustments for the many contextual changes present in the online classroom. As readers begin to create and implement their own online assessments, try to keep in mind the way that assessments should ultimately reflect course competencies and learning objectives, and should provide for exemplary methods for gauging learning and knowledge. While much of the information on assessments and grading considerations discussed in this section are derived from empirical research, some suggestions are also based upon the authors' own experience, as well as interviews with online psychology students and instructors.

TESTING

Issues surrounding online testing remain controversial and are frequently discussed at educational conferences and in the literature. One of the reasons for this is that for some, online testing seemingly defies our classic understanding of testing as a proctored, timed, closed-book phenomenon. Further, because we cannot directly observe our online students as they work on tests, there is a preconception that the fidelity of the testing apparatus is somehow less precise than a test that occurs in shared physical space. Nonetheless, the authors perceive that many of the criticisms of online testing either no longer apply or are not relevant to the way that online courses are delivered. For example, one of the complaints about online testing is the lack of a proctor, meaning that no human being is present to oversee the proceedings. However, students are required to log in to the testing apparatus before taking their test, helping to increase the likelihood that students are who they say they are. Also, the sophisticated software included in CMS means that we can ensure our exams are timed, and we can control elements that were previously uncontrollable in traditional testing, such as whether students are allowed to change their answers once they have responded. The following section addresses these issues and also the creation and regulation of online tests along with strategies for managing student expectations.

CREATING AND REGULATING ONLINE TESTS

One of the keys to successful online testing is selecting the rules of the testing apparatus first, and second, managing student expectations about testing. In terms of selecting the rules for online testing, consider first the learning objectives and course materials. As the instructor, are you mainly concerned with summative assessment? An instructor concerned with summative assessment would want to ensure that students retain basic knowledge such as definitions of key concepts, as well as distinguishing between different theories or different ideas (think about the early steps in Bloom's taxonomy). These types of assignments would provide a specific grade, and specific feedback surrounding that grade. Or, as the instructor, are you more concerned with formative testing? In this situation, students would answer essay questions and give feedback about how their experiences pertain to the course materials (think about some of the later stages in Bloom's taxonomy, like application and analysis). Depending upon the goals of the test, online instructors will engage in a varied approach to testing. One of the great benefits to online testing is the level and amount of options that instructors can vary, including the timer, the number of questions, the style of questions, and the grading criteria. Consider these options as this section explores the important decisions pertaining to online test creation: *content, delivery,* and *duration.*

Content

The first component to any successful online testing assessment is selecting content that meets the learning outcomes or unit objectives for that particular section of interest. The best way to determine test content is by asking, "What are the most important points that students need to know?" Note that this can include not only memory recall and learning facts, but also higher level critical thinking, such as the ability to apply, synthesize, and evaluate. Depending upon the course, there might be different learning objectives that are particularly relevant. In the discipline of psychology, the content of online testing can vary tremendously across many different levels. In an Introduction to Psychology course, for example, the content of online tests will probably involve recall and definitions of important terms or theories. But, in an Applied Health Psychology course, the content of the test will probably surround higher order questions where students will be required to synthesize theories and apply findings to real-life situations.

After deciding the learning outcomes or unit objectives that the test will meet, the next question surrounds where the content itself is derived from. Will this test be based upon textbook readings, online articles, class discussion boards, lecture slides, online videos, or all of the above? Try to choose the content delivery that is most applicable to your learning objectives. So, in the Applied Health Psychology course mentioned above, a case study video followed by test questions might be more applicable to reaching the learning outcome than a multiple choice test featuring definitions from the textbook. Alternatively, it might be advisable to engage in multiple forms of questioning to ensure that the topic is triangulated: The same test might feature analysis of a case study video, recall of definitions, as well as some kind of free-response or debate. Because of the potential for variation here, it is crucial to make it crystal clear to students the topics or assignments that will be featured on their tests, and where they can review the content prior to the test. As discussed later on in this section, when student expectations about testing content or rules are violated, there can be difficult consequences for their experience in the course and their faith in the instructor.

Delivery

After selecting the content that most appropriately matches up with the learning objectives and course unit goals, the next step is to determine the method of test delivery. Considerations surrounding the delivery of tests include the types of questions selected as well as the arrangement of the testing questions. The most common online CMS interfaces, specifically Blackboard and Moodle, offer an increasingly diverse range of testing options. So, for example, if an instructor is looking to create a quiz or test with a certain number of objective questions, the multiple choice format is not the only option available. In the online environment, it is possible to alter the type and format of questions ranging from true-false, to fill-in the blank, to calculated responses. In other words, online testing offers the same variety of questions that could be utilized on a traditional in-class test, with the added bonus that all questions can be graded automatically by the system for immediate review by students. It is possible to enter feedback for "correct" and "incorrect" choices to ensure that students will see an explanation, possibly featuring a link or a page number in the text.

First, it is necessary to choose the type or types of questions that will be delivering the assessment to the students. The online testing apparatus can be highly beneficial in the options that are offered to instructors, including the ability to grade tests immediately, and to give feedback. The online testing apparatus also offers a variety of options with regard to the organization and delivery of the questions themselves. For example, would you prefer students to read and answer one question at a time, or view the entire set of questions, work on them, and then submit the entire test at the end? Both of these options are plausible using CMS like Blackboard and Moodle. If students are allowed to view and answer the questions one-by-one, the instructor can also determine whether students are allowed to backtrack after completing a question. Some instructors choose to prohibit backtracking to ensure that students cannot look up answers after answering and return to change a specific question. Again, the usefulness of this limitation really depends on the types of questions being asked. If the question asks for a definition of an important construct, then it is possible that students who have time remaining might take a moment to look up the answer in their textbook and return to change their response. If the question involves analyzing a case study or making an argument to support a specific point, then backtracking is probably not going to have a massive effect on student performance.

Second, the online testing apparatus also offers the option of question randomization, as well as the selection of questions from a test bank. Randomization refers to questions being delivered to students in a random order for each test. Often, this is done in traditional classrooms by delivering multiple forms of the same test to ensure that students will not be motivated to cheat or copy each other's papers. The benefit in the online learning environment is similar in that students who do communicate regarding test questions will be unclear about which questions came in what order. So, for example, one student who emails another stating that "I think the answer to question 10 is A" will probably be speaking about a different question than their classmate sees for number 10. Letting the class know from the beginning that questions will be randomized will help to ensure the fidelity of the test.

In addition, if an instructor becomes especially concerned that students might be sharing information about the tests (and if the instructor believes that this can be damaging to the assessment protocol), then consider that it might be worth having all test questions randomly selected from a test bank uploaded into the CMS. Many psychology textbooks offer predetermined test banks of questions that can be linked with the online test bank in a few easy steps. Usually this will involve asking the CMS to "create a pool" of test questions, which can then be downloaded from the textbook CD or website, and uploaded into the CMS. Once there, it is possible to ensure that each student receives a certain number of questions that are randomly selected from the testing pool. The testing pool will usually correspond with a specific text chapter, or a specific topic. It is also possible to create your own testing pool by manually entering all of the questions, and then asking the CMS to select questions at random. One cautionary note is that by using a test bank, it might be possible that students in the same course will respond to totally different tests with different series of questions. In one of the few research studies ever published that investigated student perceptions of online assessment, the only significant student concern surrounded questions selected at random from test banks (Dermo, 2009). In this survey conducted with 130 undergraduate students at the University of Bradford, England, students specifically identified their concern that questions selected at random from test banks are unfair due to the potential of receiving questions with varying levels of difficulty.

Therefore, questions in a test bank should be similar enough to ensure that their random selection does not influence the fidelity of the testing apparatus. Based upon study findings, Dermo (2009) recommends using item analysis or other statistical procedures that measure reliability to ensure that the questions in the test bank manifest similar levels of difficulty. An additional consideration of test banks surrounds instructor review of material. When students respond to different questions, it can be more challenging for the instructor to review the correct answers, since students might respond to different combinations of hundreds of questions. Nonetheless, random selection from a testing pool can help to deal with security concerns, or concerns about test questions being copied and pasted, or worries that all students are familiar with the same questions and are somehow distributing these to students in subsequent classes. It is important to bear in mind that this procedure may seem unfair or unpleasant for online students, who may perceive fairness issues when test banks are used. More research ought to be conducted on perceptions of online assessment to determine any other potential limitations posed by the random selection of testing questions.

Duration

After deciding upon the content of the test and the delivery of the questions, it is time to consider the duration of the test itself. Usually, the content and question delivery will help to inform decisions regarding test duration. The first issue for duration surrounds whether the test will have a timer, or be available up until a certain due date. For many tests or quizzes that focus on summative, lower-order questions (such as matching definitions and identifying key names or terms), a timer ensures that students do not have the ability to look up every answer in the textbook or their notes. In this situation, students would have about 1 to 2 minutes per question to come up with the correct multiple choice, true-false, matching, or fill-in response. An example from an Introduction to Psychology course or a lower-level social psychology course might look something like this:

6.1 SAMPLE QUIZ QUESTION FOR AN INTRODUCTORY PSYCHOLOGY COURSE

Which of these theories addresses the congruency of attitudes and behaviors?

A.   Social Comparison Theory
B.   Self-Evaluation Maintenance Model
C.   Cognitive Dissonance Theory
D.   Social Identity Theory

(You probably already know that the correct answer here is "C").

In this style of testing, affording less than 1 minute per question might induce stress for students who are slow readers or who have test anxiety. On the other hand, allowing for any more than 1 or 2 minutes per question might provide students with ample time to look up the answers in their notes or books, therefore reducing the validity of the testing apparatus to measure memory recall and learned information. In this example, the test could be available for the duration of one week, and it is launched when the student clicks on it and the timer begins. After the timer expires and the test is submitted, the students' grades are entered and they are able to view the test, the questions they got wrong, and their instructor's feedback. One of the limitations here is that, in the authors' experience, students can sometimes experience problems with timed tests, ranging from test anxiety, to having "lock-outs" or other browser issues. Depending upon the CMS, the type of test, and the student's operating system, students taking timed tests might get "booted" from their timed test for clicking outside of their testing window or running other programs. Recommendations for testing rules to reduce problems with timed tests are discussed in the next section on "Managing Student Expectations."

When tests are more formative in nature, or they ask for more complex analysis, discussion, synthesis, and evaluation-type questions, it might be useful to employ essay questions and remove the timer, instead making the test available for a certain number of hours or days. Tests that address these types of questions usually feature some kind of a prompt (such as a research article, case study, example, debate-type question, or other type data) that asks students to respond in essay or short-answer form. In the previous summative example, the test is available and the timer launches when the student opens the test. In this example, the test might be available for the duration of the semester, or for a shorter period of time, such as one week. When this type of test becomes available, students can take the appropriate amount of time to formulate their answers, such as a 6-hour period, a 24-hour period, a 72-hour period, or a week-long period, and so forth. So long as the test is submitted by the time the deadline occurs, it is accepted and graded by the instructor. However, once the deadline for submission passes, the test would be late or may not be accepted at all (this comes down to the instructor's discretion). This type of testing tends to be more prevalent as students move up to upper-level psychology courses that require analysis and critical thinking. For example, an upper-level or graduate social psychology class might have an essay test or exam where students are required to respond to this type of question:

6.2 ESSAY QUESTIONS FOR AN UPPER-LEVEL PSYCHOLOGY COURSE

Human beings are social animals. Drawing on theories and research, describe instances in which other people are seen to be important in affording individuals:

- *Greater self-understanding*
- *A guide for behavior, and*
- *Opportunities to boost esteem or feel better*

A question such as this might require extensive research and preparation time, as well as time spent writing the response itself. Therefore, it should be made available within a scope of time to ensure that students have the opportunity to prepare properly. The authors recommend giving online students at least 72 hours to respond to a complex essay question such as this, or more if there are additional essay questions as well. When assigning this type of essay exam or essay test, ensure that students save their work on their computer and copy and paste into their CMS. There is nothing worse than entering all of the information onto the CMS, only to drop the internet connection and lose everything. Losing all of one's work on an essay test is what many students would refer to as an "Epic Fail" in that the consequences are disastrous and stressful. By saving the work on their own computer, students can ensure with better certainty that they will not have to start again from scratch due to a technical problem. In addition, students should be encouraged to proofread for appropriate college level spelling, grammar, and composition, and run their exam through Turn-it-In prior to submission (antiplagiarism software is discussed later in the "Troubleshooting" section of this chapter).

EXAM RETAKES: TO RETAKE OR NOT TO RETAKE?

One of the more compelling issues discussed among online educators is whether students should be allowed to retake their tests and exams, particularly when they do not do well the first time around. It is undeniable that deadlines are created for a reason, and allowing students to flout those deadlines by retaking previous exams seems unfair to the students who studied on time and succeeded in those exams the first time around. On the other hand, all students deserve the opportunity to succeed, and sometimes they have problems or issues in their testing experience that require additional attempts to ensure their retention of information. In many ways, the decision to allow students to retake their exams boils down to a question of fairness. Is it fair to the rest of the class if certain students retake their exams? If not, would it be fair if *everyone* in the class would be allowed to retake their exams? In other words, only allowing certain students (usually those who did not do well the first time) the opportunity to retake exams for a better grade might seem unfair. If all students are afforded the opportunity, then this certainly seems more equitable. On the flipside, deadlines and timelines are present in online education for a reason, mainly because online students need to be motivated and structured in order to succeed. Allowing students to retake tests seemingly implies that the instructor is less committed to deadlines, and in turn, it might make the students take the deadlines less seriously if they know that they can just retake the test if they are not happy with their score.

Is there a universal determination of whether students should be allowed to retake their online tests? The authors would argue, definitely not. In fact, there is almost no scholarly research published on the topic of student performance and test-taking in online classes, meaning that once again, it is up to the online instructor to use his or her best judgment when making decisions about test retakes. From the authors' perspective, if students are going to be allowed to retake tests, a few limitations ought to be put into place: (a) First, all students should be afforded the same opportunities, not only students who do poorly on their tests. Allowing retakes only for students who do poorly sets the wrong example that people who succeed receive fewer rewards than people who fail. In this respect, consider the importance of fairness and equality. (b) Limit the time, number, and scope of retakes. Provide one or two opportunities to retake the exam, as opposed to 10 opportunities. Granting so many opportunities to retake an exam again seems to suggest that the instructor is not very serious about deadlines or the validity of the testing instrument. If students are allowed to retake their tests, ensure that they are allotted the same time (where appropriate) and not more time than other students were given when they first completed the test. (c) Finally, do not review the test until all retakes are completed. Although this seems obvious, instructors can sometimes make mistakes or forget that others have not yet finished their retakes when reviewing the test questions. Clearly, this is a problem and can severely compromise the test itself. It is important for students to review exams, tests, and quizzes with the class, but also necessary to ensure that this does not occur until after all tests have been completed.

Additionally, it seems that the instructor's protocol for retaking exams could benefit from remaining consistent with the protocol applied to dealing with late or missed exams. Students can miss exams for a variety of reasons, including but not limited to life events such as family or health emergencies, technological issues, or just simple negligence, laziness, or forgetfulness. Generally speaking, an instructor who allows students to retake their exams might also be more lenient to students who want to take the exams that they missed. The authors suggest that instructors use caution and common sense when determining who gets to take an exam after the due date. For example, a consistently high quality student who had a medical emergency and can supply a doctor's note is surely more worthy of a make-up test than a student who has no explanation other than "I forgot" and has a track record of missing assignments. Keep in mind similar notions of fairness as you determine who receives a make-up exam. If all exams are available early in the semester, this ensures that students have plenty of time to take them, and no excuses if they do not take their exams on time, even if a technical problem or other issue arises. Regardless of the decision, definitely try to make sure that all students are aware of the protocol of retakes and make-ups from the start.

MANAGING TESTING EXPECTATIONS

Expectation management is one of the most important components of online assessment. Students must know exactly what to expect and how to prepare, and because of the lack of physical proximity, online instructors need to be clear and articulate communicators when it comes to assessment. First, the testing rules themselves should be clearly explained. The authors recommend a combination of video or audio (such as YouTube lecture or podcast) explaining the testing rules, along with the text-based explanation of them (posted in a link, the online syllabus, or a discussion board). The testing rules will depend on the type of delivery and duration of the test itself. For example, in a timed multiple-choice test taken in the Blackboard CMS, there are a number of rules that students must follow, which ought to be clearly communicated.

In addition, remind students where the content is coming from and outline or provide links to the specific chapters, assignments, lectures, or activities that they will need to review. Try to make sure all of these rules are *clearly stated* in multiple places where students can view them. When students experience testing problems, it can become a highly charged, stressful, and even emotional situation. For example, just the other day Dr. Neff received the following email from a student in her online class:

> *Clearly, I am not having a good day. When this email was returned twice, I just lost it and just started crying. Not because it didn't reach you, but because I am just overwhelmed right now. My husband figured it out—wrong email address. I need a break! Sorry for rambling!*

It turns out that the student panicked when her timer ran out and she was unable to complete her exam, and was trying to email the instructor for help; however, she had entered the wrong email address and so the emails to the instructor were not being received. This kind of an account is unfortunately not unusual, and demonstrates the anxiety and emotion that some students experience during testing. One way to mitigate this anxiety is to ensure that students are provided with as much information as possible so that they know what to expect. The other is to remain as supportive and responsive as possible when students do experience a problem. Imagine a student who bursts into tears during a class and how an instructor would comfort that student. It can be much more challenging to provide support to the same student who is on the other side of a computer terminal. Still, it is entirely possible to provide help and support to this student by acknowledging that you are here to give support and help. In fact, Dr. Neff's response looked something like this:

> *I am so sorry to hear you are experiencing stress because of this exam. Just breathe. We will resolve the situation. Start by explaining what happened? What is your operating system and when did the exam start to have problems?*

A supportive, proactive response goes a long way to diffusing the tension of this type of a situation. Remember the importance of communication in establishing a supportive rapport with students? This is especially true with online testing. In this example, after asking and answering a few more questions, Dr. Neff was able to help the student retake her quiz. Afterwards, the student was so relieved with the steady and quick resolution:

> *THANK YOU! I'm sorry for ranting. I'm just suddenly felt overwhelmed and I crashed. I'm not overwhelmed by your class; I absolutely love it!! I'm enrolled in three other classes and I was up most of the night. It all got to me for a moment. Now I'm breathing normally!!!*

This is exactly the kind of resolution that an instructor would want to see after solving problems for a student who is experiencing stress with online testing. Often when students do not receive helpful feedback from their online instructor, they can experience frustration and this can lead them to lash out, or discourage their motivation in the class. Online instructors want to avoid this stress as much as possible by communicating a feeling of warmth, help, and empowerment.

An additional issue surrounding student expectations of online testing is that many students use their book and notes as a guide during the test itself. While some instructors would prefer this not to be the case, it is inevitable that online students will use their books, notes, and any other resources in front of them when they engage in online testing. Why? Well for one thing, they can. Usually, students who want to succeed will use all of the resources available to them, and since there is no one forcing them to put their textbooks away, the book will most likely stay open. For this reason, asking students *not* to use notes can feel futile and unenforceable. Therefore, it is better to assume that students will be using their books and notes, and to plan accordingly. How can one do this? On a multiple choice test it is necessary and important to ask questions about definitions, dates, names, key terms, and such, then a timer is a handy way to ensure that students will still have to learn the material *before* they take the exam. As discussed earlier, 1 to 2 minutes per question on a timer is cutting it very close for a student who needs to look up every answer. Consider rephrasing some questions so that students are required to apply, discuss, and compare and contrast, as opposed to simply identify key constructs. For example, instead of a question asking *"What is the definition of gender?"* ask students *"How do gender and sexual orientation differ from each other?"* These types of questions require slightly higher order thinking, and again, will still require an application of knowledge above what is directly printed in the textbook. In this respect, multiple choice or true-false questions that ask for a higher level of analysis, such as comparing, analyzing, and applying, not only avoid problems with textbook and notes, but also seem to be a better indicator of knowledge and learning.

For many essay tests, the use of books, notes, and outside resources is actually encouraged, if not required. The essay example given earlier asks for the student to review the relevant research and theory, which can only be done by using outside sources. In this respect, for instructors who are concerned about student book and note use, an essay test is a great way to mitigate any potential issues. Essay tests certainly measure important aspects of learning such as the ability to synthesize knowledge, compare theories, and apply research and theory to real life phenomena. Consider then creating multiple tests and administering them throughout the semester: Some should be timed tests with multiple choice questions, and there should be other essay tests that require the student to demonstrate a deeper level of knowledge.

Sometimes the poor management of student testing expectations can lead to a number of student complaints. At the same time, many of these complaints are not necessarily avoidable, and might arise even when the instructor works hard to manage testing expectations. Some of these complaints are discussed below, with an emphasis on how to achieve a resolution.

I Can't Find This Anywhere in the Assigned Course Materials!?

It can be frustrating when students study the assigned content, only to find content on their quiz, test, or exam that they do not recall seeing or learning. Sometimes, this can be the student's oversight in missing a particular point during the reading or lectures. Other times, this can be the instructor's oversight, due most likely to the set-up of the course schedule and execution of exams and tests. During a traditional in-class test, it might be easier for students to voice concerns and for the professor to review the question on the spot and make a decision: "I'm sorry class, that question didn't belong on the quiz, you will get points back for it if you answered incorrectly." A statement such as this would be very useful for diffusing the problem. In the online learning environment, this situation can become trickier, in part because students take their exams and tests at many different times before the due date. A student might notice the mistake or problem early on and let the instructor know, or a student might not notice the mistake until right before the deadline. To ensure fairness, so that all students receive the same or similar unmodified assessment, many CMS interfaces do not allow the instructor to change the content of the test or quiz after students have begun to take it. Thus, for the online teacher, a question that does not belong can sometimes feel like a thorn in the side as it confuses and frustrates the students.

How to deal with this situation when it turns out that it was in fact the instructor's mistake? At the very least, try to avoid these kinds of errors by reviewing all of the course content before the course is launched. Remember, prepare, plan, and test from earlier chapters? This is where a steady review of all of assessments can greatly reduce problems that create student frustration. If the mistake has already occurred, first rectify and mitigate damage as soon as possible by emailing the entire class, or posting an announcement or similar reminder on the discussion board that a certain question did not belong and that points will be returned once the testing period has been closed. Owning mistakes like this is crucial to ensure that students continue to have faith in their instructor, and really, they will respect you more than if you tried to hide the mistake itself. Second, after notifying all students, be sure to make the changes to the grade itself in a timely fashion. Students who do not see the update to their grade may continue to stew in frustration that due to no fault of their own, their grade is a few points lower than it should be. Due to the continuous nature of online courses, many students find it hard to change their mental space—in other words, once something goes wrong and they are working from their home computer, they might stew in their upset and frustration all weekend long, while the instructor is quite unaware of the problem. Tackling and addressing their issues head on, and letting them know of your intention to help can be very beneficial in remanaging their expectations!

There Is More Than One Right Answer, Which One Do I Choose!?

While the previous question dealt more closely with content, this issue really revolves around question structure and delivery. Again returning to the analogy of a traditional class, a multiple choice question with a few possible answers will probably be brought to the professor's attention during the exam itself, at which point he or she can make an announcement surrounding the question, such as "For question 12, there are two possible answers, students who select either will be given credit for this." Once again, it is more challenging to correct these mistakes in the online environment. If a student emails with a complaint like this, the instructor should first try to decide, "Are both response options correct, or is one option better?" If one of the options really is better, then the instructor should inform that student and provide an explanation. It might also be useful to email the class and state that "for Question 12, there is only one answer so please choose the better response option." If upon evaluating the question the instructor believes that the student might have a point about the response options, then make sure to let the class know that both options will be accepted, and then after all students have completed the quiz, provide a brief review explaining why both answers were accepted. The key here, as above, is *not* to leave them hanging! Again, a student left to fester in this violation of expectations and frustration, with no professor response or intervention, can become angry, stressed, anxious, and overwhelmed. It would be preferable for any instructor to help students to avoid descent into this state of mind. One of the easiest ways is to immediately tackle your mistakes head on. They will appreciate this more than if you bury your head in the sand.

I Got Locked Out of My Test, How Can I Complete It?

Possibly one of the most common issues with online testing at the present time is the phenomenon of test lock outs for timed online tests. Students can find that they are booted from timed tests for a variety of reasons mentioned in the earlier section, such as running other programs, clicking outside of the testing window, clicking save, print, refresh, copy, or losing their Wi-Fi or internet connection. Most colleges and universities that offer online courses have some kind of policy in place to deal with test lock-outs, the concern being that a student who is locked out of the test may have an advantage over other students who are not locked out. Specifically, a student who is locked out will need to have his or her test cleared by the instructor or administrator before being allowed back into the CMS to retake the test. At the time of going to press, it is not possible to reopen a test in Blackboard; rather, if a student is locked out, that student must retake their entire test again. In between the time of clearing the test and retaking the test, it is entirely possible that students may review their notes and textbooks for the answers of questions that they have already taken, and change their answers to get a better grade.

How to deal with this situation? One of the issues here is that not all students who are locked out of exams and tests are doing so intentionally. A lost internet connection or a technical problem with their CMS can boot a student out of a timed multiple choice test, much to their panic and frustration. While we sincerely hope that the majority of our students are honest, hard-working individuals, there is always a possibility that students lock themselves out intentionally to view the questions and look up the answers. Based upon their experiences, the authors recommend the following four-step protocol for dealing with test lockouts: Troubleshoot a screen shot, allow one lockout per student, record their answers, and create a make-up quiz.

Troubleshoot a Screen Shot

Any student who is locked out of their exam must send a screen shot of the error message to the instructor so that the instructor or technical support/administrators can analyze it. For example, an error message in Blackboard might look like this *"Access Denied; User does not have privileges to perform the desired action"* followed by a series of numbers and letters. By taking a screen shot and sending it to the instructor, it is possible to ensure that students are not being deceptive about the error message that they receive. If a student does not send a copy and screenshot of the error message, then that student will not have his or her test unlocked.

Once the screen shot of the error message is received, the instructor can send this to the institution's technical support department for their review, or make an executive decision about it. If it is determined that the error message was legitimate and not indicative of a student who was not following the testing procedures, then the instructor should begin to troubleshoot with the student. What is his or her operating system and web browser? Was he or she running other programs or opening other windows during the test? Is there a problem with his or her Wi-Fi connection? All of these will help the instructor to understand what the problem might be. It is important to identify this to ensure that the student is not repeatedly locked out of exams.

One Lockout Per Student

If the instructor decides, based upon the screen shot and troubleshooting, to reopen the test, it is wise to ensure that students are not afforded multiple opportunities once they are locked out. The rule of one lockout per student helps to ensure that students are not intentionally locking themselves out to have a chance to review the questions. It also ensures that the instructor or administration must troubleshoot with this student to ensure that the testing process runs smoothly for them during the semester. Repeated testing issues, especially lockouts, can become extremely stressful and anxiety provoking for students. In order to facilitate this, make sure that all students know from the start of term (i.e., in their course orientation, syllabus, etc.) that only one lock-out will be allowed, after which they will not be allowed to retake or reopen any exams, no matter the circumstances!

Record Their Answers

After a student is locked out, and before his or her test is reopened, make sure to record all of their answers, which can be found by downloading his or her attempt into the gradebook, copying and pasting it into a Word document, or just making a note of his or her choices on a piece of paper. Once the exam is completed, the instructor can go through and ensure that the student kept his or her answers the same. If the student changed an answer, the instructor should contact that student and let him or her know that the original answer must stand. Also, let them know that changing their answer might have constituted cheating. While it could be due to an honest mistake, a student who is reminded of this will be less likely to change answers in the future, and the instructor can make a note about the behavior of that particular student.

Create a Makeup Quiz

Finally, if these options are unsatisfactory, it might be beneficial to create a makeup test, exam, or quiz for all of the students who were locked out of their original test. This way, they will be given new questions and will not have had the opportunity to see the items on the test. However, there are still some issues with this approach, notably the time and effort required to create, launch, and review a separate test. Also, what happens if students become locked out on their makeup test? The authors would argue that the first lockout was their one lockout for the semester, and that now their grade must stand if they are locked out again.

A final note regarding this issue is that the technology that facilitates online testing is constantly evolving: Although systems like Blackboard have had these types of protocols in place for the last few years, it is entirely possible that as online education continues to become more prevalent, software designers will find more effective ways of dealing with online testing that do not involve test lockouts. At the time of going to press, however, this seems to be the current condition of the common CMS testing interfaces.

Why Did I Get It Wrong? Posttest Reviewing

One of the other issues that online students often have is that they crave a review of their tests, similar to what happens in a traditional class. Once again, it can become so frustrating to be unsure or confused about why points were deducted. For multiple choice tests and the like, it is possible to deliver feedback with every question that students see, depending upon whether they have entered the correct or incorrect answer. Likewise for essay tests, it would be useful for the instructor to provide feedback. After all, feedback and communication are key to student growth and success. Rather than expecting that students will understand what they did wrong, please ensure that some kind of comments or feedback are relayed to the class as a whole. For example, if the entire class has issues with a certain question, it would be good to post an announcement explaining why a certain answer choice was correct, and where students can find more information in their text or lectures. In psychology courses, scaffolding is very important: Students need to learn and retain certain core constructs so that they can move on to more complex applications, syntheses, and theories. Thus it is vital to ensure that all students demonstrate an adequate level of knowledge when they leave your course, especially if they plan to continue to upper level courses or graduate courses. For this reason, it is imperative to allot specific time to review tests and quizzes, and take as long as is required to address student concerns.

Assessment of Online Discussion Boards

As discussed throughout this book, communication is key to facilitating online courses, and to boosting online student learning outcomes in psychology. Thus, it is hardly surprising that discussion boards serve as a key activity and assessment in many online courses. The previous chapters (especially chapter 5) have already discussed the creation and implementation of discussion board activities, including the selection of questions and the moderation of student comments or debates. The following section deals with the administrative, assessment side of discussion boards, specifically, how to effectively administer and grade student performance, and how to manage student expectations. While this section does refer specifically to discussion boards, many of the grading strategies and criteria in the following section can also be applied to written work submitted online in general.

Assessment Frameworks

The first step in the successful assessment of student discussion boards involves the instructor selecting an effective framework that helps to promote the goals of the course. The *assessment framework* is best understood as the criteria upon which student discussion performance will be graded. Assessment frameworks can range from rules dictating the frequency and quantity of posts, to specific recommendations for the qualities of the posts themselves, to encouraging students to make posts that help to enhance discussion and community knowledge. The instructor can decide exactly which types of assessment criteria matter most, and these are often closely related to the learning objectives for the course. For example, when students are asked to analyze or assess the findings presented in a research article, the frequency of posts might become less relevant than the ability to critique comments from fellow students and apply content to other relevant research, or to one's real life situation. Likewise, when students are asked to construct knowledge surrounding a topic, or to create or shape interventions, then the frequency of posts and their ability to enhance the discussion might be of central importance. Consider all of these elements and how they might pertain to discussion activities, as well as how long grading might take, as we review the relevant literature on assessment frameworks in greater detail.

Anderson (2008) provides a number of different examples of discussion board assessment frameworks, with a particular highlight on components of feedback and community building. Assessment and grading are envisioned as a mechanism of student support by Anderson (2008), who argues that timely, concise feedback delivered during assessment serves as one of the "most effective" methods for motivating and engaging with students (Shepard, 2000, cited in Anderson, 2008, p. 352). Thus, when grading discussion boards, instructors should ensure that their framework will enable them to provide feedback in a timely way, as close to the actual assignment due date as possible. Second, as we know from previous chapters, the creation of an online learning community is of utmost importance to student performance and can only occur when users share a discourse and construct knowledge together. Thus it is vital that any assessment framework benefits students who work to foster a sense of community (Anderson, 2008; Palloff & Pratt, 1999).

Assessment frameworks for online student discussions in psychology can vary wildly depending upon the instructors' goals and learning objectives for the course. Anderson (2008) discusses the efficacy of contrasting perspectives on assessment, one used by Levine (2002), and one utilized by Dabbagh (2000). Levine (2002) uses the following assessment framework in graduate education courses: Students should focus only on the questions posted; they should make at least two substantial posts; and posts will start at the beginning of the week and continue until the end of the week (such as a Monday through Sunday schedule). Further, Levine (2002) finds it important that students go beyond saying "ditto" or "I agree" with another student, to engaging in discussions that build knowledge and meaning, through synthesizing, expressing observations, discussing a personal experience, or posing follow-up questions.

Dabbagh (2000) takes a contrasting approach by including heightened specifications surrounding the distribution and quantity of posts. For example, he highlights that posts should be evenly distributed during the discussion period, as opposed to clustered during the same day/time, and also dictates that posts should be a minimum of one short paragraph and a maximum of two paragraphs. He also makes allowances for "proper etiquette" including language, typing, grammar, which could also be reworded and presented as "netiquette" as discussed in chapter 2. Like Levine, Dabbagh (2000) also asks students to go beyond a simple "I agree" and explain how and why they agree or disagree with their classmates using examples from the reading or from their own experiences.

The different approaches by Levine (2002) and Dabbagh (2000) highlight the many variable areas of online discussion assessment. Instructors should feel free to select the assessment criteria that works best for them, their students, course goals, and learning objectives. In other words, there are no right or wrong choices in assessment frameworks, and instructors should trust their instincts and use their best discretion when selecting their assessment criteria. Based upon the evidence presented by Anderson

(2008), as well as the authors' experiences and input from other online psychology professors, four key criteria emerge that appear central for discussion assessment frameworks:

1. *Quantity and Distribution of Posts*: The first consideration when grading online discussion boards surrounds the number of posts students will be required to make to receive credit, as well as their distribution. This issue does beg the question, how many posts does a student need to make to demonstrate his or her understanding or expertise in a subject area? While there is no right or wrong answer here, the type of question and the subject area might help to advise the number of required posts. For example, if students are being asked to apply research findings to their own lives, then multiple posts might be required to ensure that the entire question is answered. However, if students are asked to make an argument in support of a point, perhaps only one or two posts are necessary.

A good general heuristic for the quantity of posts that has worked for the authors is as follows: Students should make more than one post, but not more than five. More than one post is set as the minimum to ensure that an actual discussion takes place, as opposed to isolated individual comments. No more than five posts are suggested due to the grading constraints placed upon the instructor. Reading and assigning a grade for each post will increase the level of work exponentially, when we compare 25 students making two posts each (50 total) with 25 students making five posts each (125 total). Given that instructors would want to grade posts in a timely fashion to ensure feedback is delivered, setting a ceiling for the number of posts makes practical sense.

Once the instructor has decided upon the quantity of posts, it might be wise to set up rules regarding the distribution of posts. As suggested by Dabbagh (2000), for example, students should not make all of their posts at the same time, but rather should wait to post after reading the replies and comments from other students. Setting rules like these helps to facilitate actual discussion and discourse, and reduces the likelihood that a student will only access the discussion board once to make isolated posts. While managing the distribution of posts sounds good in theory, in practice it becomes more challenging to implement. What is a reasonable time for posts to be distributed across: An hour, 1 day, 2 or 3 days? Again, there is no correct answer here, and instructors are encouraged to use discretion. If a discussion board becomes available to students on a Monday, with all posts due the following Sunday, then a student who makes all posts on the Monday and Tuesday might miss the more exciting and engaging discussion that happens later on during the week. Likewise, a student who makes all posts on Saturday and Sunday might be too late, making posts when nobody is around to read them or comment before the assignment ends. Recalling past findings discussed in this book that many online students tend to wait until the last minute to complete their assignments, it might be good practice to encourage students to space their posts between the beginning, middle, and end of the week. So in the Monday–Sunday example provided, students who are assigned two posts must make one post between Monday and Wednesday and the other post between Thursday and Sunday. This will ensure a greater exposure to classmates' posts, and should help to boost discussion. Thanks to the technology afforded by sophisticated CMS interfaces, it is very easy for the instructor assigning grades to view the date and time that the post was made.

2. *Quality of Posts*: In addition to addressing the quantitative requirements for a successful post, a good assessment framework should also highlight what is qualitatively viable for full credit. While again this will vary hugely from instructor to instructor, there are a number of features of good discussion posts that may become relevant, including application of concepts to real world situations, critiquing research findings, synthesizing concepts and research, expressing opinions and feelings based upon the assignment, and asking additional questions. Depending upon the type of assignment and instructor goals, it becomes imperative to specify (a) the question(s) that students are to address and (b) what is required for a successful answer. Clarity in directions is key to ensuring that students can succeed, and also vital for managing student expectations. Also consider that if a discussion question is multipart (such as two or three questions) or if it is multiphase (such as making an observation and then asking follow-up questions), students should be instructed whether they should include their responses in the same post, or across multiple posts, and should be reminded to answer all parts of the question!

It also might be worthwhile at this juncture to include limitations on the length of the post. Sometimes in higher education, students can confuse quantity with quality, but instructors know that in terms of online discussion, this is not always the case. It might be worthwhile to explain this, while setting a floor and ceiling for the expected length of a post. For example, "The post should answer this question in at least three sentences, but not longer than two paragraphs." This forces students to remain succinct, to avoid tangents, and to ensure that they focus only on answering the question that they are provided with. From a discussion-based perspective, posts that are too long might actually hinder discourse by either changing the direction of the conversation or stifling it with a burden of too much text. Depending upon the type of assignment, some students might also choose to utilize alternative media, such as videos, flyers, or other multimedia to express their ideas. Make sure to mention at the outset whether the use of non-text-based media is appropriate, and whether this can take the place of an actual post. The authors feel that so long as the multimedia addresses the question and is viewable by the other students in the course, its use could help spur student excitement and discussion.

3. *Discussion Enhancement and Focus:* After detailing the qualitative and quantitative rules for posting, consider how to enhance the discussion itself. As mentioned in this section, discussion can be enhanced when students space their posts throughout the week, when posts do not contain too much text, and when multimedia is integrated into posts. Students can also be evaluated in terms of how their posts fit in with the larger discussion. This is where unconstructive comments like "I agree," "yes," or "ditto" should be discouraged. Rather, students should be encouraged to engage in a variety of alternative strategies to boost discussion, including: The asking of follow-up questions pertaining to the material; expressing how a classmate's comments relate to their own opinion or beliefs; seeking clarification and expansion of ideas; and applying a classmates' comments to relevant research, theory, or real-world situations. While the allocation of points for these kinds of discussion promoting posts is at the instructor's discretion and would depend upon the grading rubric (discussed in the following section), it is clear that instructors should reward students who make an effort to enhance discourse and communication with their classmates. For example, instructors might want to take into consideration the number of replies that a single post generates. If a student posts an idea for an intervention and only one other student responds, how does this compare with a different student posting an intervention and eliciting multiple replies, further questions, and applications to previous studies? It is for the instructor to decide whether the response of other students can serve as a benchmark for the quality of the post, and for the ability of the post to enhance discussion.

At this juncture, the level of focus of the discussion and related posts might also become relevant. Specifically, do the posts stay on topic? It might be challenging to conduct a discussion about research on cognitive dissonance when a student continuously interjects comments about relational satisfaction, for example. In other words, the level of student focus becomes important when assessing whether posts contribute to enhancing the discussion. Generally, online instructors would desire that their students stick as closely as possible to the topic or discussion question. Often tangents can take on interesting and unexpected meaning and even fuel their own discussions, but perhaps these conversations are better housed in the "virtual lounge" or other parts of the discussion board. A discussion forum about cognitive dissonance should really only house comments relating to cognitive dissonance, and so on. Keeping this focus is important for the instructor's ability to grade and assess posts effectively, as well as for student development of understanding and knowledge on a specific topic. While it is true that instructors should refrain from controlling the discussion board, perhaps a simple comment or interjection aimed toward steering the conversation back to the question at hand would not go amiss.

4. *Composition and Netiquette:* Having considered the many substantive elements of discussion assessment, from quantity and distribution of posts, to quality, discussion enhancement and focus, the final assessment area of online discussion surrounds the more stylistic elements of writing style, composition, and tone. First, consider institutional standards and requirements for composition. Is formal written language required? Or are net-speak, abbreviations, and incomplete sentences permitted? Grading criteria regarding composition should be left to the instructor's discretion as well as any policy put forward by the academic institution. Anderson (2008) cites that the issue of formal composition remains "hotly contested" among online educators, some of whom find that the medium lends itself to a different type of language and expression than the traditional spoken or written word (p. 354). In this respect, a research paper might require full sentences, grammatical accuracy, and correct spelling, but a discussion board post that takes on the qualities of a text-based internet chat may not require the same attention to detail. While again this decision rests with the instructor, consider, does the composition of the post meet the standards required by written work at the academic institution? The authors recommend requiring the same level of quality as expected in all written work across online courses, not to make students feel uncomfortable on the discussion board, but to help improve their writing and overall ability to communicate online. Net-speak might seem natural for an online discussion, but encouraging psychology students to use incorrect grammar and incomplete sentences will not benefit them in the long term when they are seeking to compose publications or write theses or dissertations.

After choosing an assessment strategy for composition of language, decide how to ensure that students attend to netiquette while on the discussion board. Recall from previous chapters that netiquette outlines the rules of engagement for online communication, and can include regulations for polite, respectful interactions. Netiquette should be included in the course orientation materials and students should be very clear about maintaining a respectful and nonthreatening tone in their postings. Students should be encouraged to explore their differing opinions, but should do so in the context of a respectful, open, nonjudgmental environment. Assessing student posts for adherence to netiquette procedures is vital to ensure that bullying and threatening language have no place in the online discussion board. For many students, netiquette will be a welcome structure for communication, and assessing grades by their adherence to netiquette should not serve as a problem. Envisioning netiquette as an element of assessment can help to ensure that discussions can be conducted smoothly and openly, without students having fear of reprisal or negative feedback. Netiquette may be especially beneficial to new online students, or individuals who are not accustomed to online communication. For example, by encouraging constructive criticism and feedback instead of disagreement and disorder, netiquette can make the entire online discussion board a more pleasant, learner-focused place.

GRADING RUBRICS

The single most effective way to assess student discussion boards is through a *grading rubric*, which is best understood as the visual representation of the discussion assessment framework, made available to students prior to their completion of the assignment. The many assessment criteria discussed above would be housed in the grading rubric, with points assigned to each element to arrive at an overall score on each discussion board assessment. Using a grading rubric has many benefits. First, by examining the rubric prior to completing the assignment, students can be clear on what is expected of them. Given the importance of managing student expectations when it comes to online grades, this is a very positive step in the right direction. Second, rubrics can greatly help instructors to clarify the grading process. Rubrics are used across online and traditional psychology courses, in contexts like the grading of a student poster presentation, or when assigning grades for free response questions on tests. What makes rubrics for online discussion boards distinct is their ability to organize and simplify the many components required for the task of accurately assessing discussion board performance. Third, rubrics can be programmed into many CMSs such as Blackboard and Moodle, so that the rubric grid or grading criteria will be posted and displayed alongside the assignment itself. When students work on the assignment and when the instructor does the grading, the rubric should be programmed to appear as a handy guide. Fourth, rubrics can help to reduce confusion and student grade appeals. Students who disagree with their assigned grade can approach the instructor and explain how their comments meet the rubric's expectations. While this may or may not lead to a change in that student's grade, it will open a dialogue where students and instructors can share their expectations surrounding performance.

RUBRIC DEVELOPMENT

As alluded to above, the assessment of online discussion assignments is a unique task and therefore requires a unique grading rubric for analysis. Unlike a traditional discussion, paper, test, or quiz, online discussions are required to meet a number of grading criteria, including the four central assessment components: quantity and distribution of posts; quality of posts; discussion enhancement and focus; and composition and netiquette. The arrangement of these components and their allotted points can be configured entirely at the instructor's discretion. To first create a rubric, consider the four steps to rubric development originally presented by Stevens and Levi (2004) in *Introduction to Rubrics*. First, *reflect* on the assignment itself and how the expectations of the assignment will be communicated to students. Will students be provided with a discussion prompt or a specific question to respond to? What will the requirements be for quantity and distribution of posts? Second, *list* all of the learning objectives for the particular assignment. In addition to demonstrating knowledge and understanding of the concepts, will students need to show that they can synthesize different theories and studies, make applications, demonstrate critical thinking, or all of the above? Third, after deciding the main objectives the assignment will reach, *group and label* the objectives and expectations according to differing levels of student performance. What components are required for an excellent performance? How about a good performance or a basic performance? Begin to visualize how these criteria (think: distribution of posts, quality, discussion enhancement and focus, composition, and netiquette) would differ across highly successful and unsuccessful students. As the differing levels of performance begin to take shape, the final step is to *apply* these labels to your grid. Your grid is the graphical representation of grading criteria and points for various performance levels.

Constructing the Grid

Imagine your grid as a two-dimensional space or table where the y-axis (vertical) features the grading criteria that you selected in your listing stage. It might feature four categories, each related to the four main areas of assessment. Perhaps the categories would be more focused on the qualitative elements that reflect higher order thinking, or perhaps there would be a greater emphasis on following quantitative rules regarding length of posts, distribution of posts, number of posts, and grammatical composition. The x-axis (horizontal), should feature the varying performance levels from the labeling stage, ranging from "excellent, good, average, poor" or "distinguished, proficient, basic, and nonperformance," or some alternative combination of these. For ease of use and clarity, try to limit each axis to the top four criteria. Instructors can decide to allocate points for the overall performance, or for each specific assessment criterion. In the first case, overall points would be awarded based upon the entire performance of where the student landed—excellent, good, average, or poor. But, what happens if a student falls into the excellent category for two criteria, and the good category for two criteria? In this type of a situation, it makes a greater amount of sense to award points on an individual basis. In other words, a student who scores excellent in one category and good in the other would have points assigned to reflect this. Based upon this description, a successful rubric grading based off the four assessment criteria mentioned in this chapter might look something like what is shown in Figure 6.1.

Criteria	Excellent (3)	Good (2)	Average (1)	Poor (0)
Quality of Posts	Learner demonstrates excellent understanding of material, clearly integrates readings into posts	Learner knows the material well enough to identify key points and incorporate into posts	Learner makes some connections to the reading although knowledge of material is questionable	Learner does not seem to understand material or incorporate into posts
Distribution and Quantity of Posts	Posts are well distributed throughout the week; more than the sufficient number of posts	Posts are distributed satisfactorily throughout the week; more than or exactly the sufficient number of posts are made	Posts are only somewhat distributed through the week; less than or exactly the sufficient number of posts	Posts are not distributed throughout the week; does not meet the sufficient number of posts
Discussion Enhancement & Focus	Learner does an excellent job to ask follow-up questions, give feedback or apply student comments; stays very focused on questions	Learner does a good job to ask follow-up questions, give feedback or apply student comments; stays somewhat focused on questions	Learner makes some attempt to enhance discussion by asking follow-up questions, giving feedback or applying student comments; learner focus could be improved	Learner makes no attempt to enhance discussion and uses "I agree" or other types of follow-up; learner posts do not remain focused on topic
Composition & Netiquette	High quality grammar, spelling, composition; student is polite and respectful	1-2 mistakes with grammar, spelling, composition; netiquette is sufficient	3-4 mistakes with grammar, spelling, composition; netiquette is questionable	More than 4 mistakes with grammar, spelling or composition; problem or violation of netiquette.
Grading	10-12 = A	7-9 = B	4-6 = C	1-3 = D

Figure 6.1 *Sample Grading Rubric—Lower Level Psychology Course.*

This rubric serves only as an example, and based upon it, instructors can pick and choose their grading dimensions and the qualities that apply to their assignment. A note about grading: The grading criteria should be displayed somewhere on the rubric, or in the syllabus, such as, 10–12 points = A, 7–9 points = B, and so on, then students will know the number of points available, and what is expected of them if they are to receive an A on the assignment. In the above example, only a total of 12 points are available. This means that students who score lower than 6 points will effectively fail, unless the assignment is graded on a curve. Some instructors prefer to have a greater number of points available, which can be altered at their discretion. Alternatively, some would prefer that each category does not hold the same weight. Even though composition and netiquette may be important, they may only constitute 10% of the overall grade, whereas the quality of the post might count for 40%. In this example, instructors can calculated a weighted grade based upon a rubric by multiplying the score on each section by its weight. So, a student with the following scores would see grades adjusted as shown in Figure 6.2.

The score of 3 on quality of posts would be multiplied by 4 (for 40%) to arrive at 12, the 2 on distribution by 2 (for 20%) to arrive at 4, the 3 for discussion by 3 (for 30%), and the 1 for netiquette and composition by 1 (10%). The score would then be totaled as: $(3 \times 4) + (2 \times 2) + (3 \times 3) + (1 \times 1) = 26$ out of a total of 40 points. In case you were wondering how we arrived at 40 points, use this simple rule. Multiply the total points available in each category (excellent = 3, in this case) by the weight and then sum for the total. $(3 \times 4)= 12, (3 \times 2) = 6, (3 \times 3) = 9, (3 \times 1) = 3$, and when these are summed the total is 40. This is only an example of one of many ways to weigh and calculate grades using rubrics. Instructors who utilize other strategies and techniques will still be able to integrate them with their rubric.

The rubric above shows that it is possible to clearly assess learners on many important criteria of online discussions. Notice that arbitrary

Criteria	Excellent (3)	Good (2)	Average (1)	Poor (0)
Quality of Posts (40%)	3			
Distribution and Quantity of Posts (20%)		2		
Discussion Enhancement & Focus (30%)	3			
Composition & Netiquette (10%)			1	
Grade:				

Figure 6.2 Grading Rubric Calculations.

specifications can be incorporated into the rubric, such as the number of grammatical mistakes that qualify for each category or the number of posts that qualify for each category. Also consider that double-barreled categories can make it difficult to assign a grade. For example, take discussion enhancement and focus. These are two separate constructs being graded in a single box, not ideal for the validity of the measure! Let's say a student does a great job asking follow-up questions, but does not stay focused on target. In this case, how should the student be graded on this criterion? It would be possible to average scores across two categories to come up with a grade in this situation. While it might be time consuming, averaging across two categories may also be a fair way of assessing students using this system. Alternatively, instructors can simplify by picking and choosing the criteria that are most relevant to learning outcomes in the course. A good balance might want to include: protocol requirements (such as length, distribution, number of posts), the extent to which discussion has been promoted by the post (such as frequency of student replies, focus on the topic, giving good feedback, etc.), and finally, knowledge and understanding of the topic (including critical thinking, communication of ideas, application to the field, theory synthesis, etc.). The exact distribution of these in a grading rubric in psychology may depend upon the type of course itself (training, scholarly, or research-based), the instructor's preferences regarding grading and protocol violations, the program goals and learning objectives, and the level of the course.

Consider, for example, how a higher level psychology instructor would be more concerned with critical thinking, advanced knowledge, and theoretical or practical applications, as opposed to the stylistic elements of the post, or the mechanical facets of the discussion. This type of a rubric may be much more qualitatively focused, with one large category to encompass technical elements that include length of post, distribution of post, number of posts, grammar, spelling, and writing style. In the following example, the "communication of ideas" section can be used to measure how discourse was facilitated and whether students gave constructive feedback or asked follow-up questions. This example should help clarify how instructors can specifically tailor rubrics to meet their learning goals (see Figure 6.3).

"Fish Bowl" Approach to Online Discussion Assessment

When assessing online discussion boards, instructors might also seek alternative methods for simultaneously grading and enhancing quality of the discussion between students. While the methods for ensuring higher level critical thinking in discussions are covered elsewhere in this book (see

Criteria (% of score)	Excellent (3)	Good (2)	Average (1)	Poor (0)
Understanding Key Concepts (30%)	Learner demonstrates high levels of expertise and excellent knowledge of key theories, concepts or research studies	Learner demonstrates good proficiency and some knowledge of key theories, concepts or research studies	Learner demonstrates average proficiency and basic knowledge of key theories, concepts or research studies	Learner demonstrates below average proficiency and limited knowledge of key theories, concepts or research studies
Critical Thinking (30%)	Learner demonstrates excellent proficiency in assessing, analyzing and making applications from theory to practice	Learner demonstrates good proficiency in assessing, analyzing and making applications from theory to practice	Learner demonstrates average proficiency in assessing, analyzing and making applications from theory to practice	Learner demonstrates poor proficiency in assessing, analyzing and making applications from theory to practice
Communication of Ideas (20%)	Learner communicates ideas very clearly and effectively asks for clarification or follow-up	Learner communicates ideas with good clarity and asks for some clarification or follow-up	Learner communicates ideas with average clarity and asks for minimal clarification or follow-up	Learner communicates ideas with poor clarity and does not ask for clarification or follow-up
Technical Elements (20%)	Learner adheres to all technical rules including number of posts, length of posts, grammar and spelling rules	Learner does not adhere to one of the following: number of posts, length of posts, grammar or spelling rules	Learner does not adhere to two of the following: number of posts, length of posts, grammar or spelling rules	Learner does not adhere to three or more of the following: number of posts, length of posts, grammar or spelling rules

Figure 6.3 *Sample Grading Rubric—Upper Level Psychology Course.*

chapters 3 and 5), it is sometimes useful to ask the entire class to observe a discussion or interaction between a few students, dubbed the "Fishbowl Approach." This approach, taken from the traditional classroom, is best utilized in online simulations or role-plays, debates, or at any time when the instructor seeks to improve student responses to open-ended questions or encourage them to express themselves and appreciate each other's ideas (Douglas & Johnson, 2010; Opitz, 2008). In the traditional classroom the "observation" of the discussion literally involves the rest of the class sitting still and watching like traditional observers, but in the online learning environment, observation can be extended to include reading an asynchronous discussion thread, or viewing a live video, audio, or text-based chat session, either streaming or recorded. When two students interact, the rest of the class observes, and can either make notes, comments, or assign grades via peer review.

To develop your "Fishbowl," Opitz (2008) recommends first creating your grading rubric, based upon the goals and expected outcomes of the activity. Using the rubric approach outlined above, think about what you hope to achieve by asking students to observe the discussion: Should the observers create insightful follow-up questions? Or should they be asked to comment on the types of communication styles used? Will the discussion focus on a specific course topic and if so, which one? What is the end product, a specific theory, quote, idea, or suggestion? Will student reflections on the fishbowl be graded as well? Once the rubric has been developed, encourage the class as a whole to discuss the goals of the assignment first, so that everyone is on the same page. Next, says Opitz (2008), give your thought provoking question, or specific problem to be solved, to the discussants. Who gets to be the discussant? It might be useful to solicit brave volunteers for the first few runs of this activity, knowing that all students will serve as discussants at some point during the semester. During the fishbowl exercise, encourage observers to focus on both the discussion process and products. The discussion *process* highlights how higher level ideas are expressed and shared; the discussion *product* refers to the content and thinking developed by the discussion. After the fishbowl exercise is over, Opitz (2008) recommends acknowledging the efforts of the discussants, and any potential nervousness and anxiety they might have experienced. For the final step, observers will be assessed according to the criteria in the rubric, including their comments and feedback on process and products, their follow-up questions, their peer grading of the discussion, and any other important criteria determined by the instructor.

Managing Discussion Expectations

Undoubtedly, online psychology students enter the online classroom with differing expectations surrounding the level of interaction and engagement expected of them to succeed. Just as some students will enter the course with the intention of making posts every day, or even several times per day, others will enter the course under the assumption that one post per day is sufficient. To reconcile these different expectations, not to mention varying levels of comfort and familiarity with technology, keep a list of rules for the discussion board handy and email it to students before their first discussion assignment. This list should include chosen criteria for the four key elements of discussion board assessment: quantity and distribution, quality of posts, discussion enhancement and focus, and writing and composition. These components should also be included in rubrics for discussion assignments and posted on the discussion board throughout the semester. Common concerns for students being assessed via online discussion board are discussed below, along with possible solutions.

How Is My Grade Being Calculated?

Even when provided with a list or rubric for assessment by their instructors, online students can still experience confusion surrounding the exact calculation for their grade. While some instructors balk at the thought of making the online discussion grading process so objective, the reality is that some students do expect to see a standardized system where their grade will be calculated according to a specific formula. Using an exact method to calculate grades should greatly reduce grade complaints and student frustration. By enabling them to know exactly what percentage or weight each grading criterion counts for, students will be less inclined to question their grades, and email instructors questions about their grades, or vent their frustration to the instructor, their classmates, their friends, or the internet. The objectivity of grading itself does not necessarily cancel out the many subjective and individual ways in which students communicate their ideas, express critical thinking, or make applications or follow-up questions. Instead, it offers a canvas for students to paint their thoughts and ideas, and the instructor can use the rubric and weighting scale to assign grades to these. For example, in the above rubric, 20% of the weight is assigned to communication of ideas, 30% to critical thinking, and so on.

It is important for students to know how their grades are calculated to ensure that their expectations of assessment are not violated. There is a certain element of fairness here that should remain intact, so that a student who adheres to the necessary rubric criteria can see this reflected in the grade, and so on. A failure to accurately communicate how grades will be calculated and assigned can lead to the following problem regarding debates over points.

I Deserve More Points! Can I Make a Few More Posts to Get There?

Sometimes students do not get the grades they want. This is true the world over in education, and yet in the online classroom, concerns over grading can be especially common. Earlier in this book, the authors discussed how feelings of anonymity may be responsible for the online students' ability to ask questions or make requests for grade changes that would not really happen in the physical classroom. Sending an email with the hope of affecting change requires much less effort and commitment than approaching an instructor after class and asking him or her face-to-face. In terms of online discussions, a disconnect can sometimes arise when students believe that they are adhering to the grading rubric with their posts, even when they are not. A student might believe that an adequate application to past research has been made, whereas the instructor will find that this application was incorrect, unclear, or unfounded. In this situation, a simple email to clarify the confusion, or leaving a follow-up post for this student might help them to see where they went wrong. Commonly, this type of comment will be followed by an email or post by the student requesting clarification and correct the mistake in order to receive credit. This can also occur often when students make mistakes regarding grammar, spelling, and composition, and upon losing points they might ask to re-post with grammatical corrections to earn back the points that were lost.

Should students be allowed to modify, correct, and improve their discussion posts for additional points? On the one hand, a significant part of the learning process deals with students who seek to improve themselves, and by giving them this opportunity they can learn where they went wrong and demonstrate a commitment to positive change. On the other hand, it would seem unfair to students who submit adequate, correct posts the first time to allow those students who submit an incomplete or below-par assignment the chance to correct it for additional points. Allowing students to make corrections and additional posts after the submission date might remove the motivation for students to complete and submit the assignment to the best of their ability the first time around. Whatever your stance, the *can I submit extra/more/again??* issue should be addressed by the instructor at the beginning of the term, and the same rule should be used to apply to all students.

A cautionary note to instructors who decide that students can correct their posts after the fact for grade changes: This can double or even triple your workload. If the instructor is required to reassess all older posts, and compare these with newer posts to determine a new grade, this can become an extremely time-consuming process. However, if you still would like students to have the opportunity to correct their mistakes, consider grading these changes according to the entire semester, not one assignment. In other words, it might help to inform students who correct their posts that at the end of the semester the instructor will review their posts and determine if their corrections merit an increase in their overall course grade. In this approach, the changes may or may not actually translate to concrete grade changes. This strategy makes it possible to assess improvements based upon the instructor's feedback, while ensuring that the instructor is not overwhelmed with work, and that students still maintain motivation to submit on time the first time around.

I'm Having Trouble with Posting and Now I Missed the Deadline: What Should I Do?

While online orientation should ensure that students are proficient at using the discussion board, occasionally things go wrong and students may miss a deadline, or experience technical problems with the discussion board. Will they be allowed to submit a late post? Once again, the instructor's decision here should be reflective of his or her overall course policy. If students are allowed one late assignment, then perhaps that student could make the post after the assignment was due for partial credit. Some online instructors will not give extensions for technical problems that lead to missed assignments, such as the discussion board not displaying a post, or kicking a student out of the CMS (which although rare, does happen). If you are the type of instructor who does not give these extensions, let the students know unequivocally during orientation. If you are the type of instructor who does grant these extensions, just ensure that a student is not taking advantage of your kindness by constantly making excuses to submit assignments late. The authors favor a "one time" policy where students who have a technical problem or miss a discussion once will be allowed to make up the assignment, but repeated mistakes will not be met with the same amount of leniency.

I Would Like More (or Less) Feedback!

The process of giving discussion board feedback and communicating with students via asynchronous posting is discussed elsewhere in this book; however, at this juncture it does seem relevant to consider some basic ground rules for feedback giving when using a discussion board rubric. For example, *do* explain to students how their grades have been calculated based upon the varying criteria in the rubric. *Do* make comments on posts, asking for clarification, expansion, or application if you feel a student's post was insufficient. *Do* give positive feedback and encouragement to student posts. *Do* use warm, ingratiating language and try to foster a spirit of community. *Do not* take center stage on the discussion board, be too critical, or feel the need to respond to every single post.

An online criminology student interviewed for this book gave the example of a professor who was a semiretired expert in his field of criminal profiling. While the students were initially excited to be taught by an expert, they became concerned and almost wary of posting when the instructor met every single post made on every discussion board with a follow-up question, criticism, or request for clarification. While online instructors should absolutely feel entitled to make comments as they see fit, in this particular instance students became fearful of making posts, often waiting until one minute before the due date in hopes that their own posts might escape the critical eyes of the instructor. Given the importance of open dialogue, community, and shared discourse, the overly critical, overly feedback-focused approach did not foster discussion—in fact, it had the opposite effect. While this is only one example, it does suggest that commenting and questioning every single post made by every student might be a bit extreme, and at the very worst it can stifle discourse completely by creating a culture of fear.

Just as making too many comments and criticisms can stifle a discussion, being an absent instructor can also stifle the discussion because students might not feel like anyone is even reading or caring about what they have to say. Therefore while it is important not to take control or take center stage, it is important to be present and to let students know that their posts are important and that you are keeping up with their dialogues. The authors suggest doing what feels most natural, and also, trying to achieve a balanced level of involvement. One handy heuristic used by the authors is that instructors should make some kind of a comment on 25 to 50% of all posts or comments: Less than this feels uninvolved; more than this can feel overbearing. Select different categories of posts to comment on across the spectrum of student performances. For example, highlight and give positive feedback to the most successful, top scoring posts. This will make those students feel good, and show the rest of the class what they need to do to succeed. When discovering a post that asks a question, that requires a follow-up, or that needs clarification, make sure to address it in order to facilitate discourse and knowledge building. Finally, try to restrain criticism to the few posts that are the most problematic. And even when giving out criticism, keep it constructive. Rather than telling a student that his or her posting was poor, subpar, or unacceptable, tell that student that his or her ideas could have been communicated more clearly.

ASSESSMENT THROUGH E-PORTFOLIOS

The concept of a portfolio that highlights previous work, research activities, and educational background is hardly new to those of us who have attended graduate school in the social sciences. Not surprisingly, the idea of collecting and displaying a portfolio of one's own work and past achievements has been translated to the web and to the online classroom through *e-portfolios*, broadly defined as a body of "electronic evidence assembled and managed by a user" including written text, videos, podcasts, images, blogs, wikis, web-links, and any other type of electronic file (Wikipedia, 2012c). In the context of online psychology assessment, a student might be asked to create an e-portfolio on a specific topic throughout the semester, collecting relevant articles, videos, and websites, while producing and incorporating thought papers, reflections, journal entries, research proposals, study materials, and measurement scales. Such a collection of materials might lead to a full-blown research paper, scholarly article, master's thesis, or dissertation. Alternatively, the e-portfolio might serve as an accumulation of materials and past works over the course of several semesters, reflecting the student's identity and growth toward meeting her or his program requirements. This type of e-portfolio can demonstrate many achievements including a video of the student teaching in the classroom or working in the field; links to their related blog posts, wikis, or Facebook posts; links to teaching or workplace evaluations; websites they created about themselves or their research; podcasts they have created; reflection papers or thought pieces; published works or other written content. This e-portfolio can then be utilized in the job or graduate school application process.

Are e-portfolios a useful and viable assessment technique? Research conducted by Driessen and colleagues (Driessen, 2008; Driessen, Muijtjens, van Tartwijk, & van der Vleuten, 2007) indicates that the use of e-portfolios can increase student motivation and stimulate self-reflection and metacognition. In this respect, e-portfolios can be utilized to serve as an integral part of the learner-centered approach to assessment, encouraging student growth, awareness, and critical thinking. While portfolios seem to offer a valuable assessment platform, does an online, electronic portfolio offer more to the user than a paper portfolio? E-portfolios tend to be perceived as more user friendly than regular portfolios, due to the ability to easily share information and to incorporate links, multimedia, and make use of the other web 2.0 technology (Woodward & Bablohy, 2004). Further, while traditional portfolios must utilize a linear structure, e-portfolios afford the opportunity to transmit information through a "network" structure, courtesy of the use of links and the differing combinations of multimedia elements (van Wesel & Prop, 2008). It also appears that students spend a greater amount of time on e-portfolios compared with traditional portfolios (Driessen et al., 2007). In a study comparing students in the same context using either e-portfolios or traditional portfolios, van Wesel and Prop (2008) found that learning outcomes were significantly higher when students used e-portfolios.

Based upon this review of literature, it seems that e-portfolios can function as a valuable assessment platform in online psychology courses.

To assign an e-portfolio, first decide whether the duration will be course specific (either for an entire semester or for a few weeks of the semester). If you are a mentor or administrator in a psychology program, then the portfolio will probably incorporate work across many semesters. Second, for class assessment, help students decide the topic, as well as the desired end product (i.e., is it a research paper, journal article, thought piece, or a thesis?). Third, provide students with a list of acceptable content for their e-portfolio and select a certain number of required elements. A sample prompt might read something like this: *Students must submit six of the following to their e-portfolio before they draft their research proposal: Journal entry, thought paper, podcast, PowerPoint presentation, video, article, wiki, blog, Facebook post, web-link.* Once the duration, topic, and specific content has been decided upon, it's up to the student to gather the material and present it in a meaningful way. Many CMSs now incorporate e-portfolio hosting or software, which enables easy storage of data and easy sharing of the contents of the portfolio with the instructor and the class. One of the most prominent software platforms for creating and managing student portfolios is www.eportfolio.org, which offers instructors the opportunity to assign portfolio projects with grading rubrics and comment and score students' work online.

TROUBLESHOOTING: REDUCING ACADEMIC DISHONESTY ONLINE

Issues with academic dishonesty undoubtedly come to mind when discussing the assessment of online students, due mostly to the absence of face-to-face conduct during assessments. For example, without direct visual contact, how can we tell if students are who they say they are? How do we know they are not cheating? These types of questions are only natural. First, we need to come to a consensus about what academic dishonesty actually means. The authors encourage online educators to imagine academic dishonesty through the lens of Gallant (2008, p. 10) who envisions academic dishonesty itself as being best understood as having five separate components:

1. *Plagiarism*: Using another's words or ideas without correct citations. In online courses where students submit written work electronically, the direct "cut and paste" from websites, as well as the submission of papers purchased from paper mill websites, would both constitute plagiarism.
2. *Fabrication*: Making up numbers, information, data, or results and reporting them. In online psychology courses this could include students who fabricate data for their research papers.

3. *Falsification:* Altering or manipulating data, results, information, or numbers and reporting them. Again, in online psychology courses this type of academic dishonesty seems especially relevant to research papers and assignments.

4. *Misrepresentation:* Falsely representing oneself or one's efforts. In online courses, issues of misrepresentation are possible if the instructor is not able to verify whether the student completing the assessment is the same as the student listed on the roster.

5. *Misbehavior:* Acting in ways that are counter to instructions or expectations. In online courses this could include collaboration on assignments such as papers or tests when such collaboration was forbidden by the instructor.

IS ACADEMIC DISHONESTY MORE LIKELY TO OCCUR IN ONLINE CLASSES?

Since the first studies conducted on student-reported academic dishonesty by Bowers (1964), it appears that overall, its prevalence has been steadily rising (McCabe 2001–2002, 2005). In general, anywhere from 50% to 75% of students report engaging in some kind of cheating (Burrus, McGoldrick, & Schulmann, 2007), with some studies showing that forms of academic dishonesty associated with technology are increasing, such as "copy and paste" forms of plagiarism. One study by McCabe (2005) showed that this type of plagiarism increased from 10% of students in 1995 to 41% of students in 2005. In this respect, both technology and the internet can help to enable academic dishonesty by potentially obscuring the true individual enrolled in the class, by providing access to materials that can be easily plagiarized, by facilitating collaboration between students, or affording the opportunity to purchase written materials from online paper mills (Epilon, 2007).

The U.S. government in particular has highlighted issues of misrepresentation by passing the Higher Education Opportunity Act of 2008. This act asks that all institutions that offer online courses "*have a process through which the institution establishes that the student who registers in a distance education or correspondence education course or program is the same student who participates in and completes the program and receives the academic credit*" (HEOA: Issue 10, 2009). While the HEOA law in particular highlights concerns over misrepresentation, the authors encourage taking a broader view of academic dishonesty that incorporates the many contexts (falsification, fabrication, plagiarism, and misbehavior) as well.

In spite of the potential temptations afforded by the online environment, and the possible issues surrounding misrepresentation, there has yet to be any research published to confirm that online students are more likely to engage in plagiarism than students in traditional face-to-face courses (Burrus et al., 2007; Varvel, 2005). In fact, the research that has been conducted tends to demonstrate no significant differences between incidents of academic dishonesty in online versus traditional classroom students. For example, Grijalva, Nowell, and Kerkvliet (2006) surveyed nearly 800 online college students and found that the prevalence of cheating in online courses was equivalent to the amount of cheating in an in-person course. Research has also demonstrated that online instructors do not perceive that online students participate in academic dishonesty more frequently than students in a face-to-face classroom. In their interviews of 256 online instructors in the University of Texas system, McNabb and Olmstead (2009) found that the perceptions of academic dishonesty in online versus on-campus courses did not differ. This lack of any significant perceived difference was found across a number of dimensions including the likelihood of cheating and the opportunities that students have to cheat. While faculty members at some institutions may maintain that online courses are more prone to academic dishonesty, these faculty members are usually individuals who have never taught a class online (McNabb & Olmstead, 2009).

Strategies to Reduce Academic Dishonesty

Although research has not indicated that academic dishonesty is more prevalent in online courses, numerous online educators have nonetheless developed strategies to reduce cheating, plagiarism, and problems of misrepresentation. Olt (2002) developed three key strategies to reduce online academic dishonesty: policing, prevention, and virtue. Policing refers to punishing students who participate in academic dishonesty, whereas prevention refers to reducing opportunities to engage in academic dishonesty, and virtue encourages students to strive for academic integrity. Using focus groups with online educators, McNabb and Olmstead (2009) developed a similar system for reducing academic dishonesty, comprised of course design, communication, and collaboration. For *course design*, it appears that some assignments lend themselves to plagiarism or cheating better than others, and that instructors should be encouraged to select assessments that make academic dishonesty unlikely. These assessments should include critical thinking, opportunities for interstudent collaboration to promote authenticity and honesty, and rubrics to clarify the grading criteria so students do not become confused. According to the focus groups, the assignments that best promote honesty are ones that emphasize student individuality and identity, and encourage them to explore and analyze issues as opposed to focusing on memorization or grades. Second, *communication with students* is vital to ensure academic honesty, and includes providing grading rubrics, an academic honesty policy that students should agree to (or an honor code), and perhaps a lesson communicating what constitutes academic dishonesty and how to avoid it. These findings are echoed by others in the field who have discussed promoting academic honesty by making students acutely aware of the definitions of plagiarism, cheating, and falsification (such as Sewell et al., 2010). Finally, *collaboration between students* was identified as a key factor in promoting academic honesty, although it was more challenging to describe. The underlying idea here is that students who have a stake in the outcome of a project, and who are required to demonstrate an honest, authentic self to their classmates should be less likely to cheat. In this respect, when students can encourage each other to develop ideas and take pride in their own original content, academic dishonesty should be less likely.

Judging by these studies, it appears that different types of assessments may perhaps require different strategies to promote academic honesty. For example, much has been made over online testing, specifically, issues over misrepresentation. Recall, federal regulations require all accredited institutions that offer online education to put a process in place to ensure that students are who they say they are. At some institutions, this means giving the tests at an on-campus proctored location, or even using a remote proctoring service as described in a case study by Bedford, Gregg, and Clinton (2009). In this study, the authors asked a small group of students to evaluate, adopt, and install Remote Proctor, an electronic device that verifies the user's identity using biometric and photographic information. The researchers concluded that due to its low cost and functionality, this technology "may be a valuable resource to colleges and universities when determining that students are actually doing their own work" (Bedford et al., 2009, p. 237).

Proctor-U has made huge advances in the field of remote proctoring, by using a web-cam to identify users. Proctor-U (www.proctoru.com), which promises the use of "Real People, Real Proctoring," has seen exponential growth since its inception in 2008, now offering real-time proctoring services to over 100 colleges and universities, including Columbia College, University of California at Irvine, University of Texas, and even for Marine and Army personnel completing their education online while stationed in Iraq and Afghanistan. In 2011 alone, Proctor-U saw the volume of online tests and exams that it proctors rise from 20 to 30% every month. Proctor-U works by logging in and connecting to the student's computer screen via the internet web-cam, and requesting photo identification and answers to a variety of security questions to ensure that the student is who he or she claims to be. The company claims that this will help to reduce cheating, academic dishonesty, and misrepresentation, and judging by the massive increase in utilization of these services during the last year, higher education tends to agree. Proctor-U argues that their real-life proctors "can see the student, see what they are doing, and know who they are monitoring... while adhering to the highest accreditation standards in the industry" (Proctor-U, 2012).

What if an on-campus location is not an option, and technology such as Remote Proctor or Proctor-U is not available? Consider the following scenario: An individual accesses his or her online banking website by typing in a name and password, and perhaps answering some security questions or entering an access code. The same individual then enters online banking and makes a payment to a credit card company, or transfers funds to another account. Can we assume that the person who logged in is the same person who owns the account? According to the world's financial institutions, Yes! If entering specific log-in criteria is an accepted method of managing our money, then similar protocols should also be accepted methods of logging in to online courses. However, bank account websites do get hacked, just in the same way that online courses can get hacked, or users can give their information to other parties and ask them to sign in. Currently, a universal strategy has not been adopted across online educators or institutions to deal with issues of misrepresentation. Rather, it is assumed (just like in the banking scenario) that a user with a unique name and password is logging in as themselves. Perhaps in the not too distant future, institutions will be able to check the IP address of the computer being used in the online course, to confirm that it belongs to, or resides with, the actual user of the course. Likewise, software that incorporates biometric information, such as an online scanned finger print, may only be a few years away (Bedford et al., 2009).

In their (2009) article on "Best Practice Strategies to Promote Academic Integrity in Online Education," the WCET Working Group on Academic Integrity and Student Verification (2009) does not directly provide instructions for dealing with student misrepresentation, but they do highlight security concerns surrounding student and instructor passwords. For example, they argue that students should use "secure logins" to access all course documents, and that instructors should "use a robust user name and password to protect their computer-based gradebook, and keep a printed copy in a secure place in case students are able to hack into the computer system" (WCET, 2009, p. 3). While unlikely, security concerns are something that all online professors should remain wary of. Many simple steps can help to improve instructor security. For example, when logging into the online course from a public or remote location, always ensure that the last thing you do on that computer is log out from your class. Also, make sure that you clean your work and home computers for spyware or other malicious software that may expose your hard drive to risk or viruses. If you believe you might have been hacked, report it to the academic institution and your CMS provider immediately.

In many ways, the relevant literature shows that differing strategies to reduce academic dishonesty can be implemented depending upon the nature of the assignment itself. For example, we all know that the discussion board is the heart of the online courses, but are there a specific set of rules that can help reduce academic dishonesty specifically for online discussions? According to Olt (2009), yes, "it is possible to deter plagiarism of discussion board threads through design and facilitation" (Olt, 2009, p. 222). Based upon a review of the relevant literature and discussions with other online instructors, Olt (2009) developed seven key strategies for reducing plagiarism in online discussions:

1. *Ensure that discussion questions encourage higher order thinking skills.* As mentioned throughout this chapter, questions that engage higher order thinking skills require more complicated, in-depth responses than can be afforded by simply cutting and pasting an answer from another source. Olt (2009) cites the three different higher order thinking skill questions proposed by Bradley, Thom, Hayes, and Hay (2008), including *course link questions* (asking students to link a course topic or idea with another source), *brainstorming questions* (asking questions that help lead to ideas or resolutions to problems), and *direct link questions* (asking for analysis or synthesis of a topic, idea, or article).

2. *Relate discussion to the course as a whole.* Olt (2009) cites some findings to reinforce the notion that students will plagiarize less when they perceive their assignment as meaningful and useful (such as McLafferty & Foust, 2004). The argument here is that if students believe they are improving their own learning and abilities, they will be less likely to copy and more likely to express their own original ideas.

3. *Rotate the curriculum.* Students sometimes share answers, or record them and pass them on to future classes. By changing the questions instructors can easily ensure that this does not happen. Olt (2009) cites comments by Born (2003) on the importance of rotating and varying questions, prompts, and articles each term.

4. *Encourage interactivity.* Recall the research discussed throughout this book highlighting the importance of an online "sense of community" to enhance online learning. According to Olt (2009), the

trust and respect involved in this type of community in and of itself serves as a deterrent to academic dishonesty (the author also cites work from McLafferty & Foust, 2004, to support this point).

5. *Ensure that instructors take an active role in online discussions.* According to Mandernach, Forrest, Babutzke, and Manker (2009), instructor interactivity is "the key to promoting students' critical thinking" (p. 54). Olt (2009) cites this study, as well as an article by Thomas (2002) explaining how instructors have the potential to promote critical thinking. Olt (2009) argues that to do this, instructors should always respond to direct questions from students, intervene to clarify issues, redirect when questions go astray, ask probing questions to encourage students to think more deeply, and introduce new ideas to promote discussion (p. 225).

6. *Ensure the workload is manageable.* When students become stressed and overwhelmed, they may become more likely to plagiarize. Grijalva, Nowell, and Kerkvliet (2006) refer to this as "unintentional cheating" where students engage in academic dishonesty in a moment of panic, and may resort to copying and pasting or improper citations. Olt (2009) does remind instructors that "it is not possible to quantify the ideal number of discussion questions in an online post," but generally students should be required to make one post of their own, and respond to a few other posts from their classmates. Making this requirement too strict or extreme may encourage students to revert to plagiarism in order to complete their assignments on time.

7. *Assess discussions and provide feedback.* When instructors provide feedback, especially formative feedback, this can encourage students to develop more thorough and detailed comprehensions of their course materials. Olt (2009) reminds us that formative feedback can help foster trust and sense of community between instructor and students, which can in turn lead to reductions in academic dishonesty.

Thanks to programs like Turn-it-In (www.turnitin.com) and Plagiarism Detect (www.plagiarismdetect.com), it has become very easy for instructors to scan written work for plagiarism, ranging from discussion board posts to longer papers that are submitted in online courses. These types of antiplagiarism programs, which are already integrated into the most common CMSs like Blackboard and Moodle, scan the written document for its level of "originality" after it is submitted. The term *originality* here refers to the percentage of the text that is the student's original work, compared to the percentage of the text that has been derived from other sources. These programs will highlight exactly where the text from other sources has been derived from, including specific websites, research articles, textbooks, or other student papers. Note that instructors have a variety of ever growing options with antiplagiarism software, including that they can separate the "works cited" from the sources without any citations. In this respect, the originality report might indicate that the paper is 78% original, with the remaining 22% all derived from sources that are cited correctly in the text. In this case, the student has not plagiarized and the software will indicate this by highlighting the "works cited." This previous breakdown is very different from a student whose report is 78% original, with 22% of the paper being copied directly from another source without any citations. The authors have seen limited cases of plagiarized papers submitted through Turn-it-In, including one that was comprised almost entirely of excerpts directly copied and pasted from Wikipedia.

In addition to using antiplagiarism software, the WCET Working Group on Academic Integrity and Student Verification also presents a number of tips that can help to reduce academic dishonesty in written work. These include requiring an annotated bibliography and submission of all sources, requiring an abstract, requiring a submission of draft and bibliography prior to the submission date, requiring students to create a project plan that is approved by the instructor before they write the paper itself, and not allowing last minute changes in topic of the paper (WCET, 2009, p. 3). Also, several suggestions have been made for examining a work that might be plagiarized, including comparing the writing style of the paper to the student's past discussion board posts, comparing the writing throughout the paper for consistency, noting any strange or jargony sentences that do not fit with the flow of the paper, and highlighting writing that reads more like a textbook or news article and less like a student paper (p. 3). If the instructor notices any of these trends in the paper, then it might be worth investigating further.

What is an online instructor to do when plagiarism is suspected, such as when the antiplagiarism software produces an originality report that is unsatisfactory? First, please refer to the institution's academic honesty policy. Some institutions require immediate notification when a plagiarized work is submitted by a student, including emailing a copy of the originality report to the dean or other administrators for their review. Other institutions will allow the instructor to first attempt to resolve the situation, usually by emailing a copy of the report to the student and explaining that proper citations were not utilized. Unfortunately, as instructors we can never be sure if the plagiarism occurred due to lack of knowledge about proper citations, or if it was intentional cheating, or "accidental" cheating due to stress and lack of time to finish the assignment. It might be useful to email the student and explain the problem, and ask them to resubmit the paper using their own words and proper citations. When an originality report appears problematic, communication between the instructor, student, and academic department is of central importance. Note that policies on plagiarism can vary wildly: In some institutions, a plagiarized paper yields an immediate F in the course. In other institutions (including the California Community College system, for example), students may receive a grade of zero on their plagiarized work, but this work does not constitute them receiving a failing grade in the course. Always check with your academic department for their most up-to-date policies for dealing with potentially plagiarized written work. If your academic institution does not have a policy in place for dealing with suspected plagiarism in online courses, at the next faculty meeting ask your department chair to create one!

Just as discussion boards and written work can benefit from certain protocols aimed to reduce academic dishonesty, cheating during online testing can also be reduced by using many of the tips already discussed in this chapter. According to the WCET Working Group on Academic Integrity and Student Verification, the likelihood of cheating or academic dishonesty on testing is reduced when a test bank of questions is used, so that not all students have the same test. In addition, use randomized question orders and forced-completion so that students cannot go back and retake the test or change their answers; showing only one question at a time can also reduce cheating. The WCET study also suggests password-protecting exams to help ensure that the person enrolled in the course is the one taking the exam. In addition, it is possible to utilize a web browser lock-down program during testing so that students cannot access the internet on their computer while they are taking a test or exam (WCET, 2009, p. 3). Instructors can also benefit from waiting until the entire class completes the exam before giving any feedback to students. Finally, WCET (2009) suggests that instructors assume that all tests will be open book, and select questions accordingly.

While it is true that the strategies discussed in this chapter may not curb online academic dishonesty completely, they can help to empower instructors to adapt their assessments to the new rules of the online environment. Keep in mind that technology and the online classroom is constantly improving and evolving, and as we see antiplagiarism software already incorporated into the CMS, in only a few years we might see remote proctor and biometric log-in information used to deal with issues of misrepresentation. Future directions and advanced applications will be discussed in the following chapter. As instructors, students, and the technological interface all become more familiar with the many components of academic dishonesty and how to reduce it in online courses, perhaps the perception that academic dishonesty is more likely in online courses will begin to wane. After all, no published research has documented any differences in the likelihood of academic dishonesty across face-to-face and online courses, and yet, concerns seem to be readily voiced about issues of plagiarism and misrepresentation pertaining to the online environment. In some ways, these continued concerns over online courses reflect a larger and less understood stigma regarding online learning that may be present in higher education. The nature of this stigma, and how to go about reducing it at your academic institution, is discussed in the following chapter.

SUMMARY: BRINGING IT ALL TOGETHER

This chapter provided tips and tricks on how to ensure quality online assessment, with a focus on reaching goals for course objectives and student learning outcomes. As you select your course assessments, try to ask, how does test/paper/discussion/element help to meet my unit objectives, student learning outcomes, and overall program goals? Also keep in mind the tips for managing student expectations and concerns that arise out of assessments. Student success, retention, comprehension, and critical thinking should all be enhanced when their expectations can be managed, and their problems can be mitigated. Sometimes problems surrounding academic honesty arise that can be unique to the online classroom, and it is important to be aware of these potential pitfalls and address them efficiently. We hope our discussion of online academic dishonesty and the potential tips presented to reduce it become useful tools in your online assessment arsenal. Keep the channels of communication open between yourself, the administration, and the student when you suspect that academic dishonesty might occur, and look for potential solutions. We have come very far at this stage in the book, from managing a course, communicating with students, implementing technology, creating activities, and handling assessment and testing. In the following chapter we continue facing forward as we explore what the future holds for the online teaching of psychology.

CHAPTER 7

ADVANCED APPLICATIONS AND FUTURE DIRECTIONS IN ONLINE PSYCHOLOGY

Based upon the previous six chapters, it is only natural to wonder, what does the future hold for online education in psychology? What other applications are there beyond traditional undergraduate modalities? This chapter seeks to address these questions and more by discussing the many extensions, applications, and future directions that are offered by the online teaching of psychology. First, the "Purpose" section discusses how the online teaching of psychology fits nicely with notions of "giving psychology away" by opening up access and opportunities for new and traditionally underrepresented groups in higher education. Applications of professional development to applied areas are also discussed. Next, the "Implementation" section deals with graduate education; specifically, how online education can enable the dream of a PhD, followed by a discussion of faculty acceptance and the job hunt for individuals with online PhDs, featuring a review of relevant research as well as anecdotal material. Finally, the "Troubleshooting" section helps to set a course for moving into the future by detailing theory and research surrounding online faculty development as well as future considerations of online psychology education, including K-12 online education, accreditation, and demographic and economic trends.

PURPOSE: "GIVING PSYCHOLOGY AWAY"

In 1969, then president of the American Psychological Association George Miller gave a rousing presidential address calling for his audience to "give psychology away to the public" (Miller, 1969). While it may have taken many years for this idea to catch on, it is undeniable that the discipline of psychology has moved forward a great deal from the laboratory experiments in the ivory tower of the 1960s, to focus much more broadly on improving people's lives through applied research, practice, and training (see Donaldson & Berger, 2006). In his 2004 paper asking "Does Psychology Make a Difference in People's Lives?" social psychology icon Philip Zimbardo highlights how learning about psychological principles can benefit people's lives, especially topics on parenting, psychological stress, lifespan development, psychological therapies, self-directed change, and prejudice and discrimination, to name a few (Zimbardo, 2004). The article then goes on to discuss the many professional fields in which learning about psychology can further professional development and success, including criminal justice, education, and health. The article closes with the author advising us, "may the positive forces of psychology be with you, and with our society" (Zimbardo, 2004, p. 348).

Just as Miller encouraged us to "give psychology away" and Zimbardo highlights the many ways in which psychology can improve not only individual lives but our world as a whole, we argue that online education reflects the next great frontier in the quest to give psychology to the world. Never before have individuals across the globe had such easy access to so much information about psychology. If we consider that the dissemination of psychological information can lead to a better world, then opening up access to it via online courses promises to better society and improve the human condition! While there may be some resistance to online education within traditional academic institutions (discussed later on in this chapter), it is undeniable that opening up access to psychology can have massive benefits for potential learners, and that as educators, would should champion the opportunity to reach a more diverse sample of individuals, including traditionally disadvantaged minority groups and older adults.

OPENING UP ACCESS TO HIGHER EDUCATION: MINORITIES AND OLDER ADULTS

Online psychology courses can harness the power to break down cultural and social barriers and unite people. For example, Enger (2006) states that while "students from underrepresented minority cultures are particularly vulnerable to feeling isolated from the majority culture on many campuses[,] online education has the potential for mitigating this problem" (p. 7). The online learning environment can break down what Enger refers to as "cultural barriers" through a "social process" connecting individuals with common interests and goals, regardless of their backgrounds (p. 8). Enger (2006) cites her own experiences as an online educator to discuss how the web offers a much more "color-blind" world than afforded by traditional learning, what one of her online students describes as " 'faceless' yet culturally integrated" (p. 8). While Enger argues for the benefits of the online learning environment in general to increasing minority enrollment, access, and participation in higher education, it is worth considering how the specific discipline of psychology can further enhance this experience. If online education itself can break down barriers, then online education that focuses on understanding and reconciling cultural differences should be especially effective. In other words, a psychology course in this type of environment has the potential to entice, excite, and bring a diverse community of individuals together. Just as online education has the potential to attract minority students, minority students have the ability to greatly enhance and broaden discussions on psychological topics including minority influence, social identity, sense of community, and health disparities, to name a few.

In addition to enhancing access and participation for minority students, online education in psychology also offers the potential of engaging older adults (aged 50+). In one of the only empirical research studies published to date on this topic, Gaumer-Erickson and Noonan (2010) compared online learning satisfaction and success in an asynchronous online graduate education course across 136 adults in three age categories: Early career (21–35), midcareer (36–49), and late career (50–65). While there was no difference in the self-reported technological abilities of the three age categories, mid- and late-career adults perceived themselves to be less technologically skilled than early-career learners. Late-career learners also asked significantly more technology-related questions than early-career learners. Late-career adults demonstrated significant increases between pretest and posttest scores on course related knowledge (the competency test was taken before and after the course), while mid- and early-career learners demonstrated no significant differences in learning. Late-career learners were also statistically more likely than early-career learners to be satisfied with their learning experience, specifically that the course held their attention and they believed that the online courses could be an important resource in the future.

Taken as a whole, these results are promising for adult learners. It appears that older adults are not only open to online education, but they can actually thrive, succeed, and find satisfaction in online educational settings. Empirical research on the experiences of older adults in online higher education is extremely limited (see Paulson & Boeke, 2006), Gaumer-Erickson and Noonan (2010) argue that their findings fit with previous studies showing that "older adults prefer highly specific, short-term learning opportunities based on their interests and job requirements" (p. 394). It seems thus that the learning needs and higher educational goals of late-career learners might be fundamentally different from those of early-career learners, who might be more concerned with developing a depth and breadth of knowledge as opposed to obtaining specific vocational training. This was one of the very first studies to empirically assess the educational experiences of late-career learners, and consequently, more research is needed to "identify the needs, interests and necessary online supports of this age group" (Gaumer-Erickson & Noonan, 2010, p. 395).

ONLINE EDUCATION FOR PROFESSIONALS: EMERGING TRENDS IN THE APPLIED HEALTH FIELD

Just as online psychology courses have the potential to open up access and build communities among diverse populations, professionals are finding that online courses are increasingly valued and sought after. This trend has been especially pervasive in the health and nursing fields, where many professionals have expressed their needs to continue their education and training online (Berman & Novotny, 1999; Ellery, McDermott, & Ellery, 2007). Indeed, the United States is facing a potential shortage of nurses and nurse educators, with 76% of nursing schools claiming that the shortage of faculty was their central reason for rejecting students (American Association of Colleges of Nursing, 2003). According to Holly (2009), the Director of the Doctor of Nursing program at the New Jersey School of Nursing, training America's nurses online offers an ideal solution to this growing problem by affording flexibility, access, cost-effectiveness, and the potential to increase the number of ethnic minorities in the profession. Furthermore, online learning would help nurses reach important standards for informatics training, including achieving comfort and familiarity with the new technologies utilized in the profession (Holly, 2009). Aside from the ease of use, access, cost-effectiveness, and technological skills involved, online nursing courses also offer the added benefit of making it easier for instructors to "support critical thinking and clinical judgment skills" using online modules and high-end clinical technologies.

Indeed, it appears that many nurses and health care professionals are looking to pursue their education in the online classroom (Cobb, 2004). For example, one survey of Wisconsin public health professionals showed that a whopping 92% indicated that they were interested in online health education courses (Milwaukee/Waukesha Public Health Consortium, 2006). To understand the needs of these professionals, Zusevics and colleagues (Zusevics, Gilmore, Jecklin, & Swain, 2009) surveyed 145 Wisconsin public health employees to determine their preferences surrounding online course offerings. Just under half of the respondents were content with receiving continuing education credits for their participation in online courses, whereas 24% were interested in pursuing an online PhD and another 28% were looking to complete an online master's of public health. In terms of the preferred subject of study, the most common interest was courses that address emerging health needs (52%) followed by epidemiology (46%), public health law (46%), health and policy administration (44%), and environmental health (42%). In terms of online course technologies, participants were most comfortable with using asynchronous learning (46%), email communication (46%), and online exams (41%). Furthermore, over half of respondents had already engaged in some form of online health training, and an additional one-third were interested in participating in technology training/online course orientations. These results demonstrate a promising trend where public health employees are open to, and seeking out, opportunities to enhance their qualifications and education in the online environment.

Online public health education becomes even more vital when considering how rural, underdeveloped, or underprivileged parts of the world struggle to obtain access to appropriate education and training. One example comes from rural Australia where only about 36% of regional health care centers offer access to palliative oncology specialists (Koczwara, 2010). Koczwara and colleagues (2010) sought to create an online program in palliative oncology to train local specialists who could provide care to individuals in rural areas in response to worrying trends that individuals who live further from a cancer treatment center are at risk for poorer cancer outcomes. The authors developed a 7.5 hour online training session in palliative oncology for 501 users. In program evaluations completed by 90 of these users, 91% indicated that their learner needs were partially or entirely met, and 75% planned to review or change their cancer practice as a result. The authors concluded based upon these evaluations that "the online program is effective in meeting learning needs of Australian health providers, reaching higher numbers with high acceptability" (p. 317). These results indicate potential for online health education to improve the expertise of providers in hard-to-reach areas, and could indirectly improve health outcomes of those patients in need.

IMPLEMENTATION: ENABLING "THE DREAM OF A PHD"

Online education in the psychological sciences has the potential to broaden our world in so many ways, from delivering access and opportunities to traditionally underrepresented learners, to training health professionals to give the care that the public needs. As indicated by the Wisconsin public health study, approximately 25% of health care professionals were interested in obtaining a PhD online. Indeed, the demand for online PhDs is rising, especially in psychology and related fields, although it remains unclear exactly how many online PhDs are granted each year. In fact, "the exact number of colleges and universities in the United States that offer online education degrees is difficult to determine because new online programs are launched on an ongoing basis" (Betts, Hartman, & Oxholm, 2010, p. 16). According to the National Center for Education Statistics (Parsad, Lewis, & Tice, 2009), in 2006–2007, over 12 million students were enrolled in online courses at 2- and 4-year postsecondary academic institutions. Of the 1,810 institutions surveyed that offered graduate or first-professional degree programs in 2006–2007, 82% of public 4-year institutions and 46% of private not-for-profit 4-year institutions offered graduate level online education, with approximately 51% of public 4-year institutions and 21% of private not-for-profit 4-year institutions awarding online graduate or professional degrees (data was not available on public 2-year colleges, private for-profit 2-year colleges, and private for-profit 4-year colleges). According to the statistics from the NCET report, 25% of graduate or professional degree programs were completed entirely online. These findings indicated that a significant percentage of academic institutions in the United States offered online degrees, with approximately 2.4 *million* students enrolled in online graduate education (Parsad et al., 2009). The data were not specific about degree program areas, so it is unclear how many of the online graduate degrees awarded were in psychology and related fields. However, given the popularity of a psychology-related degree, it is possible that at least some of these 2.4 million students are participating in graduate education towards a doctoral degree in the psychological sciences.

How can we compare the perceived quality and standards of an online PhD with a PhD acquired through traditional face-to-face courses? Is an online PhD somehow less worthy, indicative of lower quality and reduced expertise? Not necessarily, although some members of higher education and academia have reinforced an attitude that online PhDs are somehow inferior. For example, of the 2,500 academic institutions interviewed by the Sloan Consortium, only about 30% agreed that their faculty members "accepted the value and legitimacy of online education" (Allen & Seaman, 2008, p. 12). The acceptance rate is even lower for graduate-specific programs, with only 20% of institutions with doctoral/research and master's programs agreeing that faculty accepted the value and legitimacy of online education, compared with 44% of institutions that granted associate degrees. These data indicate that online graduate education tends to be less accepted than online undergraduate education. Even in light of this, 74% of public institutions and 70% of all doctoral/research institutions agreed with the statement that "online education is critical to the long-term strategy of my institutions." Thus it seems that while online graduate education may be less accepted than online undergraduate education, online education remains an important part of the future at graduate institutions.

While the future of online graduate education is ramping up, individuals with online PhDs have faced some skepticism and resistance in their attempts to land academic jobs. In their 2005 survey of 109 academic search committee chairs, Adams and Defluer (2005) found that 98% would prefer to hire a candidate with a traditional degree compared to one with an online degree. A similar bias against online PhDs for faculty hiring was also uncovered in surveys of 28 academic hiring committees (Flowers & Baltazar, 2006), although for some respondents, the applicant's PhD granting academic institution was deemed more important than whether the degree was obtained in-person or online. This, of course, brings up the additional question regarding the legitimacy of PhDs awarded from fully online institutions. One of the largest fully online institutions, the University of Phoenix (which has over 400,000 students across its undergraduate and graduate programs), has been accredited via the Higher Learning Commission (http://ncahlc.org), which accredits more than 1,000 academic institutions across the United States. Only time will tell if accreditation can help to reduce the bias against fully online institutions and the degrees that they confer.

Not all news is bad news when it comes to obtaining academic jobs with an online PhD. For example, Guendoo (2008) found that community colleges are much more accepting of hiring faculty members with online PhDs, bucking the trend of previous studies on perceptions of online PhDs in higher education. In this survey of 52 administrators from the 145 largest community colleges in the United States, 89% did not view having an online PhD as harmful to a candidate's credibility, while 94% disagreed with the statement, "I would not hire a candidate with an online degree for a faculty position even if the degree came from a reputable academic institution." Further, 91% of respondents strongly disagreed that "online doctoral programs have too many drawbacks to make them credible" (Guendoo, 2008). When contrasted with previous studies on public and private institutions, these findings on community colleges offer a stark contrast in attitudes about the quality of online PhDs. While there are many possible explanations, it is clear that faculty and administrators at public institutions tend to have more favorable attitudes toward online education in general, especially given that more than half of all community college students have been enrolled in at least one online course (Allen & Seaman, 2008). Guendoo (2008) offers other possible explanations, including that community colleges may be less resistant to change and development than academic institutions with long histories of tradition; that community colleges are driven by the idea of access and openness, and it would seem counterproductive to offer many online courses only to not accept a faculty member with an online degree; and finally, community colleges may not be as concerned with doctoral degrees obtained online or in person, because typically a master's degree is sufficient for hiring.

While it may seem like a small step, this survey of community college administrators serves as a promising harbinger for change. Resistance to new ideas and practices has always been prevalent in higher education, and it is only natural that new and nontraditional practices are first met with trepidation, followed usually by trial periods, and, if successful, then met with acceptance. As educators, psychologists, and supporters of online learning, is it possible to help improve attitudes about online degrees? Absolutely. The first way to do this is to ensure that your own courses at your institution reach the highest possible standards of quality and excellence. Tips for enhancing graduate education are discussed below. Second, consider how to address the documented concerns that faculty members with online degrees might lack face-to-face experience, research training, and time spent with other academic peers (deemed "academic socialization") (Adams & Fleur, 2005). As more and more students and educators become involved in online education, it would make sense that online graduate degrees will become more accepted, and that people will become more aware of the skills and rigor required by online education. Consider the many ways in which technology has shaped higher education, and how resistance has ultimately given way to acceptance, integration, and appreciation. For example, technology has afforded huge developments such as researching online using PSYC-INFO instead of microfiche or the library card catalogue. Or being able to analyze data much more quickly and efficiently using computer terminals and data-analytic packages like SPSS. Technology also affords little things, like being able to send an email to your professor, watch a video streaming on YouTube in a classroom, or better yet, empowering students to write and produce their own multimedia content. The advancement of technology has only helped to spur on developments in higher education, and online education is surely the next great frontier.

Part of the resistance to online education surrounds the continued absence of the types of program rankings that are available for traditional universities and colleges. Without these kinds of rankings and standards, how can we know if a potential employee's degree came from a high quality program? In response to this information gap, in early 2012 *US News and World Report* issued its first ever "Top Online Education Program

Rankings" of 196 online bachelor's degree programs and 523 online master's degree programs in business, engineering, nursing, education, and computer information technology, based on surveys of roughly 2,000 institutions. Online bachelor's degree programs were rated across three core elements: student engagement and assessment, student services and technology, and faculty credentials and training. As opposed to generating a numerical rating for each program, *US News* instead issues an "Honor Roll" for online undergraduate and graduate programs that rank in the top third of all three categories. Interestingly, none of the for-profit online universities (think: University of Phoenix, DeVry University, American Public University, all with very high enrollments) made it onto the honor roll. For online bachelor's programs, Westfield State University in Massachusetts was ranked number one for faculty training and credentials, Bellevue University of Nebraska was ranked number one for student engagement and assessment, and Arizona State University was number one for student services and technology. The online bachelor's degree honor roll includes Pace University of New York, Florida Institute of Technology, Westfield State University, and the University of Florida. For the full honor roll for online bachelor's programs and complete ranking methodologies, visit http://www.usnews.com/education/online-education.

In terms of online graduate programs, ratings and honor roles were issued for master's degrees in business, nursing, education, engineering and information technology. Notice that online doctoral degree programs have not yet been rated, nor do the rankings offer a psychology-specific category. However, given that this is new in 2012, we should expect a greater range of ratings to emerge in the future. Both education and nursing programs are of interest for those who teach psychology online. In terms of education, Northern Illinois University was ranked highest for faculty credentials and training, University of Northern Colorado was rated highest for student engagement and accreditation, Syracuse University was rated highest for student services and technology, and Pennsylvania State University-University Park was rated as having the most selective admissions process. For online nursing master's programs, George Washington University was rated the highest for faculty credentials and teaching, Loyola University, New Orleans was rated highest for student services and technology, University of Northern Colorado was rated best for student engagement and action, and Delta State University was rated as most selective. For the full 2012 honor rolls, please visit http://www.usnews.com/education/online-education/education for education, and http://www.usnews.com/education/online-education/nursing for nursing.

Making Online Graduate Education Great!

Hundreds of highly respected, accredited educational institutions offer online graduate programs and professional training around the globe. Universities that have worldwide reputations, such as Stanford University, MIT, Harvard, University of Chicago, University of New South Wales in Australia, or the Open University UK, offer the educational benefits of a diverse range of faculty teaching online from all over the world, with students reflecting a similar level of variation. Further, the 2012 issuance of online graduate program rankings and honor rolls from a reputable organization like *US News and World Report* helps to validate the legitimacy of online graduate education. It seems likely then that the notion that a graduate, professional, or doctoral degree conferred online is somehow inferior will become an idea of the past, as we see the ways that learning from anywhere at any time opens up new possibilities, new opportunities, and new pathways for learning, especially in applied contexts. One of the best examples of this comes from the University of New South Wales online master's in cross-disciplinary art and design program. Not only does this program reflect an innovative and cutting edge approach to the discipline where students can learn collaboratively online, but this program attracts both teachers and learners from at least four different continents. This type of online learning truly integrates diverse perspectives, outlooks, and attitudes in a way that traditional education simply cannot offer.

Before delving into how to manage the transition from online undergraduate to graduate education, let us consider a few anecdotes from coauthor Dr. Stewart Donaldson, who currently serves as Dean of the School of Social and Behavioral Sciences at Claremont Graduate University. In recent years, he has experienced unconventional requests from students increasingly seeking to tailor their graduate experiences to meet their personal needs and interests. The first example is Charles, a mid-career professional who has dreamed of pursuing a PhD in applied psychology with a concentration in applied research methods and evaluation, but who unfortunately lives in the Midwest and has been unable to move to California due to life constraints and financial challenges. Rather than giving up on his dream, Charles has managed to create an experimental arrangement where an online teaching assistant attends every course he is enrolled in, and records and streams this course to him via the web. Charles has regular online remote meetings with his advisors and is essentially able to replicate the same graduate experience found at the University, without leaving his home and office in St. Louis, Missouri. Through the laptop in each classroom or meeting, he is able to ask questions and interact as if he was actually present. Opportunities like this might seem unusual for now, but as more and more educational institutions experience demand from these kinds of individuals, remote online learning might soon become a naturally accepted modality for graduate students.

It is important to note that in this example, Charles is not enrolled in an online graduate degree program, but rather is able to remotely access courses that are taking place in-person in California. Thus while he is technically receiving his degree "online," he might be missing out on the many benefits that a fully online program would have to offer, including online asynchronous discussions, and online versions of tests. One of the interesting trends that occurred since Charles was given permission to try this experimental program was that other students soon became interested in the potential to complete some of their graduate coursework online. In this respect, a "hybrid" online program where students attend some classes in person and take other classes online might reflect a massively popular modality for graduate learning in psychology in the future.

For example, a graduate student in psychology named Yumi found out about Charles' remote coursework, and petitioned to take one semester of remote online courses so that she could pursue her research goals of working in Japan following the recent earthquake and tsunami that wreaked devastation in the region. She sought to understand coping with trauma and to take a hands-on approach to the psychology of rebuilding one's life following extreme change. While a student in a traditional graduate program would only be able to travel to conduct research after coursework was finished, or would have to take a break from learning, an online course option would enable Yumi to work and conduct research in the field without having to sacrifice her learning. By enabling the dream of researching in applied contexts while simultaneously learning about research, psychology and applications, online graduate programs can greatly enhance student abilities and insights in a highly immersive and functional way. In this respect, a graduate program that offers online options to students could help to make a huge impact upon the world, which is one of the central goals for many individuals who obtain an applied psychology PhD. Imagine the opportunities across the world to do research to make positive changes, whether we are talking about New Orleans in the aftermath of Katrina, to understanding the HIV pandemic in Sub-Saharan Africa, or the quest for statehood in Palestine. Having students who have worked hands-on in these environments not only makes for better students, but for more diverse and enriching programs, and better quality research being published from your institution.

Another example surrounds the ability for nontraditional individuals to engage in innovative, multidisciplinary research and training. Dr. Donaldson was recently contacted by two individuals, Matt and Christina, highly qualified business consultants in Australia who were pursuing a joint PhD together online from a university in Europe. He was contacted as an expert in positive organizational psychology to provide some insight into their desired choice of a research topic. As it turns out, Matt (living in New York) and Christina (living in Melbourne, Australia) had been directly contacting experts from all over the globe to gain insight for their joint PhD research. Now at first glance, it sounds a little bit strange to imagine: Two individuals doing a PhD together, online, and on a different continent from where they are located, who are contacting experts on a third continent to obtain some kind of feedback. Still, we need to consider that as high-level working professionals, Matt and Christina would probably not have the opportunity to complete a PhD in the traditional sense. By creating their own program, and focusing specifically on a research topic that is relevant to their work environment, they might be able to gain insight that they would not have gained in the traditional graduate research environment. While the success of their program remains to be seen, this example makes it clear that online graduate education can open access to working professionals to conduct organizational research in ways that they might not have previously been able to. Theoretically, the work being conducted by individuals directly in these relevant fields might actually help to push the discipline in new, innovative, and exciting ways.

Based upon these examples, online graduate education can provide older adults with the flexibility and access to live the dream and obtain their PhDs, while empowering applied psychology students to travel to where they are needed most to work for positive change. Online graduate education can also help open access to working professionals, who might bring their own unique knowledge to innovate and create new perspectives. All of these potential features of online graduate education share one thing in common: They can help to push the discipline of psychology *further.* Access from diverse individuals, helping to solve global problems in applied settings, and organizational research from the very individuals usually targeted by these efforts, all offer the benefit of broadening the field of psychology by developing research programs in new arenas using nontraditional frameworks. It seems that online graduate education might be especially useful for applied psychology, as it has the ability to attract individuals who already work and participate in actual fields, from health and well-being, to organizations, to clinical and counseling worlds. Thus while the traditional academy might find these new innovations and research opportunities a little bit strange, we argue that this perceived strangeness might have the benefit of opening up psychology, much in the tradition of "giving psychology away." Further, doctoral research conducted at this level in applied perspectives might have much more to offer us in terms of diverse target populations, opposed to traditional doctoral research, collecting surveys of other graduate students on campus.

TRANSITIONING TO ONLINE GRADUATE EDUCATION

Based upon a decade of experience delivering graduate education in psychology and distance/online graduate level professional development courses, Dr. Donaldson will make several recommendations for managing the transition from traditional to online graduate education, highlighting that the incorporation of online elements can sometimes become a gradual process. In other words, if your university currently does not offer an online graduate education in psychology, consider how engaging in some of these steps might help pave the way for future distance and online programs. If your university does already offer online graduate education in psychology, think about how integrating these elements might enhance student learning in your program.

Webinars and Online Broadcasts of Department Speakers

Webinars provide an excellent first step into incorporating online learning components into courses. Many universities already offer webinars of important lecturers, guest speakers, or professional training initiatives. In a webinar, online students from around the globe view a talk or a lecture on a digital hosting interface (Elluminate live! is often used), and are able to make comments and ask questions which the lecturer will then respond to, sometimes with the help of a moderator who controls the online dialogue. In some webinars, students can ask questions via text only, whereas in others, students will be visible to the lecturer via their webcam (to ensure that they aren't falling asleep, among other things!). Webinars can benefit online graduate education because in many ways they mimic the interaction and level of focus required in a traditional classroom environment, with the added benefit of attracting students and scholars from across the globe. For example, the International Positive Psychology Association sponsors a webinar series that provides psychology college students and professionals all over the world with the opportunity to learn about the latest cutting edge research in positive psychology (see Donaldson, Csikszentmihalyi, & Nakamura, 2011). Below is an illustrative screenshot of a webinar in action. In this example, the moderator (Dr. Fetterman) ran an exercise for the on-site participants while the off-site participants did a similar exercise on the whiteboard area. Then Dr. Fetterman explained the results, and the off-site audience could see the results of their exercise on the whiteboard.

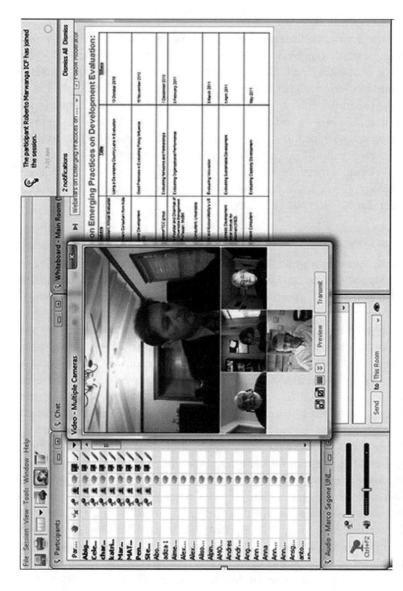

Figure 7.1 *Sample Webinar Screen Shot.*

Often, the comments, questions, and feedback that occur during a webinar can exceed those found in a traditional class. Particularly for new online programs, webinars are a great way to manage the transition to online education, as they portray similar experiences to sitting in a live lecture without leaving home. Sometimes it can also be beneficial for psychology departments to stream important lectures from their faculty online. Not only can this help further the education of those viewing the lecture, but it can also help to raise the profile of the institution and attract potential students or extramural funding.

Online Professional Development Workshops in a Variety of Formats

After managing hundreds of workshops over the past decade, online professional development in psychology is something Dr. Donaldson has become very familiar with. The workshops can serve as a natural precursor to distance, online, and traditional graduate degree programs, where participants receive online training in a relevant area, usually spanning the course of a day to one week. For institutions that have yet to offer distance and online degrees, professional development workshops provide a great opportunity to test the waters and gauge the success of future online course offerings. He has provided and overseen many online professional workshops, open for public enrollment, in positive psychology, applied psychology, organizational psychology, evaluation and applied research methods, quantitative research methods, qualitative research methods, mixed methods designs, culturally competent applied research and evaluation methods, grant proposal writing, data-analytic presentations, the psychology of evaluation, and meta-analysis, to name a few. These professional development workshops are offered in-person while simultaneously broadcast in a state-of-the-art online classroom on the web. Such workshops can potentially bring together professionals from a variety of disciplines to learn together, featuring 50 to 100 online students who interact as if they were actually present at the workshop itself. These additional students from across the globe help to add fresh perspectives and diversity to such workshops, as well as a feeling of global connectedness. Online students in these workshops typically report high levels of satisfaction, and appreciate not having to travel long distances and pay travel costs to learn from top experts. Some students have even argued this is a more environmentally friendly way to deliver professional development workshops.

Distance Education Certificates

Based upon the success of the online professional development workshops, it seems only natural to begin to enroll students in certificate training programs online. Dr. Donaldson has overseen the Certificate of Advanced Study in Evaluation since it was created in 1998, and has seen it develop from a smaller traditional onsite program to a distance education program that has now graduated more than 50 advanced evaluators. These types of online certificate programs can be extremely valuable for professional students looking for specific training in their field. For example, think back to the earlier studies cited of public health professionals who were seeking to earn certificates and training online. In the Claremont Graduate University (CGU) distance education certificate program, students complete a rigorous series of distance based courses over a 1-year period, a series online or onsite workshops, and are required to complete an evaluation practicum project supervised at distance by CGU faculty (about 100 hours working in the evaluation field) before taking written and oral Qualifying Examinations to receive their certificate. Graduates of these programs often have the option of transferring their certificate courses toward a master's or doctoral degree at Claremont and elsewhere. This type of a format could be highly beneficial for a number of professionals seeking certificates and training in the psychological sciences, from the applied health field, to counseling or clinical psychology, to applied research training. Such a format enables a great amount of latitude for training professionals without having to enroll them into a larger degree program. For students, this means a cost-effective, flexible, accessible, and time-efficient means of gaining the training they require without having to leave work, relocate, or incur other life inconveniences.

Online Option for Master's and Doctoral Courses

Finally, as discussed earlier, Dr. Donaldson has recently taken some experimental steps into online master's and PhD courses in psychology, most notably by granting Charles the opportunity to stream courses online to his office and home in the Midwest. These types of dalliances are an excellent way for an institution or program to become familiar with online graduate degrees, particularly when webinars, professional development training, and certificate courses have all been executed with success. While CGU does not currently offer any fully online master's or PhDs, the possibility has arisen for some of these courses to be delivered in an online context. One of the key considerations here is the components that become part of the online version of the course: Streaming live lectures, online webinars interacting with real-life classes, asynchronous discussion boards, papers and tests, online chat, assigned readings, and outside research. At the moment, it appears that the online graduate students at CGU engage in coursework that is very similar, if not identical, to that of their peers in the face-to-face courses. The benefit to this is that nobody can argue that this online graduate degree is somehow less worthy, when that student has participated in exactly the same courses and mentoring as other students. Likewise, incorporating certain unique online elements might further enhance the online experiences in these classes. While this is a new and unofficial program, it does seem that online educators can learn from how CGU has integrated its graduate program in psychology into the online learning environment. One of the main findings so far is that faculty are most receptive when a highly trained teaching assistant serves as the interface between the online student and the class. That is, a good high tech TA can facilitate this experience so that it enhances the online experience for both the professor and student. There is no additional workload or worries for a professor when a TA is competent and fully in charge of the technology.

TROUBLESHOOTING: FACULTY DEVELOPMENT AND FUTURE CONSIDERATIONS

As online education continues to grow and move into the graduate and professional realm, the natural question remains, where do we go from here? While it may be unclear what the future might hold, we can assume that at least in part, it will involve a greater emphasis on online faculty development and training. Recall from the Sloan Consortium report that approximately 20% of all instructors who teach online receive absolutely no online training (Allen & Seaman, 2010). Thus the next section approaches issues of faculty development and training, as well as additional future considerations for online teaching and learning, including but not limited to cultural differences, K-12 training, accreditation, and demographic and economic factors.

STRATEGIES FOR ONLINE FACULTY DEVELOPMENT

In the past few years, a number of research articles and publications have emerged detailing the resounding need for online teacher training, paired with best practices for delivering such training online (Kyei-Blankson, 2010; Ray, 2009, 2009; St. Clair, 2009; Yang & Cornelious, 2005). Due to the astounding increase in online students during the last 5 years (recall, as many as 12 million students took at least one class online in 2006–2007), there has simply not been an opportunity for many online teachers to catch up to this rapid growth. Online teachers must not only be familiar with their subject matter, but also with the vast array of technology they will be required to manage. Recall that to teach online, successful instructors must become familiar with many components discussed in this book including course design, online communication, multimedia, and assessment design, to name a few. As argued by Bates and Watson (2008), online teaching requires a completely different set of teaching skills, and training should be delivered with this in mind. In extensive interviews with 111 online college teachers from Pennsylvania, Ohio, and West Virginia, Ray (2009) found that 65% desired additional technological and pedagogical training, and that 86% believed that faculty new to online teaching should receive some kind of pedagogical training prior to the start of their online courses. This finding seems to support past research demonstrating that faculty members who teach online are not getting the training that they require (such as Lewis, 2007, who found that only 27% of online instructors received both pedagogical and technological training prior to the start of their online course).

BEST PRACTICES FOR TRAINING ONLINE FACULTY

Because research surrounding online faculty development is still in its infancy, it is challenging to reach a consensus on the best practices for faculty training. However, different models and approaches have been highlighted. In their book, *The Excellent Online Instructor: Strategies for Professional Development*, Palloff and Pratt (2011) discuss the readiness of faculty to teach online, noting that online faculty will be most successful when they possess the following characteristics: Visibility, Compassion, Communication, Commitment, and Organization. *Visibility* refers to the instructor being present in the online environment; *compassion* means that the instructor sincerely cares about students and believes in student-centered learning; *communication* refers to the instructor's ability to provide constructive feedback and communicate using appropriate technologies; *commitment* refers to the instructor's motivation and dedication to creating an academically rigorous and challenging course; and finally, *organization* means that the instructor can manage time and execute a course according to a plan (Palloff & Pratt, 2011, p. 19). Faculty who possess these five traits are deemed to have the appropriate "readiness" to begin their online training.

Palloff and Pratt (2011) cite Sherry, Billig, Tavalin, and Gibson's (2000) phased approach to online faculty development as an excellent starting point for this training. According to this approach, an online teacher in training progresses through five steps, and can benefit from receiving some kind of workshop or faculty training throughout the process (Sherry et al., 2000, cited in Palloff & Pratt, 2011, pp. 48–49). The first step, *teacher as learner,* refers to the first phase of learning how to teach online, when instructors are learning, gathering information, and collecting the necessary technological and pedagogical skills to teach online. At this phase, the best learning can come through watching or being mentored by other online instructors who have already integrated these technologies into their courses. The second stage, *teacher as adopter,* is more experimental, as online teachers are encouraged to try out new technologies and media, and share their experiences with a mentor who can give feedback about the process. The third phase, *teacher as colearner,* is where the teacher begins to make connections between technology and multimedia, and the types of assignments, assessments, and documents best used for the course. It can be useful to run ideas by potential online students and determine whether the assessments are appropriate. In the fourth stage, *teacher as reaffirmer or rejector,* the teacher forms an understanding of learning outcomes and the effects of technology on student learning. In the final stage, *teacher as leader,* online instructors are encouraged to share their experiences and train other instructors, while conducting research and evaluation to determine the success of their courses.

One key consideration here is, how long does it take for an instructor to progress through these steps? Or, put another way, what is the appropriate amount of time for faculty members to train before they start teaching online? While Palloff and Pratt (2011) remind us that every instructor's learning curve is different, they suggest at least one semester for training online faculty, noting that this depends upon "a number of factors such as faculty level of experience with technology and online learning, and whether or not courses are prewritten or need to be developed" (Palloff & Pratt, 2011, p. 59). Instructors who are familiar with technology, and who do not need to create an online course from scratch, might be able to participate in training initiatives in a couple of weeks, just as faculty members who are new to technology, and who have to write and design their own course, might require one or two full semesters of training before the course begins. As institutions become more comfortable and open to online teaching, "the program itself should be flexible enough to move an experienced faculty member directly into online courses with a minimum amount of training time" (p. 59).

BENEFITS OF MENTORING ONLINE INSTRUCTORS

An additional consideration surrounds the value of mentoring; that is, online instructors helping each other to succeed. Indeed, one of the first surveys on faculty mentoring demonstrated that faculty members can benefit from turning to their peers when they require help or assistance. In a survey of 117 faculty members who teach online, or who were transitioning to teaching online, Kyei-Blankson (2010) found that 80% said that they were likely or very likely to seek assistance from their faculty peers or colleagues when they were preparing to teach in an online environment, and that 68% perceived their faculty peers and colleagues as a useful or very useful resource for online teaching (Kyei-Blankson, 2010, p. 44). In terms of the qualitative nature of the interaction between faculty members, most them were informal and spontaneous, with conversations taking place in hallways, during office visits, or via email and phone. While most of the time it was the novice faculty members who sought assistance, in other situations, experienced faculty members "initiated the contact and willingly offered to help" (p. 45). In this study the support provided across faculty members proved highly beneficial by creating a positive learning community among faculty, making the transition to online course delivery smoother, leading to new ideas, providing a space to vent anger, and helping to ensure consistency across course offerings. The researchers concluded based on their data that "faculty perceive peer support, collaboration and interactions to be very essential" to their development as online instructors (p. 46).

Peer mediated faculty support is different from a traditional mentoring framework where an advanced or master's-level instructor is paired with a novice level instructor to provide guidance, training, and support. Palloff and Pratt (2011) argue that while this traditional framework can be useful, novice online faculty members can receive support through a wide network of individuals, including students who assist with technology, other faculty members who provide peer support, the experienced online instructor who provides pedagogical support, and the department chair or faculty mentor to provide support with content (Palloff & Pratt, 2011, p. 68). In this "networked approach," faculty members are not formally assigned to mentors but rather fluctuate in and out of relationships depending upon the instructional needs and the challenges they face at any given time. Through networking, new online instructors can receive assistance not just from one individual, but from a diverse array of people who each offer different skills and learning opportunities (Goodyear, 2006).

Based upon their literature review of technology mentoring programs, Chuang, Thompson, and Schmidt (2003) found that mentoring offers many potential recurring themes. First, mentoring can provide *visions for technology use*, by helping mentees to develop "a deeper level of understanding and a higher level of confidence in the use of technology" (Chuang et al., 2003, p. 4). Second, mentoring programs can help to *individualize technology support* by directly addressing the unique needs and pace of learners. As Palloff and Pratt (2011) argue, "given that the learner-focused approach is what we promote for online teaching, doesn't it make sense to provide the same to those who are learning how to do it?" (p. 66). Third, mentoring can help to *break down hierarchical structure* where a top-down approach is replaced by learners and mentors sharing a common goal and being motivated to learn together. Fourth, mentoring can help to *establish open dialogue and collaborative relationships* based upon a mutual respect and trust between mentor and mentee. Chuang et al. (2003) discuss how partnerships and collaborative work can evolve through an interactive mentoring experience. Along with line of thinking, mentoring can *provide mutual benefits* as the mentoring experience is dynamic and tends to evolve over time. As such, these types of relationships can help to boost self-esteem and enhance empowerment for all involved (Chuang et al., 2003; Goodyear, 2006). Finally, mentoring can help to *establish learning communities* where mentor and mentee can work together to exchange ideas while feeling nurtured and supported. The sense of community that develops from the mentoring relationship can help to reduce the feelings of loneliness and isolation that some online instructors might experience (Palloff & Pratt, 2011). Based upon these findings, it is clear that mentoring can greatly benefit online faculty members and profoundly enhance their skills, sense of community, and overall experiences as online instructors.

ADDITIONAL BENEFITS OF ONLINE FACULTY DEVELOPMENT

As highlighted by the research presented above, online faculty training can lead to well-adjusted, confident, and secure online instructors. An additional factor surrounds whether online faculty development can actually be utilized for all instructors, even those who do not teach online. Lowenthal (2008) argues that training all new faculty online could help to mitigate the many challenges of becoming a new instructor, including but not limited to the time constraints of managing work and family life and competing on-campus commitments. According to Lowenthal (2008), there are three main benefits to delivering faculty development workshops online. First, these workshops can be asynchronous, allowing faculty members to work at their own convenience. This would eliminate the inconvenience of all faculty being required to share the same time and space. Second, an online workshop is one that can be stretched over time, thereby increasing "seat time" and decreasing the feeling of "trying to change the world in a day" (Lowenthal, 2008). Third, as pointed out earlier in this chapter, teachers learn in the same way that their students learn best, so a learner-centered, community-based workshop that encourages critical thinking and evaluation will be more effective for really educating faculty than a one-off, 3-hour session. Cheiro and Beare (2010) demonstrated the benefits of online teacher training in their comparisons of the ratings of K-12 teachers who graduated from either online or traditional preparation programs from 2003 to 2009. Across approximately 11,000 teachers who were evaluated, those who graduated from online programs were significantly more likely than those who participated in traditional programs to be rated as "well or adequately prepared" by their supervisors. These findings support the argument that "a well-designed online teacher preparation program can be as effective or more effective as a campus-based program" (Cheiro & Beare, 2010, p. 788).

Lowenthal (2008) also makes an interesting argument for online faculty development to be reconceptualized as "storytelling" creating a "sense of community, which fosters collaboration, which then fosters meaning and marking" (Lowenthal, 2008, p. 352). According to this perspective, online faculty development could benefit from the digital stories of online instructors, who can make and share videos documenting their positive and negative online teaching experiences. By engaging with each other's stories, faculty members will have the opportunity to become familiar with technology, reflect and connect with each other, share their stories with millions on the web, and crucially, "reflect on best practices in action" (p. 354). Just as a good online facilitator ensures that students do not feel lonely or isolated, so too should a successful faculty development initiative reduce the feeling that online teaching is a private, individual, and solo experience. Rather, the idea of digital storytelling implies that it is possible to harness the communicative power of the web to train instructors, by providing an open, accessible, inviting, and semianonymous place for them to share and grow.

Another interesting benefit to online faculty development is the potential to break down the barriers and stigma that are sometimes associated with online learning. Faculty members and administrators can be resistant to online education due to concerns that online courses are more difficult to teach (Gerlich, 2005), that they require greater preparation and grading time commitments, that they will not be met with institutions' support and assistance, and that software, hardware, and technological issues can make life difficult. Interestingly, faculty development for online education can help to reduce these perceived barriers through education about course design, online communication, and technology training, to name a few (Kyie-Blankson, 2010). It has been consistently argued that the academic resistance to online courses "is attributed to a lack of support, assistance, as well as training by institutions of higher education" (Kyie-Blankson, 2010, p. 535; Allen & Seaman, 2008). In other words, when new faculty are not given the tools they need to succeed in their online courses, it may create a climate at the institution that does not accept the viability of online learning. It naturally follows that when an institution supports its faculty members, training them both technologically and pedagogically, and offering them mentors and guidance, faculty members at that institution will probably be more in favor of online education. Research has yet to be conducted to empirically demonstrate this relationship, and in general, research on online faculty development is very much still in its infancy (Dede, Ketelhut, Whitehouse, Breit, & McCloskey, 2009; Ray, 2009). Indeed, Hewett and Powers (2007) argue for "an increasing understanding of professional development and teacher mentorship in online environments via theoretical and empirical research" (p. 3), noting that the majority of related journals, books, and edited volumes on education and technology do not give much attention to the topic of online teacher training. Taken as whole, consider the many benefits of online faculty development, as well as the potential for conducting empirical research and evaluations on this topic in the future.

Pursuing Additional Online Faculty Training

Can an expert still become a better instructor? Definitely! Think about how technology is constantly evolving and changing, and how we can all benefit from staying abreast of these changes. What about the readers of this book who will go on to become highly successful and skillful online instructors? Absolutely! Ko and Rossen (2010) argue that for even the most seasoned online instructor, new opportunities and new training programs are always available. First, check to see what online training opportunities are available at your own institution, and sign up! If you can't find anything at your own institution or you have already participated in all of the opportunities on offer, look around at the training programs offered at other places. For example, the Sloan Consortium offers both an Online Teaching Certificate Program as well as a Blended Teaching Certificate, while many other institutions offer certificate programs in online teaching, including the University of Wisconsin, California State University, East Bay, and the author's own Saddleback College. It is also possible to pursue an online graduate degree in online education, such as from the University of Maryland or the Open University UK (Ko & Rossen, 2010). As online education becomes more prevalent, widespread, and accepted, expect the course offerings for degrees and certificates in online education to skyrocket in the next few years.

When deciding to enroll in one of these programs, what are the features to look for? Ko and Rossen (2010) address this question by advising online educators to look for a few potential features such as it being offered online, a flexible schedule, asynchronous learning, a teacher who participates regularly, and discussions assignments completed at short intervals. They also advise looking for a program that is a minimum of 6 weeks long to ensure actual development and enough time to learn and process new ideas. In terms of the content of the program, Ko and Rossen (2010) advise looking for the following: *software training, facilitative or methods training, course design, personal consultation,* and *supervised start-up.*

Software Training

Include the use of the course CMS as well as all related course technology. Because it is so important to stay up-to-date with technology, this becomes a crucial part of selecting the right training program. This software training should involve creating a demo course or course shell as a means of practicing and becoming familiar with software platforms.

Facilitative or Methods Training

Facilitative or methods training refers to being able to explore the differences and similarities between the face-to-face and online classrooms, as well as a focus on classroom management, student interaction, and preparation. The authors also suggest a program that allows learners to analyze case studies of actual online courses, and the potential to observe and critique actual online courses.

Course Design

Programs can benefit from offering hands-on experience with designing and implementing a course, including creating content and assessments that are in line with learning outcomes. A good training program should provide for these issues related to the development of the course content itself.

Personal Consultation

At some point toward the end of the program, it would be useful to have a one-on-one consultation with an online teaching expert who could help advise and give feedback on the ideal style of the course you are looking to create. Always important here is that the consultation leads to an outcome in line with your goals.

Supervised Start-up

The end of your training program should be paired with the actual start of your online course, ideally with an expert to oversee and help facilitate its launch. If the program does not offer this, Ko and Rossen (2010) suggest asking another faculty member who teaches online to serve as a mentor or to give feedback about your course. They cite an example from the University of Maryland where novice online instructors are assigned a peer mentor for their first semester of online teaching to iron out the kinks and make sure everything runs smoothly.

Even if you are not thinking about further online education through a certificate or program, keep in mind that you can always learn from your mistakes, your successes, and your experiences in general. As educators, we are in many ways committed to a process of lifelong learning, and this is especially true for the online learning environment, which is constantly growing, evolving, and changing in new and exciting ways (Ko & Rossen, 2010). Consider that we may now be on the brink of a transition to Web 3.0 where the web will know and understand our interests and will seek to provide us with content to our liking. Online educators have barely begun to discuss how the new software platforms and offerings in Web 3.0 will affect online learning. This is why it is always important to stay plugged into the trends surrounding education and technology, including reading relevant journals like *Chronicle of Higher Education, MERLOT,* and the *European Journal for Open, Distance and E-learning,* attending educational conferences like WCET and SLOAN, and networking with other online instructors via APA's Division 2 for Teaching Psychology. Does this sound familiar? Many psychologists are already participating in these kinds of academic activities as part of their research and scholarship in their specific areas—consider making online education another one of your chosen fields, like another tool in your box. Being up-to-date with current academic and applied trends and staying in touch with others will both help to maintain your sense of community with the world of online education, and push you to work to maintain and improve your online courses.

TROUBLESHOOTING: FUTURE CONSIDERATIONS FOR ONLINE EDUCATION

The emergence of Web 3.0 suggests many possible new trends for how human beings interact online, which may in turn affect the delivery of online courses in the future. As of now, it is too early to tell. A number of other future considerations for online education are present, including the impact of culture on online education, issues surrounding accreditation, as well as economic and demographic factors associated with the future rise of online education. In addition to graduate programs, K-12 programs are now increasingly likely to feature some components of online education, which are discussed in the following section.

Cultural Issues in Online Education:
Western vs. Non-Western Students

The concept of cultural issues in online education is relatively new (Guanwardena, Wilson, & Nolla, 2003), and according to researchers in this area, "the growth of cultural concerns in regard to online learning has not been accompanied by a growing number of studies in the field" (Liu, Liu, Lee, & Magjuka, 2010, p. 177). Indeed, a meta-analytic review conducted by Uzuner (2009) uncovered a total of only 27 qualitative and quantitative studies that addressed cultural differences in online learning. Much of the research that has been conducted demonstrates cultural differences between "Western" and "non-Western" students and their engagement in the online teaching and learning process (Bates, 2001; Guanwardena et al., 2003; Liu et al., 2010). For example, Bates (2001) found that "Western" students (think United States, Great Britain, Canada, and Australia) were more likely engage in critical thinking, debate, and discussion than their "non-Western" peers, who had greater respect for the instructor and found it difficult to question their teacher or express an opinion in a debate. In general, research findings that compare American and Chinese students tend to mirror the differences found between these two groups in higher education in general, including that Chinese students were less opinionated in online discussions, less likely to challenge the attitudes of their teachers, and less likely to engage in critical thinking (Thompson & Ku, 2005; Zhao & McDougall, 2008). In interviews of 17 international students from China, India, and Russia, Liu and colleagues (2010) found these international students preferred a highly structured course that emphasized exams and memorization, and that some students felt uncomfortable with interacting on the discussion board due to lack of structure and language barriers. Indeed, the preference of Chinese students for a rigid online class structure has also been supported by interviews conducted by Smith and Smith (1999).

How can online instructors broaden their own cultural sensitivity and ensure that their course would appeal to international students? Based upon their findings, Liu and colleagues (2010) recommend that online instructors can engage in a number of steps to improve their cultural competency, including participating in faculty training and awareness, providing an orientation to appropriate course conduct, offering more structured rules for the discussion board, reducing the language barrier through audio and visual aids, and assigning a wide range of activities to give international students the opportunity to practice their English. Guanwardena and colleagues (2003) suggest a multidimensional method where instructors include students in important course-related decisions on language choice, format choice, communication channels, and activity choices.

Language choice refers to using the dominant language (English in this case) and also providing materials in other languages, where possible. If you know that a certain percentage of your students are Chinese, for example, consider asking your institution to hire a translator for your key course documents. Liu et al. (2010) found that Chinese students had to triple their time spent reading when the content was in English, rather than Chinese. If it is not possible to translate course materials, using audio and visual aids such as videos, podcasts, and audio recordings can help speed up knowledge acquisition and retention time.

Format choice refers to the navigational structure of the course, such as the icons, texts, fonts, and colors. The authors cite the argument by Marcus and Gould (2000) that students from "high-power" countries may prefer a symmetrical layout with pictures of the university and faculty administrators, while students from "lower power" countries might prefer a greater amount of navigational control and a more asymmetrical layout. It is also vital to ensure that students are briefed on institutional rules at an early stage of the course, especially plagiarism and proper citations. In qualitative interviews, Liu et al. (2010) found that several international students experienced "frustration" after being punished for improper citation, when they were not briefed on the way that this is done in the United States (p. 184).

Communication channel refers to the type of discourse that occurs during the class, through asynchronous discussion boards, synchronous chats, email, or a combination of the three. It seems that offering a diverse array of communication channels might help to ensure comfort for students from a variety of backgrounds. Liu and colleagues (2010) found that synchronous chats helped international students get to know each other, but that scheduling such chats with students across the globe created significant problems. Likewise, international students also appreciated the accuracy and clarity of asynchronous discussions, but struggled to garner nuances and intentions from these conversations. Thus, Liu et al. recommend that Chinese and other international students would feel most comfortable with "a combination of both types of communication modes in order to balance the communication weaknesses of each type" (Liu et al.,2010, p. 183).

Activity choice should include culturally appropriate learning activities that can be any combination of papers, group work, and projects that address the needs and abilities of the student (Collis, 1999; Gunawardena et al., 2003). Some studies have shown that students from collectivist, non-Western cultures are more passive and hesitant than U.S. students (Zhao & McDougall, 2008), possibly hindering their success at working in a group. If group work is very important to your course, it might help to allow students the opportunity to form relationships before the group project begins (Liang &McQueen, 1999). Assigning small, diverse groups and monitoring their collaboration and communication can also help international students feel more comfortable (Wang, 2007).

Issues in K-12 Online Education: Narrowing the Gap

According to the International Association of K-12 Online Learning, approximately 1.5 million K-12 students were engaged in online and blended learning in the 2009–2010 school year, with some kind of online learning available to K-12 students in 48 of 50 states (Wicks, 2010). The most significant dimensions of K-12 online learning are whether the courses are full-time at one school or supplemental to students at other schools, the reach of the program (within a school system, across a state, nationally), the delivery of the program—most are asynchronous—and whether courses are fully online, blended, or hybrid. K-12 education is experiencing a significant transition to the online learning environment, at a growth rate so rapid "that data are at risk of being out-of-date before they are published" (Watson, 2010, cited in Wicks, 2010, p. 13), but estimates from the Sloan Consortium indicate that K-12 online course offerings grew 47% between the 2005–2006 school year and the 2007–2008 school year. It is not surprising then that many elementary, middle, and high school teachers have not been adequately prepared for this transition and have not been adequately instructed how to teach online, finding themselves paired with young learners who are highly skilled with technology. Deubel (2008) argues that the "skill sets acquired for teaching in face to face settings are not adequate preparation for online teaching or online course development" (p. 1). How many online K-12 teachers actually receive some kind of training prior to teaching online? In *Going Virtual! The Status of Professional Development for K-12 Online Teachers*, Rice and Dawley (2007) reported that of 167 K-12 online instructors, 86% received some kind of training to teach online. However, for 62% of respondents, this training did not occur prior to beginning to teach online, but rather during the first year or after the first year of teaching online.

The late start to online teacher training is problematic, considering that in order to be excellent online teachers, K-12 instructors "need to possess the same characteristics of excellence as their counterparts in higher education" as well as being able to make their content age appropriate and meet state mandates and requirements (Palloff & Pratt, 2011, p. 81). Given that learning psychology and psychological principles at the K-12 level can be an important contributor to students' decision to pursue study and careers in the discipline, it is imperative that K-12 instructors receive the training that they need before they begin to teach online, to ensure successful courses and retain students. According to the National Education Association's *Guide to Teaching Online Courses* (2010), professional development for online K-12 teachers should incorporate several elements, including the following: Appropriate communications, appropriate and timely feedback, facilitated discussions, facilitation of teamwork and multimedia projects, adaptation of curriculum and materials, and adaptation of online tools to support effective instruction. They also argue for such training to be distributed by master teachers and at least partly online, since "traditional methods of professional development—a day or two of face-to-face training—are not reliably effective" (NEA, 2010, pp. 10–11). Currently, only a handful of states offer online teacher accreditation programs, but the NEA suggest implementing state-wide teacher licensure criteria that ensures online teacher preparation (NEA, 2010, p. 23). While online educators wait on local, state, and national governments to work together with school boards to determine these parameters, students continue to enroll in K-12 online education. At some point in the near future these criteria will be decided upon and disseminated, and we will know more about the appropriate protocol for training K-12 teachers and reducing their knowledge gap.

Moving Toward National and Global Accreditation

Achieving some kind of standardized credential or accreditation for online degree programs would be hugely beneficial to improving attitudes about online education, and reducing the stigma faced by many with online degrees. Just as we cannot assume that all face-to-face courses are great, we cannot assume the same for online courses. In other words, all modalities of higher education should be evaluated and accredited by regional or national organizations to help solidify their legitimacy. The U.S. Council for Higher Education Accreditation explains that the purpose of accreditation is to ensure quality, provide access to federal funds, ease transferring, and engender private sector confidence. Thus it is vital that online degree programs can receive the accreditation that they need to facilitate successful student outcomes and provide quality instruction. Currently, the U.S. Department of Education recognizes several accreditation agencies for distance education, including the most widely accepted six regional associations: The Middle States Commission on Higher Education, the New England Association of Schools and Colleges, the North Central Association of Colleges and Schools, the Northwest Association of Schools and Colleges, the Southern Association of Colleges and Schools, and the Western Association of Schools and Colleges. By recognizing these associations, the Department of Education gives them the ability to accredit online education programs. While traditionally accreditation has been a regional enterprise, Lezberg (2003) argues that distance education changes the necessities and parameters for regional accreditation. More and more frequently, regional organizations have engaged in cooperation to determine the accreditation standards for distance education programs. Essentially, these standards had to be revised when applied to online learning, including requirements for technological expertise needed by undergraduates to complete their programs, expansion of library and information personnel, and guidelines for regional boundaries when the student resides in one state and the instructor resides in the other (Lezberg, 2003).

It also appears that accreditation has yet to become standardized on a global level. Mason (2003) argues that "one area in which educational globalization lags behind economic globalization is that of cross-border regulations" (Mason, 2003, p. 744). He cites in particular the problem that credit transfers between online degree programs are rare even at the national level in the United States, let alone when assessing our international students. According to this perspective, an international system that enables users to transfer online credits from one country to another will "open the floodgates" for the globalization of online higher education (p. 744). Further, he argues that until this accreditation occurs, certificates from professional associations will become more important than online degrees. So for example, a certificate in computer programming form Microsoft might be considered more valuable and globally recognized than an online degree from a top university. Again, this trend should have important implications for the ability to distribute our online courses to the global market and attract international students. Once they are confident they can use our credits for transfers in their home countries, they will possibly become more likely to enroll. Just as we are now managing to reach national standards for accreditation in the United States, so too should global standards emerge to guide us in the near future.

Economic and Demographic Trends Fueling Online Education

In their article on "Re-examining and Repositioning Higher Education," Betts, Hartman, and Oxholm (2010) highlight 10 economic and 10 demographic factors that are driving the enrollments into online and distance education, and will probably continue to drive online education into the next decade and beyond. As online educator, consider yourself riding the wave of the future that shows no sign of slowing down. In fact, as these trends tend to show, there is every reason to believe that student interest in online education will continue to rise in the years to come.

In terms of the economic factors, *tuition* continues to remain a huge burden for many students, while colleges are increasingly relying upon tuition fees for revenue. According to Betts and colleagues (2010), "colleges and universities are seeking innovative strategies to cut costs while keeping tuition increases to a minimum and maintaining or increasing quality" and clearly, online education represents an excellent solution to this growing problem (p. 5). Many states are also undergoing budget crises, meaning the potential for cuts to *state funding* of many colleges and universities. The authors have experienced this first hand in California, where the state budget deficit in 2011 was nearing $8 billion. As operating budgets fall, online courses provide a way of catering to the increasing numbers of students without laying off faculty of engaging in other cuts. This problem is being compounded by the *credit crisis*, which has prompted many educational institutions to put a freeze on hiring and question the creditworthiness of their students who may struggle to obtain student loans since the collapse of Sallie Mae (Betts et al., 2010). For this reason, the number of students seeking *financial aid* has increased dramatically, as FAFSA applications rose 20% between 2008–2009 and 2009–2010 alone. Colleges and universities are struggling, with many seeing a drops in their *endowments* and *fundraising* with investors and alumni lacking confidence. These reductions put more of an onus on cutting institutional costs, such as layoffs or hiring freezes, or tuition hikes.

One cost in particular is the cost of *space*: specifically, *construction, maintenance,* and *deferred maintenance,* which can be extremely costly to academic institutions. Online courses can help circumvent problems of space and problems of *energy,* including those costs related to electricity and gasoline. One of the greatest costs of university enrollments is *room and board,* and for many students, even grants-in-aid no longer cover the costs of living on campus. Online learning from home offers a much more cost efficient alternative to paying exorbitant prices to live on campus. Finally, *technology* spending has increased dramatically as institutions race to update their classrooms with multimedia, Wi-Fi, tech support, and access to digital libraries. If the institution is already engaging in technology spending, it makes financial sense to utilize that technology to facilitate online courses.

National demographic shifts have also greatly affected the need for online education, with "minorities" set to become the "majority" population by 2050. While minorities are often disenfranchised in higher education, we have already discussed how online education offers a "color blind" environment that welcomes individuals from diverse backgrounds. Indeed, *diversity* will play an important part in future online learning, as educators will seek to address gaps in educational attainment by harnessing online educational opportunities. In addition, *population shifts* should drive online education in states expected to grow during the next 20 years, specifically Florida, California, and Texas, which will account for half of the United States population by 2030. Further, there will be *decreases* and *surges* in high school graduates in certain parts of the United States. For example, California has seen increases in the number of high school students eligible for college, meaning that the number of available places in colleges and universities gets smaller. One way to integrate these students and create new spaces for them is through online learning. Further, states that experience decreases in the number of high school graduates should see a competition between in-state institutions to retain students, meaning that "higher education institutions in these states will need to develop innovative enrollment strategies to reach new student markets including online and blended delivery options" (Betts et al., 2010, p. 13).

The number of *adult learners* is also expected to rise during the next 20 years, as adults seek to obtain workplace qualifications and enhance their opportunities by acquiring a degree. Based upon evidence presented earlier in this chapter, it appears that adult learners can have very positive experiences from learning online. As *employment expectations* emerge in fields related to technology and innovation, younger and older adults alike can benefit from receiving certificates and degrees online. It is also possible that due to spiraling tuition costs, students may seek to attend higher education abroad, demonstrating the *global competition* that is ensuing in higher education. The United States ranks 13th out of 15 countries when it comes to the affordability of education. It is possible that online education can halt students from going abroad while simultaneously attracting students from around the globe. One benefit to this is that the *online program inventory* of educational institutions is growing so rapidly, demonstrating how online courses reflect "viable, sustainable, and cost effective options" (Betts et al., 2010, p. 16). Finally, just as the number of online programs are constantly expanding, so too is the general *acceptance of online degrees*.

What can all of these combined factors teach us about the future of online education? One thing is for sure: The popularity of online learning has shown no sign of waning. On the contrary, it appears that online programs have nearly unlimited potential for growth during the next 20 or so years. Online learning has already exploded into a multi-billion dollar business, expected to be worth around $52 billion worldwide in 2010 (Global Industry Analysts, 2007). As the new generation of *millenials* enters the educational landscape, we can expect that they will be increasingly likely to pursue online education, as they live, breathe, and co-exist with their laptops, phones, and other portable technology devices. All of these economic and demographic transitions occurring in the United States seem to be pointing strongly towards a future where access to quality online learning will be possible for all people, regardless of their financial situation, ethnicity, or geographic location. As psychologists, it is our duty to stay abreast of these important changes and ensure that we can get our messages out there to the people who need them most by giving psychology away via our online course offerings.

SUMMARY: CHANGE IS THE ONLY CONSTANT

While it may seem unclear what the future of online learning in psychology holds, it is undeniable that online educational hardware, software, methods of delivery, student base, and even technical support will continue to change and evolve in the 21st century. These changes have already taken place at a near-exponential rate, considering that online learning was practically nonexistent prior to the mid-1990s, and now at least 12 million students are enrolling in online undergraduate and graduate education each year. Considering that the statistics on 12 million students were derived from the most recent dataset from the 2006 school year, we imagine that current and future enrollment rates will continue to skyrocket in the years to come, driven by economic and demographic shifts in the United States and the world. As a psychology instructor, continue to pursue goals of "giving psychology away" by working with your institution to ensure that diverse populations can gain access to your online classes. Consider developing new courses, and new modalities of delivery, that appeal to not only undergraduates, but also to professionals, doctoral students, certificate trainees, and even K-12 students. Strive to push our discipline and capabilities to the limit, for innovation and advancement. In the current state of our world, rife with unrest, whispers of revolution, and upheaval by the masses, the online teaching of psychology can benefit so many lives, and possibly help to improve the human condition. As we proceed in our careers as online psychology instructors, perhaps we could all find inspiration from adopting Ghandhi's mantra to "be the change you hope to see in the world."

REFERENCES

Adams, J., & DeFleur, M. (2005). The acceptability of a doctoral degree earned online as a credential for obtaining a faculty position. *The American Journal of Distance Education, 19*, 71–85.

Akin, L., & Neal, D. (2007). CREST+ Model: Writing effective online discussion questions. *Journal of Online Learning and Teaching, 3*. Retrieved from http://jolt.merlot.org/vol3no2/akin.htm.

Alexander, M. E., Commander, N., Greenberg, D., & Ward, T. (2010). Using the four-questions technique to enhance critical thinking in online discussions. *Journal of Online Teaching and Learning, 6*, 409–415.

Allen, I. E., & Seaman, J. (2010). Learning on demand: Online education in the United States, 2009. Retrieved from http://sloanconsortium.org/publications/survey/learning_on_demand_sr2010.

Al-Shalchi, O. N. (2009). The effectiveness and development of online discussions. *MERLOT: Journal of Online Teaching and Learning, 5*, 104–108.

American Association of Colleges of Nursing. (2003). *Alliance for Nursing Accreditation statement on distance education policies*. Washington, DC: AACN Publications.

Anderson, T. (2008). Teaching in an online learning context. In T. Anderson (Ed.), *The theory and practice of online learning* (2nd ed., pp. 343–365). Edmonton, Canada: Alabasca University Press.

Anderson, T., Rourke, L., Garrison, D. R., & Archer, W. (2001). Assessing teaching presence in a computer conference context. *Journal of Asynchronous Learning Networks, 5*, 1–17.

Angelo, T. A., & Cross, K. P. (1993). *Classroom assessment techniques: A handbook for college teachers* (2nd ed.). San Francisco, CA: Jossey-Bass.

Astleitner, H. (2002). Teaching critical thinking online. *Journal of Instructional Psychology, 29*, 53–77.

Baird, D. E., & Fisher, M. (2005). Neomillennial user experience design strategies: Utilizing social networking media to support "always on" learning styles. *Journal of Educational Technology Systems, 34*, 5–32.

Bates, C., & Watson, M. (2008). Re-learning teaching techniques to be effective in hybrid and online courses. *Journal of American Academy of Business, 13*, 38–44.

Bates, T. (2001). International distance education: Cultural and ethical issues. *Distance Education, 22,* 122–136.

Bedford, W., Gregg, J., & Clinton, S. (2009). Implementing technology to prevent online cheating: A case study at a small southern regional university (SSRU). *Journal of Online Teaching and Learning, 5,* 230–238.

Bender, T. (2003). *Discussion-based online teaching to enhance student learning.* Sterling, VA: Stylus.

Berman, S. J., & Novotny, T. E. (1999). Extended degree and continuing education preference of California public health professionals. *Journal of Public Health Management Practice, 5,* 20–24.

Bernard, R. M., Abrami, P. C., Lou, Y., Borokhovski, E., Wade, A., Wozney, L., & ÖHuang, B. (2004). How does distance education compare with classroom instruction? A meta-analysis of the empirical literature. *Review of Educational Research, 74,* 379–439.

Berry, R. W. (2009). Meeting the challenges of teaching large online classes: Shifting to a learner-focus. *Journal of Online Learning and Teaching, 5,* 176–181.

Betts, K., Hartman, K., & Oxholm, C. (2010). Re-examining and repositioning higher education: Twenty economic and demographic factors driving online and blended program enrollments. *Journal of Asynchronous Learning Networks, 13,* 3–23.

Bloom, B. S., & Krathwohl, D. R. (1956). *Taxonomy of educational objectives: The classification of educational goals, by a committee of college and university examiners: Handbook 1. Cognitive domain.* New York: Longmans.

Boettcher, J. V. (1999). How many students are just right in a web course? Retrieved from http://www.designingforlearning.info/services/writing/number.htm.

Boettcher, J. V., & Conrad, R. M. (2004). *Faculty guide for moving teaching and learning into the Web* (2nd ed.). Phoenix, AZ: League for Innovation.

Boettcher, J. V., & Conrad, R. M. (2010). *The online teaching survival guide.* San Francisco, CA: Jossey-Bass.

Bond, D., Wells, P., & Holland, T. (2008). *Podcasting and its relation with student performance.* Paper presented at the 3rd International conference of e-learning, University of Cape Town, South Africa.

Borstroff, P. C., & Lowe, S. L. (2007). Student perceptions and opinions toward e-learning in the college environment. *Academy of Educational Leadership Journal, 11,* 13–30.

Bowers, W. J. (1964). *Student dishonesty and its control in college.* New York: Bureau of Applied Social Research, Columbia University.

Bradley, M. E., Thom, L. R., Hayes, J., & Hay, C. (2008). Ask and you will receive: How question type influences quantity and quality of online discussions. *British Journal of Educational Technology, 39,* 888–900.

Brown, A., Brown, C. Fine, B., Lutterbach, K., Sugar, W. & Vinciguerra, D. C. (2009). Instructional uses of podcasting in online learning environments: A cooperative inquiry study. *Journal of Educational Technology Systems, 37*(4), 351–371.

Bullen, M. (1998). Participation and critical thinking in online university distance education. *Journal of Distance Education/Revue de l'enseignement ‡ distance, 13.,* 1–32.

Burrus, R. T., McGoldrick, K., & Schuhmann, P. W. (2007). Self-reports of student cheating: Does a definition of cheating matter? *Journal of Economic Education, 38,* 3–16.

Campbell, M., Gibson, W., Hall, A., Richards, D., & Callery, P. (2008). Online vs. face-to-face discussion in a Web-based research methods course for postgraduate nursing students: A quasi-experimental study. *International Journal of Nursing Studies, 45,* 50–59.

Cardall, S., Krupat, E., & Ulrich, M. (2008). Live lecture versus video-recorded lecture: Are students voting with their feet? *Technology and Medical Education, 83,* 1174–1178.

Carlson, N. (2011, January 5). Facebook has more than 600 million users, Goldman tells clients. *Business Insider.* Retrieved from http://articles.businessinsider.com/2011-01-05/tech/30100720_1_user-facebook-pr-goldman-sachs.

Carpenter, P., & Roberts, E. (2007). Going wiki in online technology education courses: Promoting online learning and service learning through wikis. *North Carolina Council on technology Teacher Education Technology Education Journal, 9,* 58–64.

Chapman, C., Radmondt, L., & Smiley, G. (2005). Strong community, deep learning: Exploring the link. *Innovations in Education and Teaching International, 42,* 217–230.

Chiero, R., & Beare, P. (2010). Evaluation of online versus campus-based teacher preparation programs. *Journal of Online Teaching and Learning, 6,* 780–790.

Chuang, H., Thompson, A., & Schmidt, D. (2003). Faculty technology mentoring programs: Major trends in the literature. *Journal of Computing in Teaching Education, 18,* 26–31.

Clark, R. C., & Mayer, R. E. (2002). *E-Learning and the science of instruction: Proven guidelines for consumers and designers of multimedia learning.* San Francisco, CA: Jossey-Bass.

Cobb, S. C. (2004). Internet continuing education for health care professionals: An integrative review. *The Journal of Continuing Education in the Health Profession, 24,* 171–180.

Collis, B. (1999). Designing for differences: Cultural issues in the design of WWW-based course-support sites. *British Journal of Educational Technology, 30,* 201–215.

Collison, G., Elbaum, B., Haavind, S., & Tinker, R. (2000). *Facilitating online learning: Effective strategies for moderators.* Madison, WI: Atwood.

Colwell, J., & Jenks, C. (2004). *The upper limit: The issues for faculty in setting class size in online courses.* Paper presented at the Teaching Online in Higher Education (TOHE) Conference Proceedings.

Coutinho, C., & Bottentuit, J., Jr. (2007). *Collaborative learning using wiki: A pilot study with master students in educational technology in Portugal.* Proceedings of World Conference on Educational Multimedia, Hypermedia, and Telecommunications, 1786–1791, Vancouver, Canada: Extended Abstracts.

Dabbagh, N. (2000). *Online-protocols.* Retrieved from http:// mason.gmu.edu/~ndabbagh/wblg/online-protocol.html.

Dahl, J. (2005). Who owns the rights to online courses? *Distance Education Report, 9,* 4–7.

Dede, C., Ketelhut, D. J., Whitehouse, P., Breit, L., & McCloskey, E. M. (2009). A research agenda for online teacher professional development. *Journal of Teacher Education, 60,* 8–19.

DeLaat, M., Lally, V., Lipponen, L., & Simons, R. J. (2006). Online teaching in networked learning communities: A multi-method approach to studying the role of the teacher. *Instructional Science, 35,* 257–286.

Dell, C. A., Low, C., & Wilker, J. F. (2010). Comparing student achievement in online and face-to-face class formats. *Journal of Teaching and Learning, 6,* 30–42.

Dennen, V. P. (2005). From message posting to learning dialogues: Factors affecting learner participation in asynchronous discussion. *Distance Education, 26,* 127–148.

Dermo, J. (2009). E-Assessment and the student learning experience: A survey of student perceptions of e-assessment. *British Journal of Educational Technology, 40,* 203–214.

Deters, F., Cuthrell, K., & Stapleton, J. (2010). Why wikis? Student perceptions of using wikis in online coursework. *Journal of Online Teaching and Learning, 6,* 122–134.

Deubel, P. (2008). K-12 online teaching endorsements: Are they needed? *T.H.E. Journal.* Retrieved from http://thejournal.com/articles/2008/01/10/k12-online-teaching-endorsements-are-they-needed.aspx.

Dietz-Uhler, B., & Lanter, J. R. (2009). Using the four-questions technique to enhance learning. *Teaching of Psychology, 36,* 38–41.

Donaldson, S. I., & Berger, D. E. (2006). The rise and promise of applied psychology in the 21st century. In S. I. Donaldson, D. E. Berger, & K. Pezdek (Eds.), *Applied psychology: New frontiers and rewarding careers* (pp. 3–23). Mahwah, NJ: Erlbaum.

Donaldson, S. I., Berger, D. E., & Pezdek, K. (2006). *Applied psychology: New frontiers and rewarding careers.* Mahwah, NJ: Erlbaum.

Donaldson, S. I., Csikszentmihalyi, M., & Nakamura, J. (Eds.). (2011). *Applied positive psychology: Improving everyday life, health, schools, work, and society.* London: Routledge Academic.

Donnelli, E., Dailey, A., & Mandernach, B. J. (2009). Toward a philosophy of multimedia in the online classroom: Aligning multimedia use with institutional goals. *Journal of Online Teaching and Learning, 5,* 149–154.

Douglas, K., & Johnson, B. (2010). Legal education and e-learning: Online fishbowl role-play as a learning and teaching strategy in legal skills development. *Murdoch University Electronic Journal of Law, 17,* 28–46.

Driessen, E. (2008). *Educating the self-critical doctor: Using a portfolio to stimulate and assess medical students' reflection.* Maastricht, Netherlands: Maastricht University.

Driessen, E., Muijtjens, A. M. M., van Tartwijk, J., & van der Vleuten, C. (2007). Web-based or paper-based portfolios: What makes the difference? *Medical Education, 41,* 1067–1073.

Du, J., Zhang, K., Olinzock, A., & Adams, J. (2008). Graduate students' perspectives on the meaningful nature of online discussions. *Journal of Interactive Learning Research, 19,* 21–36.

Edwards, J. T., & Helvie-Mason, L. (2010). Technology and instructional communication: Student usage and perceptions of virtual office hours. *Journal of Online Teaching and Learning, 6,* 174–186.

Ellery, J., McDermott, R. J., & Ellery, P. J. (2007). Computers as a formal continuing education tool: Moving beyond intention. *American Journal of Health Behavior, 31*(3), 312–322.

Enger, K. B. (2006). Minorities and online higher education. *Educause Quarterly, 4,* 7–8.

Engestrom, Y. (1993). Developmental studies of work as a test bench of activity theory: Analyzing the work of general practitioners. In S. Chaiklin & J. Lave (Eds.), *Understanding practice: Perspectives on activity and context* (pp. 64–103). Cambridge, England: Cambridge University Press.

English, R., & Duncan-Howell, J. (2008). Facebook goes to college: Using social networking tools to support students undertaking teaching practicum. *Journal of Online Teaching and Learning, 4,* 596–601.

Eplion, D. M., & Keefe, T. J. (2007, April). Practical tips for preventing cheating on online exams. *Faculty Focus* [Online newsletter].

Farwell, T. M., & Waters, R. D. (2010). Exploring the use of social bookmarking technology in education: An analysis of students' experiences using a course-specific Delicious.com account. *Journal of Online Learning and Teaching, 6,* 398–408.

Ferry, B., Kiggins, J., Hoban, G., & Lockyer, L. (2000). Use of computer-mediated communication to form a knowledge-building community in initial teacher education. *Educational Technology & Society, 3.* [Online journal].

Flowers, J. C., & Baltzer, H. (2006). Hiring technical education faculty: Vacancies, criteria, and attitudes toward online doctoral degrees. *Journal of Industrial Teacher Education, 43,* 29–44.

Foley, B., & Chang, T. (2006, April). *Wikis as a professional development tool.* Paper presented at the American Education Research Association annual meeting, San Francisco, CA.

Fredrickson, E., Pickett, A., Shea, P., Pelz, W., & Swan, K. (2000). Factors influencing faculty satisfaction with asynchronous teaching and learning in the SUNY learning network. In J. Bourne (Ed.), *Online education* (pp. 239–269). Needham, MA: Sloan Center for OnLine Education.

Gallant, T. B. (2008). Moral panic: The contemporary context of academic integrity. *ASHE Higher Education Report, 33,* 1–12.

Gaumer-Erickson, A. S., & Noonan, P. M. (2010). Late-career adults in online education: A rewarding experience for individuals aged 50–65. *Journal of Online Learning and Teaching, 6,* 388–397.

Gaytan, J. (2005, Spring). Effective assessment techniques for online instruction. *Information Technology, Learning and Performance Journal, 23,* 25–33.

Gerlich, R. N. (2005). Faculty perception of distance learning. *Distance Education Report, 9,* 8.

Gibson, J. W., Tesone, D. V., & Blackwell, C. W. (2001). The journey to cyberspace: Reflections from three online business professors. *S.A.M Advanced Management, 66,* 30–35.

Global Industry Analysts. (2007, September 17). Study: E-Learning Spending on the Rise. *Chief Learning Officer,* Retrieved from http://clomedia.com/articles/view/study_e_ learning_spending_on_the_rise.

Gonen, Y. (2010, April 15). New York City to introduce online courses in public schools. *The New York Post,* p. 11.

Goodyear, M. (2006). Mentoring: A learning collaboration. *Educase Quarterly, 29,* 51–53.

Goodyear, P., Salmon, G., Spector, J. M., Steeples, C., & Tickner, S. (2001). Competencies for online teaching: A special report. *Educational Technology, Research and Development, 49,* 65–72.

Grijalva, T. C., Nowell, C., & Kerkvliet, J. (2006, March). Academic honesty and online courses. *College Student Journal, 40,* 180–185.

Grosseck, G. (2008). The role of Del.icio.us in education: Creating significant learning experiences. Retrieved from http://www.scribd.com/doc/2413801/The-Roleof-Delicious-in-Education.

Guendoo, L. M. (2008, Fall). Community colleges friendlier to online Ph.D.s. *Online Journal of Distance Learning Administration, 11*(3). Retrieved from http://www.westga. edu/%7Edistance/ojdla/fall113/guendoo113.html.

Gunawardena, C. A., Wilson, P. L., & Nolla, A. C. (2003). Culture and online education. In M. G. Moore & W. G. Anderson (Eds.), *Handbook of distance education* (pp. 753–776). Mahwah, NJ: Erlbaum.

Haney, C., Banks, C., & Zimbardo, P. G. (1973). Interpersonal dynamics in a simulated prison. *International Journal of Criminology and Penology, 1,* 69–97.

Hampel, R., & Stickler, U. (2005). New skills for new classrooms: Training tutors to teach languages online. *Computer Assisted Language Learning, 18,* 311–326.

Hara, H., Bonk, C. J., & Angeli, C. (2000). Content analysis of online discussion in an applied educational psychology course. *Instructional Science, 28,* 115–152.

Harasim, L., Hiltz, S. R., Teles, L., & Turoff, M. (1997). *Learning networks: A field guide to teaching and learning online.* Cambridge, MA: MIT Press.

Hewett, B., & Powers, C. E. (2007). Online teaching and learning: Preparation, development, and organizational communication. *Technical Communication Quarterly, 16,* 1–11.

Higher Education Opportunity Act of 2008, Public Law 110-315. Retrieved from http://www2. ed.gov/policy/highered/leg/hea08/index.html.

Holly, C. (2009). The case for distance education in nursing. *Journal of Online Teaching and Learning, 5,* 506–510.

Howell, S. L., Saba, F., Lindsay, N. K., & William, P. B. (2004). Seven strategies for enabling faculty success in distance education. *Internet & Higher Education, 7,* 33–49.

Hrastinski, S. (2009). A theory of online learning and as online participation. *Computers & Education, 52,* 78–82.

Huang, W. H. D. (2010). Case study of wikis' effects on online transactional interactions. *Journal of Online Teaching and Learning, 6,* 1–14.

Huba, M. E., & Freed, J. (2000). *Learner-centered assessment on college campuses: Shifting the focus from teaching to learning.* Needham Heights, MA: Allyn & Bacon.

Jaldemark, J., Lindberg, J. O., & Olofsson, A. D. (2006). Sharing the distance or distance shared: Social and individual aspects of participation in ICT-supported distance-based teacher education. In M. Chaib & A. K. Svensson (Eds.), *ICT in teacher education: Challenging prospects* (pp. 142–160). Jˆnkˆping, Sweden: Jˆnkˆping University Press.

Jenner, S., Zhao, M., & Foote, T. H. (2010). Teamwork and team performance in online simulations: The business strategy game. *Journal of Online Teaching Learning, 6,* 416–430.

Johnson, C. M. (2001). A survey of current research on online communities of practice. *Internet and Higher Education, 4,* 45–60.

Jonassen, D. H. (2000). *Computers as mind tools for schools: Engaging critical thinking.* Upper Saddle River, NJ: Merrill/Prentice Hall.

Jones, J., Warren S., & Robertson, M. (2009). Increasing student discourse to support rapport building in web and blended courses using a 3D online learning environment. *Journal of Interactive Learning Research, 20,* 269–294.

Ke, F., & Hoadley, C. (2009). Evaluating online learning communities. *Education Technology Research and Development, 57,* 487–510.

Kearsley, G. (2000). *Teaching and learning in cyberspace.* Toronto, Canada: Nelson Thompson Learning.

Keefe, T. J. (2003). Using technology to enhance a course: The importance of interaction. *Educause Quarterly, 1,* 24–34.

Kitsantas, A., & Chow, A. (2007). College students' perceived threat and preference for seeking help in traditional, distributed and distance learning environments. *Computers & Education, 48,* 383–395.

Ko, S., & Rossen, S. (2010). *Teaching online: A practical guide* (3rd ed.). New York: Routledge.

Koczwara, B., Francis, R., Marine, F., Goldstien, D., Underhill, C., & Olver, I. (2010). Reaching further with online education? The development of an effective online program in palliative oncology. *Journal of Cancer Education, 25,* 317–323.

Kolitch, E., & Dean, A. V. (1999). Student ratings of instruction in the USA: Hidden assumptions and missing conceptions about ìgoodî teaching. *Studies in Higher Education, 24,* 27–43.

Kowch, E., & Schwier, R. (1997). Considerations in the construction of technology-based virtual learning communities. *Canadian Journal of Educational Communication, 26,* 1–12.

Kranch, D. A. (2008). Who owns online course intellectual property? *The Quarterly Review of Distance Education, 9*(4), 349–356.

Krathwohl, D. R. (2002, Autumn). A revision of Bloom's taxonomy: An overview. *Theory in Practice, 41,* 212–218.

Kromrey, J., Barron, A., Hogarty, K., Hohlfeld, T., Loggie, K., Schullo, S., … Sweeney, P. I. (2005, June). *Intellectual property and online courses: Policies at major research universities.* Paper presented at the National Educational Computer Conference.

Kumrow, D. E. (2007). Evidence-based strategies of graduate students to achieve success in a hybrid Web based course. *Journal of Nursing Education, 46,* 140–145.

Kyie-Blankson, L. (2010). Faculty mentoring and support among online instructors. *International Journal of Technology and Distance Learning, 7,* 41–47.

LaPadula, M. (2003). A comprehensive look at online student support services for distance learners. *The American Journal of Distance Education, 17,* 119–128.

Leppien-Christense, K. (2010, April). Podcasting tips and tricks. In S. Donaldson (chair), *Thinking outside of the classroom: Opportunities and challenges for distance education in psychology.* Symposium conducted at the 90th meeting of the Western Psychological Association, Cancun, Mexico.

Levine, S. (2002). Replacement myth. *IT Forum.* Retrieved from http://www.listserv.uga.edu/.

Levy, P. (2003). A methodological framework for practice-based research in networked learning. *Instructional Science, 31,* 87–109.

Lewis, T. O. (2007). *The preparation of faculty to teach online: A qualitative approach* (Unpublished doctoral dissertation). Virginia Polytechnic Institute and State University, Blacksburg, VA.

Lezberg, A. K. (2003). Accreditation: Quality control in higher distance education. In M. G. Moore & W. G. Anderson (Eds.), *Handbook of distance education* (pp. 425–434). Mahwah, NJ: Erlbaum.

Liang, A., & McQueen, R. J. (1999). Computer assisted adult interactive learning in a multicultural environment. *Adult Learning, 11,* 26–29.

Liu, X., Liu, S., Lee, S.-h., & Magjuka, R. J. (2010). Cultural differences in online learning: International student perceptions. *Educational Technology & Society, 13,* 177–188.

Liu, X., Magjuka, R. J., Bonk, C. J., & Seung-Jee, L. (2007). Does sense of community matter? An examination of participants' perceptions of building learning communities in online courses. *Quarterly Review of Distance Education, 8,* 9–24.

Lowenthal, P. R. (2008). Online faculty development and storytelling: An unlikely solution to improving teaching quality. *Journal of Online Teaching and Learning, 4,* 349–356.

Mandernach, B. J., Forrest, K. D., Babutzke, J. L., & Manker, L. R. (2009). The role of instructor interactivity in promoting critical thinking in online and face-to-face classrooms. *Journal of Online Teaching and Learning, 5,* 49–62.

Marcus, A., & Gould, E. W. (2000). Crosscurrents: Cultural dimension and global web user-interface design. *Interactions, 7,* 32–46.

Mason, R. (2003). Education: Out of the ivory tower. In M. G. Moore & W. G. Anderson (Eds.), *Handbook of distance education* (pp. 743–752). Mahwah, NJ: Erlbaum.

Masson, S. R. (2010). Online highway robbery: Is your intellectual property up for grabs in the online classroom? *Journal of Online Teaching and Learning, 6,* 253–263.

McAlpine, M., & Higgison, C. (2001). *Online tutoring e-book.* Online Tutoring Skills Project. Retrieved from http://www.sonet.nottingham.ac.uk/resources/otis/T4-04.pdf.

McCabe, D. (2005, June). *Levels of cheating and plagiarism remain high: Honor codes and modified codes are shown to be effective in reducing academic misconduct.* Durham, NC: Center for Academic Integrity, Duke University.

McCabe, D. L. (2001–2002, Winter). Cheating: Why students do it and how we can help them stop. *American Educator,* 38–43.

McKeachie, W. J. (1978). *Teaching tips: A guide for the beginning college teacher* (7th ed.). Lexington, MA: Heath.

McLafferty, C. L., & Foust, K. M. (2004). Electronic plagiarism as a college instructor's nightmare—Prevention and detection. *Journal of Education for Business, 80,* 186–189.

McLean, D., & White, E. R. (2009). Two approaches to using podcasting in the classroom. *Journal of Online Teaching and Learning, 5,* 336–347.

McLoughlin, C. (2002). Learner support in distance and networked learning environments: Ten dimensions for successful design. *Distance Education, 23,* 149–162.

McMillan, D. W., & Chavis, D. M. (1986). Sense of community: A definition and theory. *Journal of Community Psychology, 14,* 6–23.

McNabb, L., & Olmstead, A. (2009). Communities of integrity in online courses: Faculty member beliefs and strategies. *Journal of Online Teaching and Learning, 5,* 208–221.

Means, B., Toyama, Y., Murphy, R., Bakia, M., & Jones, K. (2009). *Evaluation of evidence-based practices in online learning: A meta-analysis and review of online learning studies.* Retrieved from www.ed.gov/about/offices/list/opepd/ppss/reports.html.

Merriam-Webster Dictionary. (2012). Copyright. Retrieved from http://www.merriam-webster.com/dictionary/copyright.

Mevarech, Z. R., & Kramarski, B. (2003). The effects of metacognitive training versus worked-out examples on students' mathematical reasoning. *British Journal of Educational Psychology, 73,* 449–471.

Milgram, S. (1963). Behavioral study of obedience. *Journal of Abnormal and Social Psychology, 67,* 371–378.

Miller, G. (1969). Psychology as a means of promoting human welfare. *American Psychologist, 24,* 1063–1075.

Miller, M. V. (2009). Integrating online multimedia into college course and classroom: With application to the social sciences. *Journal of Online Teaching and Learning, 5,* 395–423.

Milwaukee/Waukesha Public Health Consortium. (2006). Planning for an accredited school of public health at UW-Milwaukee. *Public health professionals' continuing education survey.* https://www4.uwm.edu/publichealth/people/.../PHreport_FNL.pdf.

Mintu-Wimsatt, A., Kernek, C., & Lozada, H. R. (2010). Netiquette: Make it part of your syllabus. *Journal of Online Teaching and Learning, 6,* 264–267.

Moore, G. (1989). Three types of interaction. *The American Journal of Distance Education, 3,* 1–6.

Moore, M. G., & Anderson, W. G. (2003). *Handbook of distance education.* Mahwah, NJ: Erlbaum.

Morgan, C., & O'Reiley, M. (1999). *Assessing open and distance learners*. London: Kogan Page.

Morris, L. V., Finnegan, C., & Sz-Shyan, W. (2005). Tracking student behavior, persistence, and achievement in online courses. *Internet and Higher Education, 8,* 221–231.

Morris, L. V., Xu, H., & Finnegan, C. L. (2005). Roles of faculty in teaching asynchronous undergraduate courses. *Journal of Asynchronous Learning Networks, 9,* 65–82.

Munsey, C. (2008). Charting the future of undergraduate psychology. *APA Monitor on Psychology, 39,* 54.

National Education Association. (2010). *Guide to Teaching Online Courses*. Retrieved from http://www.nea.org/technology/images/onlineteachguide.pdf.

Olaniran, B. A. (2009). Culture, learning styles, and Web 2.0. *Interactive Learning Environments, 17,* 261–271.

Olt, M. R. (2002, Fall). Ethics and distance education: Strategies for minimizing academic dishonesty in online assessment. *Online Journal of Distance Learning Administration, 5*(3), 1–6.

Olt, M. R. (2009). Seven strategies for plagiarism-proofing discussion threads in online courses. *Journal of Online Learning and Teaching, 5,* 222–229.

Opitz, C. (2008). *The fishbowl*. Retrieved from www.edutopia.org/pdfs/coop_math.../bowman_fishbowl_method.pdf.

O'Shea, P. M., Baker, P. B., Allen, D. W., Curry-Corcoran, D. E., & Allen, D. B. (2007). New levels of student participatory learning: A wikitext for the introductory course in education. *Journal of Interactive Online Learning, 6,* 227–244.

Ouzts, K. (2006). Sense of community in online courses. *Quarterly Review of Distance Education, 7,* 285–296.

Palloff, R. M., & Pratt, K. (1999). *Building learning communities in cyberspace: Effective strategies for the online classroom*. San Francisco, CA: Jossey-Bass.

Palloff, R. M., & Pratt, K. (2005). *Collaborating online: Learning together in community*. San Francisco, CA: Jossey-Bass.

Palloff, R. M., & Pratt, K. (2009). *Assessing the online learner*. San Francisco, CA: Jossey-Bass.

Palloff, R. M., & Pratt, K. (2011). *The excellent online instructor: Strategies for professional development*. San Francisco, CA: Jossey-Bass.

Parker, K. R., & Chao, J. T. (2007). Wiki as a teaching tool. *Interdisciplinary Journal of Knowledge and Learning Objectives, 3,* 57–72.

Parker, M. A., & Martin, F. (2010). Using virtual classrooms: Student perceptions of features and characteristics in an online and a blended course. *MERLOT Journal of Online Learning and Teaching, 6,* 135–147.

Parsad, B., Lewis, L., & Tice, P. (2009). Distance education at degree-granting postsecondary institutions: 2006–2007. *National Center for Education Statistics*. Retrieved from http://nces.ed.gov/pubsearch/pubsinfo.asp?pubid=2009044.

Paul, R., Elder, L., & Bartell, T. (1997). *California teacher preparation for instruction in critical thinking: Research findings and policy recommendations*. Dillon Beach, CA: The Foundation for Critical Thinking.

Paulson, K., & Boeke, M. (2006). *Adult learners in the United States: A national profile*. Washington, DC: American Council on Education.

Pelz, B. (2004). My 3 principles of effective online pedagogy. *Journal of Asynchronous Learning, 8.* Retrieved from http://sloanconsortium.org/jaln/v8n3/my-three-principles-effective-online-pedagogy.

Penny, L., & Murphy, E. (2009). Rubrics for designing and evaluating online asynchronous discussions. *British Journal of Educational Technology, 40,* 804–820.

Poirier, C. R., & Feldman, R. S. (2004). Teaching in cyberspace: Online versus traditional instruction using a waiting-list experimental design. *Teaching of Psychology, 31,* 59–62.

Preece, J. (2000). Sociability and usability in online communities: Determining and measuring success. *Behaviour & Information Technology, 20,* 347–356.

Pyke, J. G., & Sherlock, J. J. (2010). A closer look at instructor-student feedback online: A case study analysis of the types and frequency. *Journal of Online Teaching and Learning, 6,* 110–121.

Ray, J. (2009). Faculty perspective: Training and course development for the online classroom. *Journal of Online Teaching and Learning, 5,* 263–276.

Renninger, K., & Shumar, W. (2002). *Building virtual communities: Learning and change in cyberspace.* New York: Cambridge University Press.

Rice, K., & Dawley, L. (2007). *Going virtual! The status of professional development for K–12 online teachers.* Retrieved from http://edtech.boisestate.edu/goingvirtual/goingvirtual1.pdf.

Rideout, V. J., Foehr, U. G., & Roberts, D. F. (2010). *Generation M²: Media in the lives of 8- to 18-year-olds* (Kaiser Family Foundation Report). Menlo Park, CA: Kaiser Family Foundation.

Roach, R. (2006). Higher education software giants merge in multi-million dollar deal. *Diverse Issues in Higher Education, 23,* 28.

Rose, R., & Smith, A. (2007). Online discussions. In C. Cavanaugh & R. Blomeyer (Eds.), *What works in k-12 online learning* (pp. 143–160). Washington, DC: International Society for Technology in Education.

Rosen, L. D. (2010). *Rewired: Understanding the iGeneration and the way they learn.* New York: Palgrave Macmillan.

Rovai, A. P. (2002). Development of an instrument to measure classroom community. *The Internet and Higher Education, 5,* 97–211.

Sadera, W. A., Roberston, J., Song L., & Midon, M. N. (2009). The role of community in online learning success. *MERLOT Journal of Online Learning and Teaching, 5,* 277–284.

Salmon, G. (2003). *E-moderating: The key to teaching and learning online.* London: Routledge Falmer.

Sandars, J. (2007). The potential of blogs and Wikis in healthcare education. *Education for Primary Care, 18,* 16–21.

Schallert, D, Chiang, Y., Park, Y., Jordan, M., Lee, Haekyung, L., & Song, K. (2009). Being polite while fulfilling different discourse functions in online classroom discussions. *Computers and Education, 53,* 713–725.

Sewell, J. P., Frith, K. H., & Colvin, M. M. (2010). Online assessment strategies: A primer. *Journal of Online Learning and Teaching, 6,* 297–305.

Shea P. (2006). A study of students' sense of learning community in online environments. *Journal of Asynchronous Learning Networks, 10,* 35–44.

Shea, V. (2004). *Netiquette.* San Francisco, CA: Albion Books.

Shepard, L. A. (2000). The role of assessment in a learning culture. *Educational Researcher, 29*(7), 4–14.

Sherry, L., Billig, S. H., Tavalin, F., & Gibson, D. (2000, February 1). New insights on technology adoption in schools. *T.H.E. Journal,* 43–46

Simba Information Marketing. (2010). *Moving online: K-12 distance learning market forecast for 2010.* Retrieved from http://www.simbainformation.com/Moving-Online-Distance-2522707.

Sims, R., Dobbs, G., & Hand, T. (2002). Enhancing quality in online learning: Scaffolding planning and design through proactive evaluation. *Distance Education, 23,* 135–158.

Smith, P. J., & Smith, S. W. (1999). *Differences between Chinese and Australian students: Some implications for distance educators. Distance Education, 20,* 64–80.

Sprague, D., Maddux, C., Ferdig, R., & Albion, P. (2007). Editorial: Online education: Issues and research questions. *Journal of Technology and Teacher Education, 15,* 157–166.

St. Clair, D. J. (2009). My experience with teaching online: Confessions and observations of a survivor. *Journal of Online Teaching and Learning, 5,* 166–175.

Steinkuehler, C. A. (2004). Learning in massively multiplayer online games. In Y. B. Kafai, W. A.

Sandoval, N. Enyedy, A. S. Nixon, & F. Herrera (Eds.), *Proceedings of the Sixth International Conference of the Learning Sciences* (pp. 521–528). Mahwah, NJ: Erlbaum.

Stevens, D. D., & Levi, A. J. (2004). *Introduction to rubrics: An assessment tool to save grading time, convey effective feedback, and promote student learning.* Sterling, VA: Stylus.

Suler, J. (2004). The online disinhibition effect. *The Psychology of Cyberspace.* Retrieved from http://users.rider.edu/~suler/psycyber/disinhibit.html.

Tajfel, H., & Turner, J. C. (1979). An integrative theory of intergroup conflict. In W. G. Austin & S. Worchel (Eds.), *The social psychology of intergroup relations* (pp. 33–47). Monterey, CA: Brooks/Cole.

Taylor, C. (2011, September 8). Twitter has 100 million active users. *Mashable Social Media.* Retrieved from http://mashable.com/2011/09/08/twitter-has-100-million-active-users/.

Teaching and Learning with Technology. (2001–2005). *Building blocks for teams.* Penn State. Retrieved from http://tlt.its.psu.edu/suggestions/teams/student/.

Thomas, M. J. W. (2002). Learning within incoherent structures: the space of online discussion forums. *Journal of Computer Assisted Learning, 18,* 351–366.

Thompson, L., & Ku, H. (2005). Chinese graduate students' experiences and attitudes toward online learning. *Educational Media International, 42,* 33–47.

Tu, C. H., & Corry, M. (2002). ELearning communities. *The Quarterly Review of Distance Education, 3,* 207–218.

Twigg, C. (n.d.). Who owns online courses and course materials? Intellectual property policies for a new learning environment. *The National Center for Academic Transformation.* Retrieved from www.thencat.org/Monographs/Whoowns.html.

US News and World Report. (2012). Online education rankings. Retrieved from: http://www.usnews.com/education/online-education.

Uzuner, S. (2009). Questions of culture in distance learning: A research review. *International Review of Research in Open and Distance Learning, 10,* 1–9.

van Wesel, M., & Prop, A. (2008, November). *The influence of portfolio media on student perceptions and learning outcomes.* Paper presented at Student Mobility and ICT: Can E-Learning Overcome Barriers of Life-Long Learning? Maastricht, Netherlands.

Varvel, V. E., Jr. (2005). Honesty in online education. *Pointers & Clickers,* ION's technology tip of the month. Retrieved from http://www.ion.uillinois.edu/resources/pointersclickers/2005_01/index.asp.

Vesely, P., Bloom, L., & Sherlock J. (2007). Key elements of building online community: Comparing faculty and student perceptions. *Journal of Online Learning and Teaching, 3,* 234–246.

Vogele, C., & Townsend Gard, E. (2006, October). Podcasting for corporations and universities: Look before you leap. *Journal of Internet Law,* 3–13.

Wang, M. (2007). Designing online courses that effectively engage learners from diverse cultural backgrounds. *British Journal of Educational Technology, 38,* 294–311.

Waschull, S. B. (2001). The online delivery of psychology courses: Attrition performance, and evaluation. *Teaching of Psychology, 28,* 143–147.

Watson, J. (2010). *Keeping pace with K-12 online learning: An annual review of policy and practice.* Durango, CO: Evergreen Education Group.

WCET. (2009, June). Best practice strategies to promote academic integrity in online education. *Western Interstate Commission for Higher Education.* Retrieved from http://www.wiche.edu/pub/13441.

Weimer, M. (2002). *Learner-centered teaching: Five key changes to practice.* San Francisco, CA: Jossey-Bass.

Wenger, E. (1998). *Communities of practice: Learning, meaning, and identity.* Cambridge, England: Cambridge University Press.

Whipp, J. L., & Lorentz, R. A. (2009). Cognitive and social help giving in online teaching: An exploratory study. *Education Technology Research and Development, 57,* 169–192.

White, B. T. (2009). Analysis of students' downloading of online audio lecture recordings in a large biology lecture course. *Journal of College Science Teaching, 38*(3), 23–27.

Wicks, M. (2010). A national primer on k-12 online learning. *International Association for K-12 Online Learning,* Retrieved from www.inacol.org/research/docs/iNCL_NationalPrimerv22010-web.pdf.

Wikipedia (2012a). *Online learning community.* Retrieved from http://en.wikipedia.org/wiki/Online_learning_community/.

Wikipedia (2012b). *Emoticons.* Retrieved fromhttp://en.wikipedia.org/wiki/Emoticons.

Wikipedia (2012c). *E-Portfolio.* Retrieved from: www.wikipedia.org/wiki/E-portfolio.

Wikipedia (2012d). *Social network.* Retrieved from http://en.wikipedia.org/wiki/Social_network.

Wikipedia (2012e). *Social bookmarking.* Retrieved from http://en.wikipedia.org/wiki/Social_bookmark.

Williams, B., & Bearman, M. (2008). Podcasting lectures: The next silver bullet? *Journal of Emergency Primary Health Care, 6,* 1–14.

Woodward, H., & Bablohy, P. (2004). Digital portfolios: fact or fashion. *Assessment & Evaluation in Higher Education, 29,* 227–238.

Yang, M., Chen, Y., Kim, M., Chang, Y., Cheng, A., & Park, Y. (2006). Facilitating or limiting? The role of politeness in how students participate in an online classroom. *Yearbook of National Reading Conference, 55,* 341–356.

Yang, Y. Y., & Cornelious, L. F. (2005). Preparing instructors for quality online instruction. *Online Journal of Distance Learning Administration, 8,* http://www.westga.edu/~distance/ojdla/spring81/yang81.htm.

Zembylas, M. (2008). Engaging with issues of cultural diversity and discrimination through critical emotional reflexivity in online learning. *Adult Education Quarterly, 59,* 61–82.

Zhao, N., & McDougall, D. (2008). Cultural influences on Chinese students' asynchronous online learning in a Canadian university. *The Journal of Distance Education, 22,* 59–80.

Zimbardo, P. G. (1971). *The power and pathology of imprisonment. Congressional Record.* (Serial No. 15, 1971-10-25). Hearings before Subcommittee No. 3, of the Committee on the Judiciary, House of Representatives, Ninety-Second Congress, First Session on Corrections, Part II, Prisons, Prison Reform and Prisoner's Rights: California. Washington, DC: U.S. Government Printing Office.

Zimbardo, P. G. (2004). Does psychology make a significant difference in our lives? *American Psychologist, 59,* 339–351.

Zusevics, K. L., Gilmore, G. D., Jecklin, R. A., & Swain, G. R. (2009). Online education: The needs, interests and capacities of Wisconsin public health professionals. *Journal of Online Learning and Teaching, 5,* 531–545.

AUTHOR INDEX

SUBJECT INDEX